THE ECONOMICS OF POVERTY

Richard Perlman
University of Wisconsin— Milwaukee

McGRAW-HILL BOOK COMPANY
New York St. Louis San Francisco Auckland Düsseldorf Johannesburg
Kuala Lumpur London Mexico Montreal New Delhi Panama Paris
São Paulo Singapore Sydney Tokyo Toronto

THE ECONOMICS OF POVERTY

1234567890 DODO 7832109876

This book was set in Times Roman by Textbook Services, Inc. The editors were J. S. Dietrich and Michael Weber; the cover was designed by Victor Bastante; the production supervisor was Angela Kardovich.
R. R. Donnelley & Sons Company was printer and binder.

Library of Congress Cataloging in Publication Data

Perlman, Richard.
    The economics of poverty.

    Includes index.
    1.   Poor—United States.   2.   Economic assistance, Domestic—United States.   I.   Title.
HC110.P6P465   301.44′1   75-34268
ISBN 0-07-049307-3

To Lois and Wayne

CONTENTS

PREFACE

No matter how rich a country may be and regardless of its political system and methods of distribution, part of its population will be at the lower end of the purchasing-power scale. In America, rich as it is, the most pressing chronic economic problem concerns the large number of people with inadequate spending capacity. This large mass of poverty, formed as it is mainly by particular population subgroups, creates serious psychological, social, and political problems.

Before discussing the causes and treatment of poverty, this book identifies the concept and details its demographic composition. The functional economic definition of *poverty* as "inadequate earnings" recognizes the short transition from low income to low spending power; the poor have little wealth. Since they also earn little from nonlabor sources, *inadequate earnings*, in effect, refers to low wage income. How low this income must be to classify the recipient and his household as poor is an arbitrary decision. The first chapter analyzes the various poverty standards suggested and used for policy action; but no matter how low the poverty line is set, the poverty count is still intolerably high.

The demographic breakdown of the poor in Chapter 2 points out the high incidence of poverty among particular population groups: the lesser educated, blacks, women, children, and the aged. The second section on the causes of poverty (low earnings) begins with a discussion of the fundamental handicap of insufficient and often misdirected education that affects all poverty groups. Then the next three chapters detail poverty among the high-incidence groups. It is a sad story of discrimination and limited opportunities. The background factors that induce poverty having been examined, Chapter 7 looks at the unhappy work experience of the poor—their high unemployment rates and characteristic underemployment when they do work. Chapter 8 appraises the effect of growth and inflation on the precarious economic position of the poor.

Chapters 9 and 10 study efforts to alleviate and reduce poverty. Manpower training and income maintenance represent the two main weapons against poverty. On the whole, efforts in these areas have not been vigorously pursued and have not been very successful. If there is any source of optimism for future gains against poverty, it lies in the facts that concerted governmental policies to solve the problem are still relatively new and important measures have not yet been adopted; these facts allow for hope in the future. This book offers no remedies of its own but confines itself to an analysis of the presently primitive art of fighting poverty—an art whose development will probably be delayed until the national preoccupation with recovery from recession abates in the wake of a prosperity that fosters public interest in those left behind.

The last chapter summarizes the main findings and conclusions. Here the needs for attacking poverty within particular population subgroups are stressed.

The writer wishes to thank his colleagues Marilyn Moon and James Moody for their careful comments on parts of the manuscript and those unknown reviewers whose suggestions improved the finished work. Needless to say, remaining weaknesses are the writer's sole responsibility.

Wayne Wendling, a doctoral student at the University of Wisconsin—Milwaukee, contributed greatly to the various stages of the book. His research efforts were a great help, but of even more value were his many incisive suggestions and comments that could only have come from close study of the material.

Lois Grebe typed numerous drafts with her characteristic patience, accuracy, and understanding.

Richard Perlman

THE ECONOMICS
OF POVERTY

Part One

Defining and Measuring Poverty

Chapter 1

The Concept of Poverty—
Attitudes and Definitions

All the numerous economic definitions of poverty contain one common element; they consider poverty a condition of having insufficient funds to maintain an acceptable standard of living.[1] The dispute is over what constitutes an acceptable standard. Obviously, we cannot conduct a sensible discussion of the issues involved—the extent of poverty, its incidence among population subgroups, the causes, treatment, and cures of poverty—until we decide what it is we are discussing; that is, until we have agreed on a working definition of poverty.

We may follow through the discussion with reference to a single definition of inadequate spending power. But other views of poverty must have some influence on our judgment of how well or badly we are meeting our national goal of poverty eradication. The key to the explanation of the

---

[1] Harry Johnson's straightforward definition is as good as any: "I define poverty in the usual sense, as existing when the resources of families or individuals are inadequate to provide a socially acceptable standard of living." Harry Johnson, "Unemployment and Poverty," in Leo Fishman (ed.), *Poverty amid Affluence,* Yale University Press, New Haven, 1966, p. 183.

variety of definitions of poverty lies in the changing attitudes toward poverty and, more specifically, toward the poor.

CHANGING ATTITUDES TOWARD POVERTY

If the Great Depression of the 1930s contributed anything at all positive to society, it was its profound effect on the attitudes of the fortunate rest of society toward the poor and their poverty. Prior to this period, and in fact since the late-eighteenth-century development of urban industrialization and the emergence of a highly visible and numerous subgroup of indigents, the poor were looked upon as objects of pity or scorn, depending on the humanity of the observer, but never as subjects for economic uplift through social action.

Some looked upon the poor as random sufferers of bad luck—those who were poor because of ill health, accident, premature death of the principal breadwinner, or mental incapacity were forced to live a life of penury and even beggary to survive. Others thought that the poor had only themselves to blame for their low estate—because of either laziness, instability, weakness of purpose, carousing, or careless budgeting, the poor wasted their opportunities for enjoying the better life available to the sober and the ambitious.

If this description seems to exaggerate the prevalent negative attitude of the time, one only has to skim through the early literature of poverty, written by supposedly learned men, to find even stronger feelings against the poor. The Poor Laws, which prevailed in England with a few liberalizing modifications since Elizabethan days, provided some skimpy public assistance, mainly to poor orphans and the physically handicapped. But Malthus argued for the elimination of even this limited form of poor relief. Speaking of the poor, he advised that a short time after public announcement that public relief would be cut off, any new families that were formed should receive no assistance. The family head "should be taught to know that the laws of Nature, which are the laws of God, had deemed him and his family to suffer for disobeying their repeated admonitions, that he had no claim of *right* on society for the smallest portion of food, beyond that which his labour would fairly purchase." Malthus saw the "principal difficulty" in eliminating extensive aid, a step needed to reduce (excess) population through starvation, to be "to restrain the hand of benevolence (private charity) from assisting those in distress in so indiscriminate a manner as to encourage indolence and want of foresight in others."[2]

While Malthus wanted to stop poor relief to clear the path for starva-

---

[2]Thomas Malthus, *An Essay on the Principles of Population,* 1817.

tion and thereby validate his circular logic that the poor were superfluous, others saw poverty as a spur to labor efficiency and an inducement to social conformity. Here are some choice quotes on the subject of nineteenth-century English vintage:[3]

> Penury and want do make a people wise and industrious.

> Everyone but an idiot knows that the lower classes must be kept poor or they will never be industrious.

> In years of scarcity . . . the poor labor more and really live better than in years of great plenty when they indulge in idleness and riot.

The same negative attitudes were imported into the United States, where observers saw poverty as the result of "misconduct" or individual "misfortune" but never as a widespread economic affliction resulting from the operation of the socioeconomic system itself and requiring social action to remedy.[4] Some modern critics claim that interpretations of the recent "culture of poverty" concept come close to Malthus's view that the poor have only themselves to blame for their poverty.

Michael Harrington's *The Other America*[5] did much to awaken social consciousness to the problems of the poor. This book is credited with an important role in stimulating the War on Poverty begun in the mid-1960s. In his book, Harrington describes the "culture of poverty," or environment of the poor who live in unstable family units, are subject to physical and mental disorders, show weak attachment to the work force with frequent periods of unemployment between marginal, casual jobs, and have children who perform badly at school and drop out early.

This life-style background seems designed to perpetuate poverty. But as one critic puts it, "Some psychological characteristics often attributed to the culture of poverty can also be viewed as a response to reality, ready to change if reality fosters or at least permits change."[6] That is, the poor should not be blamed if they show acceptance, resignation, and even accommodation to their poverty as they learn to live with their economic disabilities. Who can "blame" people for lethargy when their diets are inadequate to sustain full vigor, for family instability under torturing financial stress, for loose work-force attachment when jobs—dead-end ones

---

[3]Quoted in Theodore W. Schultz, "Public Approaches to Minimize Poverty," in *Poverty amid Affluence,* op. cit., p. 168.

[4]See Oscar Handlin, "Poverty from the Civil War to World War II," in *Poverty amid Affluence,* op. cit., for a summary of early American views in poverty.

[5]Michael Harrington, *The Other America,* Penguin, Baltimore, 1962.

[6]Elizabeth Herzog, "Facts and Fiction about the Poor," Perspectives on Poverty Symposium, *Monthly Labor Review,* February 1969, pp. 42–49.

at best—are few and far between, or for low standardized academic test scores when they are badly educated from infancy?

Of course, Harrington and other modern writers who describe the life of the poor do not mean to suggest that poverty initially stems from the attitudes and characteristics of the poor. Rather, they stress that poverty creates a vicious circle in which inadequate financial resources condition the hard life of the poor, which, in turn, builds barriers against their breaking out of poverty. But this is no chicken-and-egg problem. The fact that these social critics have been misinterpreted to suggest that the basic fault lies in the poor themselves, and that they have defenders who patiently explain their true interpretation of the time sequence of poverty, only reveals a single fact: the opinion that poverty can be traced to the nature of the poor themselves dies hard. In fact, unfortunately, it is not dead yet.

But ever since the New Deal there has been a social and political awareness of the prevalence and pain of poverty in America. Even if our national record in alleviating and reducing the problem cannot stand close scrutiny, the general view expressed by all varieties of politicians is that poverty is a matter of social concern and a fitting target for collective remedial action. These stirring lines from President Roosevelt's second inaugural address of 1937 set the tone for future public responsibility for the assault on poverty:

> But here is the challenge to our democracy: In this nation I see tens of millions of its citizens—a substantial part of its whole population—who at this very moment are denied the greater part of what the very lowest standards of today call the necessities of life . . . .
>
> I see one-third of a nation ill-housed, ill-clad, ill-nourished . . . .
>
> We are determined to make every American citizen the subject of his country's interest and concern, and we will never regard any faithful law-abiding group within our borders as superfluous.[7] The test of our progress is not whether we add more to the abundance to those who have much, it is whether we provide enough for those who have too little.

Here is a clear call for collective political action to remove or at least reduce poverty, a national charge which has been followed more or less faithfully, with some periods of neglect and many setbacks, since that time. It is interesting to note that while Roosevelt's "one-third of a nation" sounded to many like an example of political hyperbole, the fact is that—by even the minimum poverty standard established later—many more than one-third the population would have been classified as poor in 1937.

---

[7]Note the need, over one hundred years after Malthus, to deny the Malthusian view that the poor constitute a redundant population subgroup.

The designation of poverty limits and the classification of individuals as poor must be determined by objective standards by society as a whole and not by the poor themselves. A suburbanite who finds himself in arrears on his country club dues may feel poor, but his condition does not evoke our sympathy, nor does it generate much agitation for remedial social action.

It is significant that Mollie Orshansky—who, in her work with the Social Security Administration, has done as much as anyone to enumerate the poor measured by objective rigid income standards—should write that "poverty, like beauty, lies in the eye of the beholder."[8] We can question the aptness of her simile; there are no attractions in poverty. But we can agree that poverty income limits are subjective, depending on personal views of equity and humanity, and the established norms reflect consensus views on what should be the minimum purchasing standards for American households.

There are some who argue that labeling people as poor places a stigma on them. But the purpose of this classification is not to mark its members as objects of derogation but of social concern and subjects for public income-raising programs.

The setting of poverty limits, the count of the poor and the analysis of their characteristics, and the study of the causes of poverty are not meant to be intellectual exercises. Instead, all these aspects of poverty are studied and analyzed under the presumption that something is going to be done to raise the spending power of the poor.

Thus we can categorize a poor individual as a person whose economic status society should take measures to improve. We designate specific geographic regions of the country "depressed areas" for the same reason; they are places which will receive special help for economic development. Now, no one wishes to suggest that an individual specified as a target for social action for economic improvement should be called a depressed person. But because of the negative aspects of the word *poor,* there has been a tendency, at least in government circles, to replace it with the more cumbersome term *low-income population.* However, even the Department of Commerce in its Current Population Reports writes that "the terms 'low income' and 'poor' are used interchangeably."

In fact, the income measure of poverty is not a very accurate one. Low income does not always reflect inadequate purchasing power. A household having low earnings may have other assets which can be translated into purchasing power. This is especially true of older people. Income may be low, but needs can be well below those of the average household. This is true of smaller family units. Then, income has a time

[8]Mollie Orshansky, "How Poverty Is Measured," Perspectives on Poverty Symposium, *Monthly Labor Review,* February 1969, pp. 37–41.

dimension, and a family might have a low income for a brief period without being poor if their low spot is just an interval between customary high earnings levels. On the other hand, needs, particularly of large families, might be so high as to exceed relatively high earnings, and a brief high earning period might be but a favorable interlude in an economic lifetime of low income.

Despite the weakness of income as a guide to the adequacy of purchasing power, it is the measure used; if it is refined to take into account the value of assets and family size, it is probably the best single measure of purchasing power available.

DEFINITIONS OF POVERTY

The Poverty Index, or the Poverty Line

Inadequacy of Poverty Line Purchasing Power   The most well-known measure of poverty is the *Poverty Index,* or *Poverty Line,* as it is often called. In discussing the index—which is of course a measure of purchasing power adequacy or, more precisely, the upper limit of inadequacy—emphasis should be placed on the pitifully low income we have set as the minimum level for social acceptability. While there are other more generous poverty standards (which will be discussed below), it is this index which guides public antipoverty policy. The inadequacy of the index value, or Poverty Line, can best be explained by describing its construction.

The Department of Agriculture, the Social Security Administration, and the Council of Economic Advisers have played a part in the formulation and perpetuation of the index. They might not want credit for setting such a meager standard, but they share the responsibility.

For many years the Department of Agriculture has constructed food budgets at various cost levels. The "low-cost diet plan" allows for the purchase of a minimum diet just adequate to avoid nutritional deficiencies. (This plan is often used by welfare programs as the basis for food allotments. But hardly any public transfer programs provide sufficient funds or their equivalent in goods to meet even this low standard.) Furthermore, the budget assumes that the housewife will be a careful shopper and a skillful cook—attributes not necessarily associated with a poverty housewife whose home-management skills are further dulled by the discouraging oppression of chronic poverty. All meals are assumed to be cooked at home. Thus, any necessary (more expensive) eating out—for example, lunches at work—would strain the food budget even further.

These stringencies are severe enough, but the shocking fact is that the Poverty Index reaches even lower in the Department of Agriculture's food budget scale. It uses the Department's "economy diet plan," a euphemistic term which consists of food costs of only 75 to 80 percent of the "low-cost plan," and is described as applicable for "temporary or emergency use when funds are low." In other words, long-term adherence to the economy plan, even under the best of circumstances, would not provide an adequate diet for the maintenance of health for a person who began the regimen in normal physical condition.

From the two food budgets, the Social Security Administration constructed consumption indexes by the simplest technique possible. Based on past experience that low-income households spend about one-third of their income on food, they multiplied the cost of each food plan by three to arrive at the total consumption indexes.

It remained for the Council of Economic Advisers, in its 1964 Annual Report, to use the lower index, based on the economy food budget, as the Poverty Index. In fact, the Council shaved the calculations a little, reducing the estimated total budget of $3,165 to attain the much neater figure of $3,000 as the Poverty Line; no matter that the process lopped off spending power from a budget that, if rigorously applied, was designed to weaken and eventually sicken those who followed it. In short, to the Council, perhaps our most influential economic body, goes the responsibility of setting a widely accepted poverty line which is based on an eating regimen suitable for a lifeboat.

The Council was well aware of the importance of its arbitrary decision on the dollar amount of the Poverty Line. In its 1964 report it writes:

> No measure of poverty as simple as the one used here would be suitable for determining eligibility for particular benefits or participation in particular programs. Nevertheless, it provides a valid benchmark for assessing the dimension of the task of eliminating poverty, setting the broad goals of policy, and measuring our past and future progress toward their achievement.

Cutting through the verbiage, the Council suggests that one can consider the job of poverty elimination well done if every household attains a minimum spending level that assures slow starvation.

In fact, though, the poor do not actually starve, simply because, when their total income is pressed too low, they spend more than one-third of it on food. Survival dictates that the lower their income, the greater the part of it the poor spend on food.

Table 1-1 updates a 1967 study of the average budget for those at the Poverty Line by adjusting for a 47 percent change in the price level over the period 1967–1974. Note that over 40 percent of total expenditures are budgeted for food. Apart from an inadequate diet, allotments for other essentials are very thin, and almost nothing is assigned for life's small

Table 1-1 Monthly Budget, Urban Family at the Poverty Line, 1967 and 1974

Consumption item	1967	1974
Food	$122	$179
Housing	91	133
Transportation	6	9
Clothing and personal care	57	84
Medical care	—	—
Gifts and contributions	—	—
Life insurance	—	—
Other consumption (recreation, education)	9	13
Total	$284	$418

Source: Poverty and Plenty, The Report of the President's Commission on Income Maintenance Programs, 1969.

pleasures. Furthermore, the zero allowance for medical care admonishes the poor to stay healthy, quite a feat considering the substandard expenditures on physical maintenance.

Policy Peculiarities of the Poverty Line Although the poverty rate has not quite reached the status of the unemployment rate or the Consumer Price Index as a measure of overall economic welfare, it is a well-publicized statistic, and the national goal is to make it as low as possible. No one wants to contest the national goal of poverty reduction, but preoccupation over reducing the percentage below the Poverty Line can lead to strange policy proposals.

If the public limits its interest in maximizing the number who cross the line, then budgetary limitations would focus on those plans and programs which would give the greatest assistance to those households of lesser need whose income puts them close to the line. Raising a family's income level from $2,900 to $3,005—to use the original 1964 Poverty Line—would remove it from the poverty rolls. On the other hand, raising a very low income family's spending power from $1,000 to $2,700 would dramatically improve its standard of living but would have no effect on the poverty count or the percentage in poverty, the statistic in this area best known to the program-evaluating public. This is not to suggest that public decision makers by nature have a callous attitude toward the most desperately poor; but they must respond to political pressures, and these pressures are for measures to reduce the poverty count and rate.

Modification of the Poverty Index In his discussion of antipoverty policy, Lampman speaks of the need for reducing the "poverty gap" as well as the poverty rate.[9] This gap is the total shortfall of income from the Poverty Line received by all the poor. Thus, the gap for a $2,800 household would be $200 and for a $1,000 one it would be $2,000, with a total gap of $2,200 for the two families.

The goal of closing the gap is an improvement over that limited to raising families over the Poverty Line in that it places as much social value on the dollar gain in income of those well below the Poverty Line as on the same increase for higher-income recipients up to the Poverty Line.

But the two goals are sometimes inconsistent. Programs aimed at recipients of the lowest incomes and that reduce the gap the most are those that do the least to reduce the poverty rate. You cannot have it both ways, and often a choice would have to be made between programs that would reduce the gap the most or push the most people across the politically magical Poverty Line. Furthermore, Lampman's gap concept places no value on adding to the income of the near-poor, those just above the Poverty Line.[10] Thus an antipoverty program that raised incomes from $2,800 to $4,000 would have no more social value than one that raised incomes from $2,800 to $3,000. The reduction in the poverty gap and the poverty rate would be the same for both cases.

Harold Watts constructs a poverty index which has the realistic feature of assigning a higher social value to a rise in the lowest incomes than it does to the same increase to households closer to the Poverty Line.[11] He defines the "welfare ratio" as the ratio of a family's "permanent" income, that is, its long-run expected income (Y) to the poverty threshhold $(\hat{Y})$. In symbols,

$$W = \frac{Y}{\hat{Y}}$$

Changes in the welfare ratio are then constructed on a relative scale, so that equal dollar increases will increase the relative welfare ratio of the poorest more than that of those closest to the Poverty Line. For example, with a poverty threshhold at $3,000 a $500 increase in income—from $1,000 to $1,500—would increase a family's welfare ratio by 50 percent from 0.33 to 0.50. The same $500 increase for a family at $2,000, closer

[9]Robert Lampman, "Approaches to the Reduction of Poverty," *American Economic Review*, May 1965, pp. 521–529.

[10]The Social Security Administration uses the "low-cost food budget" in calculating the "near-poor" income limit.

[11]Harold Watts, "An Economic Definition of Poverty," in Daniel P. Moynihan (ed.), *On Understanding Poverty*, Basic Books, New York, 1969, pp. 325–326.

to the Poverty Line, would result in a poverty welfare ratio increase of only 25 percent, from 0.67 to 0.83.

One important feature of the welfare ratio is that it allows for a consideration of the welfare of those above the Poverty Line. The ratio does assume dwindling increases in welfare for each additional dollar above the Poverty Line, but it also suggests individual and social gains from raising families away from the Poverty Line, a feature lacking in the much-used Poverty Index or in Lampman's poverty gap concept.

Extension of the principle that the social policy goal for raising low incomes should not stop at the Poverty Line appears in Thomas Ribich's detailed description of the "average" taxpayer's attitude toward redistribution[12] or toward what in the past was popularly if sometimes critically denoted as "sharing the wealth" programs. There is some minimum income level that taxpayers feel should be received by all families. Thus, to raise the incomes of families to this level, they are willing to pay their tax share of the required amount. In other words, the satisfaction they derive from the income transfer to the poor just matches their share of the costs.

But the taxpayer receives declining psychic benefit from additional transfers of his or her income to the poor, until finally their income is raised to a level at which the taxpayer would not willingly transfer one more cent to them. The first income level would be comparable to the Poverty Index. But Ribich's contribution lies in the concept of a second, higher poverty line at the maximum level for any voluntary taxpayer income transfer. That this formula is vague, not operational, and difficult to measure does not detract from its relevance to the question of poverty and to our search for a new guideline that reaches beyond the limitations of the Poverty Index. The index implies that the guarantee of short-run physical survival constitutes the goal of antipoverty policy, and this is clearly unacceptable.

Relative Poverty

The Poverty Line has risen over the years, from about $3,000 when it was first calculated in the early 1960s, to over $4,200 in 1972 and approximately $5,300 in 1974. These increases do not signify gains in purchasing power but simply adjustments for inflation. The Poverty Line characteristic of measuring the bare essentials for survival has not changed.

But it is worth noting that Orshansky herself, whose name is linked to the Poverty Line concept, was aware that this narrow formulation fell far short of a social definition of poverty. She wrote that the line can tell us

[12]Thomas Ribich, *Education and Poverty*, Brookings, Washington, 1968, pp. 17–33.

"how much is too little," even though "it is not possible to state unequivocally 'how much' is enough."[13]

Expressed differently, the Poverty Index measures *absolute* poverty, but what is needed is a standard of *relative* poverty. In describing the concept of relative poverty, Oscar Ornatti constructed a "poverty band" consisting of three threshholds.[14] The lowest or "minimum subsistence" line, comparable to the Poverty Line, set the limit for public assistance. The middle or "minimum adequacy" line is the level at which a household would pay for nonmonetary welfare services, such as counseling and guidance. The upper or "minimum comfort" line marks the limit for public assistance of any type and presumably for public concern.

The significance of Ornatti's band for the relative poverty concept is that his threshhold levels increase over time, reflecting the growth in purchasing power of the average household. Ornatti writes, "As the general United States income level has risen, living standards have risen. Expectations have risen. Concepts of who is poor have risen. Thus, through the years, standards of sufficiency, however defined, have generally risen." Even the amount society considers the barest minimum has risen. Thus Ornatti's lowest threshold differs somewhat from the Poverty Line in that it includes a rise in real terms for the minimum survival budget. It acknowledges that even the idea of survival at a biologically determined level loses its impersonal quality in the face of social pressures resulting from the demands of the poor for something better and the guilt-fear and/or conscience-motivated response of the rest of society to provide it.

Ornatti's measurement of the change in the poverty rate over time shows marked deviation from single-index calculations. Over the period 1929–1960, the percent of households below the minimum subsistence level fell from 26 percent to 11 percent; but the percent below the minimum comfort level fell only from 48 percent to 40 percent. This upper level, a close relative of Ribich's hypothetical second poverty line in that it reflects the income limit to public concern about poverty, has proved a difficult barrier to cross. This difficulty exists both because the upper level rises faster than the other lines, since it is more sensitive to a rise in average incomes, and because the *relative* change in low incomes is sluggish over the long term. This last factor explains the weak gains made against poverty when poverty is considered relatively.

[13]Mollie Orshansky, "Counting the Poor: Another Look at the Poverty Profile," *Social Security Bulletin,* January 1965, p. 3.
[14]Oscar Ornatti, "The Poverty Band and the Count of the Poor," in Edward C. Budd (ed.), *Inequality and Poverty,* Norton, New York, 1967, p. 168.

The attitude of the poor themselves, and of the rest of society toward "how much is enough," or toward relative poverty, reflects the income level of the time and place. The frame of income comparison is not the present purchasing power of the poor with that of the average citizen years ago. It does not comfort the poor, or dull social interest in raising their income level, to point out that a family at today's Poverty Line real income would have been a high-income family 50 or even 30 years ago. Nor does the problem of poverty become any less socially pressing because less than 10 percent of all Asians and not much more than half of all Western European families enjoy standards of living above that of our Poverty Line households.

The socially compelling comparison is the current gap between the income received by those at the bottom and by those at the average level of our income scale. There is nothing in our national income data to indicate that those at the bottom are gaining on those above them. Table 1-2 shows the United States income distribution over a long period of time.

There has been a little sag in the relative income of those at the top of the scale, but only a very sharp eye could detect significant relative improvement among those at the bottom, those relevant to the problem of poverty.

Fuchs's Standard of Relative Poverty   An extreme view of relative poverty would hold that those who fell into a certain low percentile of the income distribution should be considered poor. Obviously, such a standard would preclude the attainment of poverty elimination, no matter how great the effort and no matter how low the standard, unless we reached a position of complete equality in household income levels. As long as there is an income distribution, there will always be one-third, one-fifth—or whatever cutoff level is used—at the bottom.

Victor Fuchs sets an operational level of relative poverty based on income distribution, which—though a much more difficult income barrier than the Poverty Line to cross—does not require the unrealistic condition

Table 1-2   Percent of Aggregate Income Received by Each Fifth and Highest 5 Percent of Families: 1947–1972

Families	1947 100.0	1950 100.0	1955 100.0	1960 100.0	1965 100.0	1969 100.0	1970 100.0	1971 100.0	1972 100.0
Lowest fifth	5.0	4.5	4.8	4.9	5.3	5.6	5.5	5.5	5.4
Second fifth	11.8	12.0	12.2	12.0	12.1	12.3	12.0	12.0	11.9
Middle fifth	17.0	17.4	17.7	17.6	17.7	17.6	17.4	17.6	17.5
Fourth fifth	23.1	23.5	23.7	23.6	23.7	23.5	23.5	23.8	23.9
Highest fifth	43.0	42.6	41.6	42.0	41.3	41.0	41.6	41.1	41.4
Highest 5 percent	17.2	17.0	16.8	16.8	15.8	14.7	14.4	15.7	15.9

Source: 1974 Statistical Abstract of the United States.

of equal incomes for poverty elimination. Fuchs defines a poor family as one whose income is less than one-half the median family income.[15] This relative poverty line moves upward with the growth in average national income, allowing for changing social standards on what constitutes poverty. It does have the potential weakness of all arbitrary limits, even shifting ones, of (1) perhaps being used as the ultimate goal of policy measures to the neglect of programs that would raise the lowest incomes toward the line and (2) giving the lowest priority to programs that push up incomes ever so slightly above the line.

The failure, noted above, of the lowest-income earners to make substantial movements toward the average level explains the poor record of antipoverty programs in reducing the incidence of Fuchs-type poverty. Table 1-3 compares the changes in the poverty rate using the controversial (Council of Economic Advisers—Social Security Administration) Poverty Line and the Fuchs standard. The former rises only because of changes in the price level, while the latter responds to improvement in the average standard of living as measured by median income.

The table shows distinct differences in poverty reduction for the two methods of measurement. There was hardly any change at all in the percentage in relative poverty, while the percentage below the Poverty Line has shrunk substantially over the past generation. This means that those with the lowest incomes have gained in their struggle for survival but have

[15]Victor R. Fuchs, "Redefining Poverty and Redistributing Income," *The Public Interest,* Summer 1967, pp. 88–95.

Table 1-3 Percentage of United States Families Classified Poor according to Poverty Line and Fuchs's Standard, Selected Years

Year	Median income	Percentage of families below one-half median*	Poverty Line	Percentage of families below Poverty Line†
1950	$ 3,350	20.0	$2,460	32.7
1955	4,420	20.0	2,736	25.8
1960	5,720	20.3	3,025	20.7
1965	6,880	20.0	3,223	15.8
1970	9,900	19.3	3,968	10.9
1971	10,320	19.7	4,137	10.8
1972	11,120	19.7	4,275	10.3
1973	12,050	19.3	4,520	9.7
1974	12,840	19.5	5,075	n.a.

*Percentage values were obtained by interpolation.

†Figures are for persons in poor families. They are a little higher than for families because poor families are generally of larger than average size.

Source: 1974 Statistical Abstract of the United States, Fuchs, op. cit., and Current Population Reports, "Money Income and Poverty Statistics of Families and Individuals in the United States," Bureau of the Census, U.S. Department of Commerce, series P-60, no. 99, July 1975.

made no move toward the rising expectations of an adequate standard based on an increased average standard of living. The poor have advanced, but no faster than anyone else.

We can debate which is the "correct" standard to use and can even concede that social strain is more closely associated with income disparity than with the relationship of low incomes to a stationary minimum subsistence standard. But regardless of the relevance to social problems of Fuchs's or any other relative poverty index, we must acknowledge that as of now the perhaps socially unrealistic Poverty Index serves as the guide to antipoverty policy. For better or for worse, it has the prestige of government acceptance, manifested through various agency calculations of the poverty population, and the influence of publicity through official publication and press reporting. But the calculated, if not widely circulated, data on the stagnant level of relative poverty explain why social pressures continue unabated for more active antipoverty programs, even while the "official" poverty count keeps falling.

Sociological Concept of Poverty

If the relative concept of poverty acknowledges that social satisfaction cannot be achieved by moving lowest-income families to the subsistence level, then the sociological view of poverty recognizes that man cannot live by bread alone.

While sociologists may differ on the characteristics and components of poverty, they are all concerned about the means of eliminating economic poverty—that is, of raising low incomes whether to a fixed subsistence or shifting relative standard. To them, income transfers are in themselves inadequate measures to treat the entire scope of poverty—poverty of the spirit, of social status, and of the pocketbook as well. The poor must become full participants in society. They must develop a feeling of self-esteem and achieve eligibility for important positions in social and political groups.

There is no necessary conflict between economic and sociological poverty reduction. In fact, appropriate income-raising measures can easily reduce both types of poverty simultaneously. What is appropriate is the creation of meaningful jobs which raise the holders' self-esteem as well as their incomes.

In his social construct of poverty, Dudley Jackson defines poverty as "inadequate social functioning"—not being gainfully employed, nor able to maintain a household, nor engaged in satisfying personal and social relationships.[16] It is this last that distinguishes sociological from purely economic poverty.

[16]Dudley Jackson, *Poverty,* Macmillan, New York, 1972, p. 13.

To Jackson, satisfying nutritional needs—or, by extension, the basic needs important in the Poverty Line income—through simple income transfers, satisfies only one, albeit the most fundamental, aspect of adequate social functioning. Wants would be fulfilled but the deprivation aspects of poverty—unemployment, inadequate family maintenance (through earnings), and inability to develop rewarding social relationships would remain.

Because of the basic nature of want satisfaction and its essentiality in the maintenance of health and attainment of a normal life span, poverty literature and policy prescriptions emphasize this aspect of poverty. As a practical matter, it is difficult to establish a sociological poverty line. Certainly, a dollar value cannot be put on such a line because it is not determined by money alone. But acknowledging a need for improving the noneconomic status of the poor explains the weakness of income transfer programs, even generous ones, in eliminating social pressures for further antipoverty action and the continual dissatisfaction of the now more solvent poor.

Alternatively, negative nonmonetary aspects of the life-style of the poor suggest that unqualified economic cost-benefit comparisons of various antipoverty programs may yield misleading policy signals to poverty-program decision makers. For example, a frequent test of the economic wisdom of an education or training program for the poor compares the net dollar gain in income of the poor from the program to the cost of the program. The presumption is that if program costs exceed the income gains, then the program is inefficient in reducing poverty and better results could have been achieved by a simple income transfer. But this method of calculation ignores the psychic gain to the poor, and to society as well, from the fuller development of skills and aptitudes, from the nonmonetary satisfaction of more meaningful jobs, and from the possible breakdown of the culture of poverty in which the poor feel trapped.

SUMMARY

The view that poverty was a random socioeconomic disease falling on individuals because of their own inadequacy or simple bad luck disappeared in the vortex of the Great Depression of the 1930s, which sucked the multitudes into economic disaster. Ever since that time, government has taken the responsibility for antipoverty action, although it has pursued the policy with varying degrees of enthusiasm and vigor.

An operational definition of poverty has evolved which, besides serving as a benchmark for measuring the effectiveness of governmental antipoverty programs, has also gained wide currency as *the* measure of poverty. Unfortunately, this Poverty Index is constructed on the basis of an "economy plan" food budget which is described by its Department of Agriculture formulators as a bare bones budget for emergency use only and insufficient to maintain normal health if followed for long periods of time. That the Poverty Line budget has almost doubled since its establishment in the early 1960s has no significance; since it only changed in response to price increases, the pitifully low standard of living it produces has remained unchanged.

The one attractive feature of the Poverty Line is its simplicity, both of calculation and interpretation. There is nothing vague about it; families who stay at this line are assured a life-style of economic misery, to say nothing of slow starvation if they follow the budgetary components faithfully. But a greater wonder than the means of survival adopted by those at the line is that in this great productive economy of ours, over 20 million people live below this level.

Apart from its obvious inadequacy to maintain a tolerable standard of living, the Poverty Line has other glaring deficiencies. It takes no account of the changing aspirations of the poor and expectations for them of the rest of society in response to the general rise of income in our expanding economy. The comparative living standard of the poor falls if it stays at a fixed level while everyone else's improves. Economists have suggested several measures of relative poverty, but even the easiest to calculate and comprehend—Fuchs's standard of one-half median family income—has not gained official recognition or popular acceptance.

Furthermore, any poverty index that sets a standard for economic adequacy ignores the nonmonetary needs of the poor. The culture of poverty features low self-esteem, fatalism, pessimism, and inadequate social functioning. Some but not all of these problems are solved by higher incomes. Thus the need remains, apart from statisfying their economic needs, for elevating the social status of the poor.

If we steadfastly follow the Poverty Line as the magic divider between inadequacy and economic sufficiency, we should not be surprised that social problems and pressures of poverty persist even as the number who remain on the wrong side of the line steadily and sometimes even rapidly declines. But economic analysis of poverty must take a practical approach. If statistics on the poor use the Poverty Line standard, if programs and policies are designed with reference to this unchanging real income level, we must treat the data and discuss the programs in their standardized terms even as we regret the inadequacy of the standard used.

Chapter 2

The Demography
of Poverty

The poor are classified and counted by various characteristics—age, sex, family size, educational attainment of family head, etc. The purposes of classification and enumeration are the same: to identify factors that lead to poverty and thereby aid in proposing corrective measures.

CLASSIFYING THE POOR

The General Poverty Rate

Before proceeding with the details of the background of the poor, an overview of the global poverty count will put the problem in perspective. Table 2-1 shows the strong downward trend in the proportion of the population considered poor since 1959, when poverty data were first recorded. While this trend has been slowing down in recent years,[1] the improvement in the poverty picture over the time has been undeniably substantial.

[1]Prosperous 1972 and 1973 did show substantial reductions in the poverty rate. But 1974 and 1975 data, when available, will undoubtedly show an upturn in the rate, associated with the recession.

Table 2-1 Percentage of Population below the Poverty Line, 1959–1973

Year	Percentage
1959	22.4
1960	22.2
1961	21.9
1962	21.0
1963	19.5
1964	19.0
1965	17.3
1966	14.7
1967	14.2
1968	12.8
1969	12.1
1970	12.6
1971	12.5
1972	11.9
1973	11.1

Source: Characteristics of the Low-Income Population," *Current Population Reports,* U.S. Census, P-60, no. 98, January 1975. All data in this chapter are from this comprehensive source or from the shorter, P-60, no. 93, July 1974 report.

But two factors, discussed in the previous chapter, take the edge off optimism about poverty reduction. First, the data are based on the Poverty Index calculation, thus putting a very low cutoff level on poverty. Then too, the reduction in the percentage poor makes no consideration for higher-income aspirations related to the strong, steady growth in average per capita spending power. Be that as it may, we are approaching the 10 percent level in the downward movement of the poverty rate, and since 1959, the actual number poor has fallen from about 40 million to less than 25 million people. Figure 2-1 depicts the trend in the poverty rate and the poverty count.

Classification of the Poor and the Causes of Poverty

There are many ways of breaking down the poverty count. The aim is not to multiply the poverty compartments but rather to focus on population subgroups which have a high poverty density.

High poverty rates imply that the subgroup has characteristics that induce poverty. The main cause of poverty is low earnings. At first view this statement seems a clear example of the classic error of explaining something by defining it—like saying rising prices cause inflation. But while poverty does mean low income, there are other components of income besides earnings—transfer receipts from the government being the largest supplement to low earnings.

In any case, we do not have to look far to find the basic cause of low earnings. Under our economic system, workers are paid what they are worth, in the crudest commercial sense of the word *worth* (meaning the value of their contribution to the output of the employer or purchaser of labor effort). Thus, incomes are low because earnings are low, and earnings are low when the value of a worker's services are low.

Only a fortunate few possess inherent talent that needs little training to be translated into high-paying effort. Without much training or education to develop aptitudes into marketable skills, the earning power of the rest of us would be mainly limited to what our simple physical strength and effort were worth on the market. Expressed more starkly, except for the few who are talented, the rest of us, without training and schooling, would all be poor. Thus we should expect poverty to be closely related to low levels of schooling. The low income population classified by years of schooling shows this relationship.

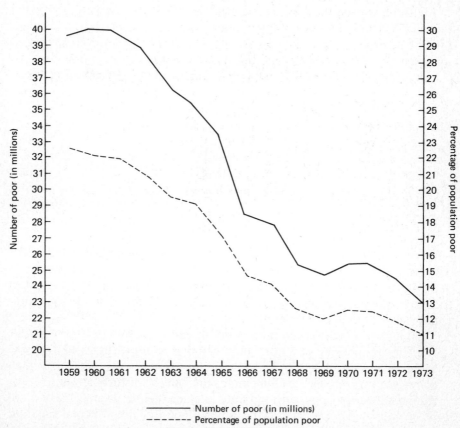

Figure 2-1   Trends in the number and percentage poor, 1959-1973.

To avoid poverty, earnings during working years must cover needs not only for these years but also for the lengthening nonwork periods of the life cycle. Our worklife as a share of total lifetime is shrinking both because we enter the labor force later, since we spend more years in school, and also because our Golden Age years stretch out longer as the average life span lengthens and the retirement age falls. We have not yet reached the stage when people retire in their senior year of college, but the trend is strong for a shorter period of work time that must cover the spending needs of a longer period without earnings.

In the case of children, this tendency toward poverty rises with increasing family size. While the poor do have more children than other families, an important factor leading to poverty among families with many children is that the earnings of the head and other household workers are unrelated to the number of mouths they have to feed. Having many children is an easy way to move many families below the poverty line.

Older people have relatively high poverty rates because their earnings during their work years, while perhaps adequate to cover consumption needs during that period, are often insufficient to make possible the accumulation of savings that will allow for an above-poverty retirement living standard. The economic problems of many aged are compounded by inadequate transfer receipts and sparse pension benefits untied to inflation, especially for those least able to finance later consumption needs from their own resources, those with low earnings and sporadic work histories.

Discrimination—or, more simply, unfair treatment—can also lead to poverty. Both blacks and women face discriminatory barriers to high earnings. In the case of blacks, bias affects every aspect of their chances to attain adequate living standards. Their early schooling is poorly financed and their families lack the resources to pay for higher education; their poverty living standard provides an unfavorable environment for economic advancement; discrimination in all aspects of work—hiring, retention, training, promotion—hampers their struggle for well-paying work. For women, the discrimination is not as all-encompassing; their educational levels are as high as men's and the family socioeconomic status of girls and boys is the same. But job discrimination alone is sufficient to keep women's earnings low and to cause high poverty rates among families headed by women.

Unemployment is another important cause of poverty. It is very difficult for purchasing power to stay effective when earnings fall to zero because of lack of work. There is no surprise in data that show high poverty rates among the unemployed, but a disturbing number of employed workers also earn too little to place their households above the poverty line. We are back to the starting point of the principal cause of poverty—inadequate earnings.

The bulk of this chapter examines the tendency toward poverty of individuals with the above-noted characteristics—those with little education, the young and the old, blacks and women, and the unemployed. Before studying the data, it is fitting to discuss the measurement standard of poverty for the individual population subgroups.

The Incidence of Poverty

A subgroup's contribution to the total poverty count depends on two factors, the size of the subgroup and the density of poverty within the group. For example, the poverty rate in the United States for those of Indonesian ancestry may be very high, but because there are few such people in the country, their high poverty rate would have little effect on the overall rate. On the other hand, while the poverty rate among whites is very low, the white poor add a substantial number to the poverty count because whites are by far the largest racial group in the population.

This size-group rate differential effect on the poverty population appears clearly in racial data. Among the total 24.5 million poor in 1972 were 16.2 million whites. The percentage of whites who were poor was 9.0 percent, significantly below the 11.9 percent overall rate. On the other hand, there were 7.7 million poor blacks, or 33.3 percent of the black population.

Thus while the *incidence* of poverty, the subgroup poverty rate, was more than $3^1/_2$ times greater for blacks, their contribution to overall poverty was less than 50 percent that of whites. Expressed in another way, 66.1 percent of the poor were white and 31.4 percent black. (The remaining poor were members of other races.)

The issue then is over which is the more important statistic, that there are more than twice as many poor whites than poor blacks or that the incidence of poverty among blacks is over $3^1/_2$ times greater. The answer to this question relates to the significance of the statistic for remedial action against poverty. That the incidence of poverty is low among whites indicates that race does not contribute to white poverty.

The high black rate suggests that there are racial reasons for black poverty. There is no mystery here; discrimination comes quickly to mind as an obvious factor inducing black poverty. Just as obvious is the policy implication. Removing discrimination, or making its practice more expensive by strictly enforced, strong equal opportunity laws, would cut deeply into black poverty. In the interim, income transfers and categorical training programs aimed at blacks would compensate somewhat for earlier lack of opportunities to develop skills and serve to raise the income levels of poor blacks.

In short, a high subgroup incidence of poverty signals antipoverty policy makers to focus their attention on the factors that induce poverty among the group. It is tempting to conclude that greater inroads on poverty would be made by designing programs for the much more numerous whites. But it is not negative treatment toward their race that makes many whites—albeit a small percentage of the white population—poor, but their low educational level, their large families, their age, or whatever characteristic *is* associated with poverty.

Even from a strictly economic point of view, the incidence of poverty is a more relevant statistic for antipoverty policy than the subgroup share of total poverty. A high incidence bodes well for extensive benefits from remedial measures aimed at reducing the subgroup's economic weakness. This does not mean that because of high incidence a scatter-gun approach is bound to hit some poverty aspects, but rather that a high incidence is likely to be associated with obvious factors inducing poverty for the subgroup in question, such as discrimination as a factor in black poverty. Thus the high incidence points to areas for high returns on the antipoverty dollar.

This conclusion arises irrespective of the size of the subgroup involved. Reconsider the hypothetical case of high poverty incidence among Indonesians. It might at first view seem, despite its high poverty rate, sheer fiscal extravagance to focus attention (expenditures) on this small population subgroup. But if there are specific causes of poverty among people of this ancestry, then corrective treatment of these factors will not involve much cost, because the number of people to be covered is small. Once again, the income-raising returns on the antipoverty dollar devoted to this small subgroup would be high.

Incidence is also the important statistic for social consideration. A high poverty rate for a definable subgroup leads to group solidarity, both in resentment and antagonism toward the rest of society. Women's liberation and black militancy have their noneconomic aspects, but low income for women and blacks and concomitant economic discrimination add strength to the movements. Then too, knowledge of high poverty incidence for particular subgroups awakens the social consciousness of the favored rest of society and leads to policies which will correct factors that limit the earnings capacity of the disadvantaged.

DISAGGREGATING THE POVERTY POPULATION

This section disaggregates the poverty population into the high-incidence components noted above. Education level, age, sex, race, and employment status breakdowns put numerical dimensions to the poverty facts we all know—that the less educated, the young, the old, households headed by women, blacks, and the unemployed and underemployed have high poverty rates. Simple enumeration is the purpose here. The chapters of

Part Two will examine the factors that relate poverty to these demographic characteristics.

Education and Poverty

There are those who claim that little schooling and low earnings levels are unrelated, but this view must argue against the close inverse relationship that exists between years of schooling and the incidence of poverty. Table 2-2 presents the data for American families. (Note the lower poverty rate, 8.8 percent, for families than for the whole population. The latter rate is 11.1 percent, which reflects the high poverty rate for unrelated individuals who are not considered as parts of family units.)

A clear pattern emerges in the crucial third column. The incidence of poverty falls as the educational level rises, crossing the overall poverty rate sharply at high school completion and ending with an insignificant rate for college graduates.

There is one interesting exception to the pattern. Note that the poverty rate for those with some high school lies above that for those with only an eighth-grade education, 11.6 percent compared to 10.2 percent.

Table 2-2 Family Poverty Rates by Educational Attainment of Head, 1973
(Numbers in Thousands)

	Total	Number in poverty	Percentage poor (incidence of poverty)	Percentage of all families at each educational level	Percentage of poor families at each educational level
All families*	55,053	4,828	8.8	100.0	100.0
Elementary school					
Less than 8 years	6,197	1,336	21.6	12.2	32.1
8 years	5,553	565	10.2	10.9	13.6
Total	11,750	1,901	16.2	23.1	45.7
High school					
1 to 3 years	8,022	932	11.6	15.8	22.5
4 years	16,824	914	5.4	33.1	22.0
Total	24,846	1,846	7.4	48.9	44.5
College					
1 year or more	14,200	405	2.9	28.0	9.8

*Data on education are for family heads 25 years of age and over. Thus subtotals would not add up total for all families.

There is no need for a lengthy explanation over one percentage point, but the data do support the view, at least superficially, that dropping out of school is bad household economics. Note the great poverty rate advantage of high school graduates (5.4 percent) to dropouts (11.6 percent).

The last two columns are included in Table 2-2 not to revive the notion that other values compare in importance with the subgroup rate in the analysis of poverty but rather to emphasize the difference in schooling received by poor and nonpoor. Note the clear tendency for lower educational levels among the poor. As we move up the schooling scale, the concentration of poor families thins out.

Again, we see a clear relationship between dropping out, or failing to finish a given educational level, and poverty. Over twice as many poor dropped out of grade school compared to those who reach the first educational plateau of grade school completion. Contrary to the trend for the population as a whole, the high school dropout rate was above 50 percent for the poor.

Education, Race, and Poverty

The racial breakdown of poverty by educational level offers important insights into the relationship of poverty to race. Table 2-3 presents the racial data for persons fourteen years old and over. (Note that the combined poverty rate, 9.8 percent, for this population lies below the overall rate of 11.1 percent, reflecting the high incidence of poverty among small children. However, it lies above the 8.8 percent family rate, shown in Table 2-2, because of the great incidence of poverty among unrelated individuals[2] who are included in Table 2-3.) Higher educational levels are not sharply defined in this table and in Table 2-2, with the college years simply classified as "1 year or more." But poverty is not a serious problem for those with even a little college, and in any case we can only study as much data as we are given.

To put it mildly, the data of Table 2-3 cast serious doubt on the argument that race is not an independent cause of poverty but is associated with other characteristics that are related to poverty, such as the low educational level of blacks. Note well that for every single educational level, the incidence of poverty among blacks is much greater than that of whites, running to almost four times as great at the high school level. Certainly, fewer years of schooling, to say nothing of their quality, play a part in black poverty, and the closeness of (the low) average school attainment between black and white poor attests to the importance of in-

---

[2]Unrelated individuals are those living alone (75.2 percent of the 16.8 million people in the group) or living with nonrelatives (24.8 percent).

adequate schooling as a cause of poverty. But if race itself plays no part, why are black poverty rates so much higher than white poverty rates at any schooling level?

The last two columns of Table 2-3 present provocative facts on racial difference in schooling levels. As expected, blacks have a relatively high proportion at low levels and a low proportion for higher education. The shares of both races at the high school level are almost identical. But how large a racial difference exists within the high school group?

The modal school attainment for whites is the high school graduate, while for blacks it is the high school dropout. We hear a great deal about the economic difficulties of the dropout, but Table 2-3 indicates that the dropout problem, at least insofar as it relates to poverty, applies almost exclusively to blacks. The data showing that the dropout proportion for blacks (28.0 percent) exceeds that for whites (19.9 percent) do not surprise us, but perhaps the racial difference in dropout poverty rates does.

At 8.4 percent, the incidence of poverty among white high school dropouts lies even below the overall national average of 9.8 percent for the population over fourteen years of age and just a little above the 7.4 percent overall white rate. For black dropouts, the poverty incidence is a hefty 31.3 percent, over three times the national average (although only slightly above the overall black poverty rate[3]) and 14.2 percentage points above the blacks who complete high school. Dropping out of high school really hurts—that is, if you happen to be black.

Education, Age, and Poverty

Everyone knows that the aged have a high incidence of poverty, but the question here is whether education has a role in the high poverty rate of the aged and whether age itself appears as an independent determinant of poverty. The answer is an unqualified yes to both questions.

Table 2-4 compares poverty rate–education levels for two age groups, twenty-two to thirty-four years and sixty-five years and over. The younger group includes all those with an opportunity to have had some college, and the older age group—the Senior Citizens, Golden Agers, or whatever euphemism we use to cover up our neglect—is the age class we associate with old-age poverty.

The incidence of poverty for the older class is more than double that of the younger group, 16.3 percent as compared to 7.8 percent, but the

---

[3]Dropout poverty rates related to the national rather than the racial average is the relevant comparison since the high poverty rate for black dropouts is a heavy contributor to the high overall black poverty rate.

Table 2-3 Incidence of Poverty among Persons 14 Years Old and Over by Educational Attainment and Race, 1973
(Numbers in Thousands)

Years of school completed	All races			Whites		
	Total	Number poor	Percentage poor	Total	Number Poor	Percentage poor
0 years of school	1,340	413	30.8	1,020	261	25.6
Elementary						
1 to 5 years	5,956	1,785	30.0	4,246	1,055	24.9
6 to 8 years	26,961	4,364	16.2	23,304	3,160	13.6
Total	32,917	6,149	18.7	27,550	4,215	15.3
High school						
1 to 3 years	32,475	3,824	11.8	27,547	2,312	8.4
4 years	53,211	3,218	6.0	48,267	2,408	5.0
Total	85,686	7,042	8.2	75,814	4,720	6.2
College (1 year or more)	37,340	1,823	4.9	34,414	1,536	4.5
Median years of school completed	12.2	9.9		12.3	10.2	
Total	157,284	15,428	9.8	138,798	10,733	7.7

incidence for those with little schooling is not significantly related to age. While poverty rates are very high for both age groups, it is worth noting that older people with only an elementary school education have a better poverty record than those in the younger age group unfortunate enough to have so little schooling. Older high school dropouts also do better.

But the pattern shifts as the schooling level advances. Poverty rates of those at high school completion and beyond are much higher for older workers.

These facts contradict the optimistic argument that older poverty, insofar as it is associated with low schooling levels, will disappear soon. This argument rests on the belief that the current aged will be replaced with more educated cohorts, since levels of educational attainment rise as we move down the age scale. No doubt the correlation between little schooling and poverty is strong—there is nothing in Table 2-4 that denies this relationship—and no doubt the current aged have little schooling. That just about 50 percent of them have only a grade school education is

Total	Blacks		Percentage of whites	Percentage of blacks
	Number poor	Percentage poor		
260	130	50.2	0.7	1.6
1,619	712	44.0	3.1	9.9
3,360	1,148	34.2	16.8	20.7
4,979	1,860	37.4	19.9	30.6
4,556	1,426	31.3	19.9	28.0
4,314	739	17.1	34.8	26.6
8,870	2,165	24.4	54.7	54.6
2,145	240	11.2	24.8	13.2
10.9	9.4			
16,254	4,396	27.0		

certainly disturbing. Finally, the future aged will surely come closer to the approximately 80 percent rate of the younger group who have at least a high school diploma; by comparison, only 33 percent of the current aged have reached this level.

But a higher educational level will not eliminate the problem of poverty among the aged, even if it will undoubtedly reduce their poverty rate. Note the relatively high poverty incidence of the older group for high school graduates and those with some college. The combined poverty rate for this educational attainment for the younger group is 5.4 percent, and for the older group it is 9.6 percent, or almost double.

Thus, though the poverty rate will probably fall sharply for the future aged as they attain more schooling than the current aged, the problem of aged poverty will remain; at least their relative poverty compared to younger people will be as great as it is today. The data carry a strong suggestion that there is more than inadequate schooling associated with aged poverty.

Table 2-4 Incidence of Poverty among 22 to 34-Year-Olds and Those 65 and Over, by Educational Attainment, 1973

Years of school completed	Persons 22 to 34-years-old				Persons 65-years-old and over			
	Total	Number poor	Percentage poor	Percentage in age group	Total	Number poor	Percentage poor	Percentage in age group
0 years of school completed	146	40	27.1	0.4	670	210	31.3	3.3
Elementary								
1 to 5 years	424	137	32.2	1.1	2,614	801	30.6	12.7
6 to 8 years	1,913	408	21.3	4.9	7,447	1,315	17.7	36.2
Total	2,337	545	23.3	6.0	10,061	2,116	21.0	48.9
High school								
1 to 3 years	4,975	793	15.9	12.6	3,042	395	13.0	14.7
4 years	16,659	958	5.8	42.3	3,919	390	10.0	19.0
Total	21,634	1,751	8.1	54.9	6,961	785	11.3	33.7
College (1 year or more)	15,255	718	4.7	38.7	2,911	244	8.4	14.1
Median years of school completed	12.7	12.2			8.9	8.2		
Total	39,371	3,053	7.8	100.0	20,602	3,354	16.3	100.0

Education, Sex, and Poverty

The poverty rate is higher for females, but as Table 2-5 shows, there is no sex difference in educational attainment. Not only do the sexes have the same 12.2 median years of schooling but there are, in addition, only negligible differences in concentration at each educational level. Proportionately fewer women are found to have completed college, but almost the same proportion of both sexes are shown to have gone through high school and beyond. These concentration rates are also the same at the lower end of the educational scale.

Thus we conclude that schooling is not a factor in the higher incidence of female poverty. Unlike blacks, women do not suffer from early discrimination which closes off educational opportunities to develop skills and earning power. But labor market discrimination is enough to raise the percentage of female poverty. Other factors do play a role in inducing poverty among women, but carrying over female labor market experience to blacks, we can forecast that the raising of black educational levels will not suffice to correct racial poverty imbalance. In fact, the current higher poverty rates for blacks at every educational level already tells us this.

Race and Poverty

No matter how we torture the data, how we correct for different variables—such as educational level, family size, location, etc.—the fact remains that blacks have much lower incomes than whites and the incidence of poverty among them is much greater. What is more, the poverty differential has persisted, with no discernible narrowing trend. Table 2-6 shows the long-run downward path in both black and white poverty rates. But the table also shows stability in the weak black position. In fact, there even seems to be a slight upward drift in the ratio of black to white poverty. But whether it is 3 or $3^1/_2$ times the white rate, the incidence of black poverty stands out as a national disgrace.

There has been substantial improvement, though, in the black poverty rate; 31.4 percent is better than 56.2 percent, even though black poverty is becoming more pronounced relatively. Apart from the fact that relative poverty carries the important social implications, is it not an ironical coincidence that, at 33.3 percent, the 1972 black poverty rate was exactly at that one-third level to which President Roosevelt, in 1937, in the depth of the Great Depression, dramatically referred in depicting the inadequacy of income and its distribution for the nation as a whole? Thus it can be said without exaggeration that blacks are in effect experiencing their own private "Great Depression."

Not only is the poverty rate relatively high for blacks but the average family deficit below the poverty line, a value indicating both the severity

Table 2-5 Incidence of Poverty among Males and Females 14 Years and Older, by Educational Attainment, 1973

Years of school completed	Males				Females			
	Total	Number poor	Percentage poor	Percentage of males	Total	Number poor	Percentage poor	Percentage of females
0 years of school completed	642	197	30.6	.09	698	216	31.0	0.8
Elementary								
1 to 5 years	3,059	803	26.3	4.1	2,897	982	33.9	3.5
6 to 8 years	13,417	1,710	12.7	17.9	13,545	2,654	19.6	16.5
Total	16,476	2,513	15.3	22.0	16,442	3,636	22.1	20.0
High school								
1 to 3 years	14,956	1,260	8.4	20.0	17,519	2,564	14.6	21.3
4 years	22,789	1,021	4.5	30.3	30,422	2,197	7.2	37.0
Total	37,745	2,281	6.0	50.3	47,941	4,761	9.9	58.3
College (1 year or more)	20,176	781	3.9	26.8	17,164	1,042	6.1	20.9
Median years of school completed	12.2	9.4			12.2	10.1		
Total	75,040	5,772	7.7	100.0	82,244	9,656	11.7	100.0

of poverty where it exists and the difficulty in reducing poverty, is also higher for blacks. While the white deficit averages $1,126 per family, for blacks an average of $1,400 would be needed to bring poor families to the poverty level.

Poverty rates are also high among people of Spanish origin. The 1972 overall rate of 23.7 percent places them almost midway between the black and white rates. But when we remove Cubans, with their low 9.1 percent poverty rate, and Central and South Americans, with their moderate 13.7 percent, we are left with 27.6 percent for those of Mexican origin and 30.0 percent for Puerto Ricans, both comparable to the black incidence.

Age and Poverty

Children Poverty among children is easy to explain. They contribute nothing to family income but add to consumption expenses. Childless families have a 6.2 percent poverty rate, and the rate rises sharply with increases in the number of children. For families with one or two children the rate is 8.8 percent; for those with three and four children, it is 14.7 percent; and for larger families with five or more children, the rate jumps to 30.3 percent (1972 data).

The Aged Few older people work, most do not have assets on which they might realize substantial nonlabor income, and many receive very low public transfer payments and pension benefits, a combination of factors that raises the odds for aged poverty and explains the high (16.3 percent) rate of poverty among the aged as compared with the overall (11.1 percent) rate.

An earlier section of this chapter pointed out that the higher poverty rate for the aged could not be explained by their lower education level alone. It was noted that while the poverty rate for workers aged twenty-two to thirty-four with at least a high school diploma was only 5.4 percent, for people over sixty-five with the same schooling the rate was 9.6 percent.

But disaggregation of the age-education data by sex shows that this weakness in aged income, which is unrelated to education, is almost entirely limited to females. Younger males with higher education have a 4.3 percent poverty rate, and for older workers this rate is 6.0 percent. The latter is admittedly a higher rate but one that poses no serious social poverty problem. For females, on the other hand, the comparable age-education poverty rates are 6.1 percent for younger women and a high 13.6 percent for older women.

These figures tell us clearly that old-age poverty is a manifestation of income differences between the sexes. Women are less able than men to

Table 2-6 Percentage in Poverty by Race of Family Head, 1959–1973

Year	Black percentage*	White percentage	Ratio of black to white poverty
1959	56.2	18.1	3.1
1960	55.9	17.8	3.1
1961	56.1	17.4	3.2
1962	55.8	16.4	3.4
1963	51.0	15.3	3.3
1964	49.6	14.9	3.3
1965	47.1	13.3	3.5
1966	41.8	11.3	3.7
1967	39.3	11.0	3.6
1968	34.7	10.0	3.5
1969	32.2	9.5	3.4
1970	33.5	9.9	3.4
1971	32.5	9.9	3.3
1972	33.3	9.0	3.7
1973	31.4	8.4	3.7

*Data prior to 1966 include nonwhite races. This difference does not distort the figures, since the poverty rate for these other races usually lies only one or two points below the black rate.

retain the higher earning capacity that advanced education produces into old age. At this point we can modify our earlier statement that broadened educational attainment would not solve the problem of aged poverty. We can, instead, state that it would go a long way to doing so if means could be found to improve the opportunities of older women to take advantage of earnings skills developed through schooling.

Whatever income handicaps may be suffered by women accentuate the incidence of older poverty because of the simple fact that so many more women than men reach old age. In 1972 there were 11.8 million female "Golden Agers" and only 8.3 million males. When both husband and wife are present in an older family, any employment handicaps that affect the woman can add to their mutual poverty. If the longer life span of women is reflected in better health at the same old age for both sexes, and if better health allows for greater employment potential, then age discrimination in employment focused on women can substantially reduce old-age family income. Data are not available for testing this hypothesis or for measuring the extent to which arbitrarily limited employment opportunities for older women drag their families, including nonworking husbands, into poverty.

Female Poverty

We have already discussed aspects of female poverty, those associated with educational level and age. Here we examine the overall differences between male and female poverty and search for other factors that lead to the higher incidence of female poverty.

We can assume that there is no difference in poverty rates by sex in husband-wife families because family members share income. But our first reaction must be one of shock at the wide gulf in poverty rates between families headed by males (5.5 percent) and those headed by females (32.2 percent). Are sexual differences in earnings potential really that great?

To approach this question, we should wonder why, among the 55.1 million families reported in 1973, the Census Bureau lists 48.3 million as headed by males and only 6.8 million with female heads. There is a simple explanation for this discrepancy: the Census Bureau is guilty of sexist reporting. Every family which has both husband and wife present is categorized as a "family with male head." Conversely, every female-headed family has the characteristic of no husband present. The Census Bureau does not consider the possibility that a husband-wife family may be headed by the woman.

If we use as the economic definition of family head the member who earns the most money, ideally, to compare family poverty by sex of head, we would want those families in which the wife earned more than the husband to be included in the family-headed-by-female category. Alternatively, we could make a narrower study by breaking out of the reported male-headed families those which had no wife present, so that these families could be compared with the reported female-headed ones.

But as Table 2-7 on family earners suggests, despite the sexist reporting of the Census Bureau, little insight into the source of female poverty would be gained by these modifications, despite their sociological merit.

Certainly the working wife's contribution to income reduces the poverty rate for male-headed households—from 6.6 percent when the man alone worked to 2.1 percent when his wife worked too. But 6.6 percent is itself a low poverty rate, so that single-worker, male-headed households do quite well without the wife's earnings.

One-worker female-headed families, though, do not have as much success in avoiding poverty. The poverty rate for these families in which the woman is the only worker is a high 30.0 percent, about four-and-a-half times the 6.6 percent comparable male rate.

But a great deal of the discrepancy in rates can be explained by the preponderance of part-time or at best less than full-year, full-schedule work effort by women. Note that the single-worker, female-headed house-

Table 2-7 Poverty by Family Earners and Sex of Head, 1973
(Numbers in Thousands)

	Male-headed families			Female-headed families		
	Total	Number poor	Percentage poor	Total	Number poor	Percentage poor
No earners	4,097	760	18.5	1,684	1,081	64.2
One earner	16,569	1,164	7.0	3,034	859	28.3
Head an earner	14,913	980	6.6	2,219	666	30.0
Worked year round, full time	11,400	449	3.9	1,097	115	10.4
Worked less than year round, full time	3,513	531	15.1	1,122	551	49.1
Wife an earner	1,096	107	9.8	X*	X	X
Worked year round, full time	486	17	3.5	X	X	X
Other relatives are earners	560	77	13.8	815	193	23.7
Two or more earners	27,583	711	2.6	2,086	253	12.1
Head an earner	27,151	659	2.4	1,812	184	10.1
Worked year round, full time	21,299	267	1.3	1,068	42	3.9
Wife an earner	21,973	472	2.1	X	X	X
Head not an earner	432	52	12.1	273	69	25.3
Total families	48,249	2,635	5.5	6,804	2,193	32.2

*X = Not applicable

holds in which the woman works full time have a poverty rate of only 10.4 percent. This is certainly higher than the comparable male rate of 3.9 percent, and there is no attempt here to gloss over the sexual difference in earnings potential; but certainly 10.4 percent is not a high poverty rate and is much closer to the comparable male rate than the global family differential by sex of head.

The high 30.0 percent rate among women earners in families they head, though, derives from their less-than-total work effort. The poverty rate for the single-worker families in which the woman alone worked less than a full schedule was an enormous 49.1 percent. The comparable figure for men in families they headed was only 15.1 percent, a high rate but not in the same class as the female rate.

Obviously, part-time work is not as great an earning handicap for men as for women. We need to know more about the differences by sex in the size of the gap from full-schedule work effort, the types of jobs held, the rates of pay, and the degree of work choice in shorter schedules to find explanations for the high poverty rate differential by sex for those who work less than full schedules. But at this stage we can conclude that households headed by women have relatively higher poverty rates partly because women earn less than men when both work full time. But the difference exists mainly because relatively more women work part time (50.3 percent of working women in households they head to 24.0 percent for men) and because the poverty incidence among families headed by a below-full-schedule working woman is so much greater than the comparable value for men.

Poverty and Unemployment and Underemployment

Certainly not having any earnings increases the odds of becoming poor and remaining in poverty. Moreover, full-time, full-year work will reduce the chances of poverty compared to the incidence among those who work less than full, permanent schedules. Table 2-8 presents overall family poverty data by employment status of head.

Table 2-8   Poverty by Employment Status of Family Head, 1973
(Numbers in Thousands)

	Total	Number in poverty	Percentage poor	Percentage of poverty population
Employed	41,780	1,989	4.8	41.2
Unemployed	1,345	263	19.5	5.5
Not in labor force	11,066	2,560	23.3	53.0
In Armed Forces	921	16	1.8	0.3
Total	55,053	4,828	8.8	100.0

The table shows that the contribution of measured unemployment[4] to overall poverty is very slight. Only 4.8 percent of poor families are headed by an unemployed worker. But of greater significance is the high incidence of poverty among the unemployed and those not in the labor force.

There is a risk of jumping to an erroneous policy conclusion here. It might seem that all that is needed is to find jobs for the unemployed and, with even greater effort, to reduce the number not in the labor force by improving employment opportunities, and the poverty rate would fall to such a low level as to eliminate poverty as an important socioeconomic problem.[5] But poverty reduction is not that simple. Poverty not only results from not working but also from being underemployed—defined here as working at less than full schedules and working at low-paying jobs.

Individuals working full year, full time have a poverty rate of only 2.8 percent, but those who work full time 26 weeks or less have a 14.6 percent rate, and part-timers have an 11.5 percent rate. The type of work performed also has its differential poverty rate. At the extreme, the rate is only 1.0 percent for salaried managers (one wonders why any of them are poor) to 10.8 percent for non-farm laborers, 30.7 percent for farm laborers, and an astronomical 51.9 percent for (mostly female) private household workers (1972 data).

What jobs have the most underemployed? What jobs can those not in the labor force become prepared to fill? If the answer to both questions is "low-wage jobs," then jobs alone will not solve the poverty problem. But we are here approaching issues best discussed in Chapter 7, on the causal relationship between unemployment, underemployment, and poverty.

SUMMARY

The overall poverty rate has been declining over the past 15 years, with a recent slowdown in the trend. But while the rate falls, the social problem of poverty remains, both because the poverty level itself sets a very low purchasing power threshold and makes no allowance for adjustment to rising expectations with rising average incomes and because poverty is strongly concentrated among particular population subgroups.

The incidence of poverty is high among the lesser educated, blacks, women, children, older people, the unemployed and nonworkers. These demographic characteristics often operate in combination to strengthen

[4]That official unemployment statistics might understate the number who should be counted is a thorny issue, treated in detail in Chapter 7.

[5]Let us hope that those who, on the basis of Table 2-8, recommend increasing the Armed Forces for the purpose of reducing poverty do so facetiously.

subgroup poverty rates. For example, while the incidence of poverty is closely related inversely to educational level, the tendency is most pronounced for blacks who drop out of high school.

Blacks have less schooling than whites, but their poverty is greatly independent of their lower educational attainment since their poverty rates are higher for every educational level. Older people are by far the least educated population age group. But since their differential poverty rate, compared to the national average, is greatest for the more educated, it is unlikely that rising future educational levels of the aged—an inevitable consequence of our expanding educational attainment—will do much to remedy their pronounced poverty status. Girls and boys reach the same schooling levels, so education plays no part in the higher poverty rate for women.

Black poverty far exceeds the white level, and the race differential in poverty rates has not diminished over time. Moreover, the average income deficit below the poverty line is much higher for blacks, indicating the severity of the difficulties facing programs designed to reduce black poverty.

Poverty is high at both ends of the life span. The incidence of poverty among children rises sharply with family size because children add to household consumption needs without contributing to income. Poverty of the aged is closely associated with female poverty. Higher-educated females are much less able to sustain their earning power into old age than can similarly schooled males. The particular aspects of female poverty are most influential in aged poverty because of the preponderance of women in the older population.

The greatest overall subgroup poverty difference occurs between male- and female-headed households. Census reporting manifests sexist bias in that it classifies all husband-wife households as headed by males and thereby considers all female-headed households as those in which there is no husband present. Nevertheless, the data indicate much higher rates for this classification of female-headed households than comparable male-headed households, in which the wife does not contribute to income. The major sources of poverty differences between the two household types lie in the higher proportion of nonworking women, in the tendency for more women than men to work less than full schedules, and in women's much higher poverty rates when both work only part time and/or part year.

As expected, the data show high poverty rates for the unemployed. But while the rate is low for those who work, finding jobs for the unemployed and those not now in the labor force who could become employable will not necessarily greatly reduce the overall poverty rate. The rate is high for those working less than full schedules and for many low-paying occupations. What is needed are good full-schedule jobs.

Putting poverty in a positive perspective, the poverty rate for thirty-five- to fourty-four-year-old white males with one year or more of college is a mere 2.2 percent. But for black women over sixty-five with less than a sixth-grade education, the rate is 52.3 percent. What a complex story of the income benefits of schooling and of race, sex, and age bias lies behind this differential!

The next section on the causes of poverty attempts to uncover this story. In addition it studies the more proximate causes of poverty —labor force participation, unemployment, and low-paying jobs.

Part Two

Causes of Poverty

Chapter 3

Education and Poverty

For better or worse, our economic system distributes earnings according to the principle that a worker is paid what he or she is worth. In this context, "worth" does not refer to the personal qualities of an individual but to the value of his productive effort to the purchaser of his services, whether to his employer or, in the case of the self-employed, to the immediate user of his services. Redistribution of income can mitigate the devil-take-the-hindmost consequences of such a distributional system, but the inequality in earnings resulting from wide differentials in value of labor services still leads to sharp disparities in income, with those at the bottom of the distribution forming the poverty population.

The value of our labor service, or, expressed more familiarly, our earning power needs development. Even genius and talent require training, study, and conditioning to achieve meaningful expression; therefore the vast remainder of us—if armed only with our undirected and unrefined native intelligence, aptitudes, and physical strength—would make very weak income generators indeed. We can liken an individual as a factor of production to undeveloped land which requires the implementation of capital to raise its productivity. There are differences in resource endowment in land, with some areas more kindly treated by nature than others; so too are there differences in native endowment among individuals, which make them more or less susceptible to economic development through capital investments. But without these investments, the best land and the most generously endowed individuals would have little earning power.

Thus, the link between earnings and human attributes is forged by human capital, the earning power embodied in the individual through investment in education and training which develops skills and aptitudes. But this investment in people takes money, and lack of human investment funds contributes to the vicious circle of poverty. People are poor because they have little invested in themselves, and poor people do not have the funds for human capital investment.

Government intervention aids in breaking the circle. Public financing of education provides investment at least through high school, regardless of the individual's ability to pay taxes for his or her share of schooling costs. That public financing of college education falls far short of the total costs publicly underwritten for lower schooling levels weakens the anti-poverty effect of governmental schooling support, since the sharpest reduction in poverty incidence by education level occurs among the college educated.

Despite the soundness of the theory that ties development of earning capacity to schooling and despite the clarity of the data showing the inverse relationship between schooling level and poverty, there are those who argue that our income distribution is unaffected by the quality and quantity of schooling received.

Before discussing this argument, which if true would prove so damaging to the view that sees the schools as an important agent of poverty alleviation, this chapter begins with a restatement and elaboration of the association between low incomes and little schooling. Then the efficiency of the American educational system in raising the earning potential of its students is examined in the context of the fundamental issue of whether education should be geared to occupational development.

Whether or not schools are designed to raise earning power, they should develop intellectual capacity. The argument that schools receive poor grades in this effort warrants our interest for two reasons: (1) if valid, it questions the need for schools insofar as their academic functions are concerned and (2) more pertinent to the present discussion, it questions whether more or different schooling can raise poverty-level incomes, assuming that intellectual development leads to higher earnings potential. Of course, if the latter relationship is denied, then the issue of whether schools perform their educational function adequately becomes irrelevant to the poverty question.

EDUCATION, WORK, AND POVERTY

Data presented in the last chapter showed an undeniably close relationship between schooling level and poverty (see Table 2-2). The incidence of poverty falls with each increase in schooling level except that it is greater for high school dropouts than eighth-grade finishers.

Occupation, Education, and Poverty

More schooling opens up opportunities for better-paying, more stable jobs. Whether schooling is really necessary for adequate job performance is an issue to be discussed later in the chapter, but at this stage, we can at least point out the connection between poverty rates, occupation, and average schooling levels. Table 3-1 reveals a sharp pattern in the relationship among the variables. Poverty rates are less for those occupations having highest educational levels. (The only occupations slightly out of place in this relationship are those of clerical workers and female household workers. The fact that their poverty rates are higher than those of workers in the occupations immediately below them in educational attain-

Table 3-1 Educational Level and Incidence of Poverty by Occupational Classification, 1973

Occupational group	Median years of schooling	Poverty rate percent*
Professional and technical workers	16.3	1.7
Managers and administration	12.9	2.3
Sales workers	12.7	3.5
Clerical workers	12.6	5.1
Craftsmen and kindred workers	12.2	3.2
Nonfarm laborers	11.2	9.9
Private household workers (female)	9.6	48.3
Farm laborers	9.4	29.7

*Poverty rates are for those who worked during the year, and are for households by occupation of longest held job of head.

Source: Data on poverty rates are from *Characteristics of the Low Income Population* and on median years of schooling from *Manpower Report of the President*, 1973, Table B-12, p. 181.

ment reflects lower earnings of women.) This pattern can be easily explained by the job stability and high earnings that characterize occupations whose workers have higher schooling levels.

Education, Poverty, and Labor Force Activity

Workers fit one of three labor force classifications: they are either employed, unemployed, or not in the labor force in that they are not "ready, willing, and able to work, plus actively seeking employment." Obviously, the chances for poverty receive a strong boost when individuals earn nothing, either because of unemployment or nonparticipation in the labor force.

There is no need to overstate the connection between low education and work instability, and it should be noted that the Labor Department reports little difference, in 1972, between educational level of the employed and unemployed. Average years of schooling for the two groups are 12.4 and 12.0[1] respectively, and it is pointless to build an argument, based on this small difference, for schooling as a means of avoiding unemployment.

Given the rising percentage of people who reach at least the high school completion level—almost 70 percent of the labor force in 1972—it is difficult for a large difference to appear in educational level by employment status. The schooling level has risen even for jobs which are more susceptible to periods of unemployment.

But a high incidence of poverty is experienced by the largest group of nonworkers, those not in the labor force; furthermore, nonparticipation is greatest for the less educated. Of course, this association partly reflects the lower education of older people, who also tend to be out of the labor force. But this interrelationship of age, nonparticipation, and low schooling does not tell the whole story of the tendency for the less educated to be outside the work force. Table 3-2 shows that participation rates are less the lower the educational level among both sexes for most age groups.

This association is looser among the younger age groups, but the higher participation rate for young male high school graduates compared with men who have some college is easily explained by the fact that many of the latter are still in college and not yet in the labor force. Similarly, the presence of young college graduates in graduate school explains the slightly lower rate for college compared to high school graduates. For women, though, the tendency for graduate study is less;

---

[1]William V. Deutermann, "Educational Attainment of Workers, March 1972," *Monthly Labor Review,* November 1972, pp. 38–42.

Table 3-2 Labor Force Participation Rates of Men and Women Eighteen Years Old and Over, by Age and Educational Attainment, March 1972

Sex and age	Less than 4 years of high school	4 years of high school	1 to 3 years of college	4 or more years of college
Men:				
18–24	75.7	83.3	64.9	81.4
25–34	73.7	97.7	94.1	95.5
35–44	93.2	97.5	97.3	99.0
45–54	90.3	95.5	96.0	97.2
55–64	75.4	86.4	88.3	89.3
65 and over	21.4	29.6	35.2	37.7
Women:				
18–24	38.5	60.0	54.7	80.5
25–34	39.7	47.3	49.9	61.5
35–44	48.3	54.3	52.6	61.1
45–54	47.0	58.0	59.0	69.4
55–64	36.3	47.8	47.6	60.9
65 and over	7.7	11.5	11.8	19.4

Source: William V. Deutermann, "Educational Attainment of Workers, March 1972," *Monthly Labor Review,* November 1972.

consequently the participation rate for young women college graduates is higher than for any other female age-education subgroup.

It is most important, in connection with the present discussion of the relationship between education and poverty, to note that participation rates in each age-sex group are lowest for the least educated with the single exception of the special case of young men with some college. Certainly low earnings from jobs with lower educational requirements contribute to the high incidence of poverty among the lesser educated; but the data of Table 3-2 suggest an additional factor—the lower labor force participation rates of the lesser educated. It is difficult to avoid poverty when you are working at a job with minimal educational requirements; it is almost impossible when you are not working at all.

THE AMERICAN SCHOOL SYSTEM AS ANTIPOVERTY AGENCY

School Purposes and Functions

The American School system would challenge the very title of this section. The purpose of schooling is education, and schools do not look upon themselves as antipoverty agencies or vocational training centers. But insofar as poverty is avoided by career preparation, it is by no means obvious that schools have no obligation to prepare their students for their later and longer worklife. Adequate preparation involves more than the provision of basic educational tools (which provide a background necessary for the attainment of occupational skills) and the development of patterns of discipline and responsibility necessary for successful work; these are functions the schools willingly assume. But adequate career preparation involves the preliminary development of occupational skills themselves—skills to be further refined by actual work experience. The school system might take issue with the recommendation that it undertake this aspect of career preparation. Educators would admit the need for vocational education and even vocational schools within the system, but—judged by the curriculum and performance of American grade and high schools and not by the lip service paid to vocational training—only a small percentage of students receive substantial occupational training or even career guidance and direction. Furthermore—and most significant—this percentage is also low for those who do not go on to college but terminate their schooling before or after high school completion. What quantity of human investment does education provide them?

In the old days, when the average American quit school by the eighth grade, the question of education's role in career preparation had little meaning. No one expects great advances to be made in the occupational development of eleven- or twelve-year-olds. Those who stayed on in school formed the academic elite who found good or at least above-poverty-wage jobs no matter how desultory their work preparation, a pattern similar to that of the college-educated today.

But over the years we have pushed the average school-leaving age upward, and compulsory education confines the young to school during important years for career development. While there is little economic loss from inadequate preparation for work to those twelve years old or under—those who typically terminated their schooling in bygone years—a slow work start associated with floundering in school at sixteen and seventeen can be permanently damaging to the prospects for meaningful jobs for many of today's youth. Furthermore, the large number forced to attend school almost through high school reduces the prestige value of school at this level and pushes into college the education that will lead to good jobs, regardless of lack of specific preparation for them.

All the above does not argue that schools should confine education to adequate vocational preparation but that the increase in years of schooling attained, either in response to legal compulsion or social pressures, into the early years of maturity obligates education to include this function. In a brief essay on education and problems of youth employment, Mincer suggests that the scope of modern education may be too much for schools to undertake and that the cooperation of other institutions must be enlisted. It really does not matter under what organizational structure occupational preparation is provided as long as it is offered to the young before it is too late to help them toward better jobs.

According to Mincer, " . . . education of the young involves transmission of knowledge, socialization, identification, and encouragement of talent, preparation for work and orientation toward future personal, household and public responsibilities."[2] On the surface, education satisfying these goals would result in excellent preparation for a politician. But whether it will allow the student a wider selection of occupations that will push his or her earnings above the poverty level depends on the schooling system's interpretation of the function "preparation for work." If it means nothing more than acquainting the student with the work setting and its requirements and characteristics—or building in him or her habits of stability, punctuality, regular attendance, and discipline needed to hold a job—little will be done to ready the eighteen-year-old for a job that will yield a steady income above the poverty level. On the other hand, for schools to contribute more than a holding function for children before throwing them into the labor market as young men and women—where, it is hoped, luck and the natural process of maturation will lead them to good jobs—requires a conscious effort to develop occupational aptitudes and skills, at least during the last years of high school.

Career Planning in the Schools— International Comparisons

A U.S. Office of Education study claims "that over 80% of the nation's youth, leaving or graduating from [high] school, are unable or ill-equipped to enter the labor force."[3] Since 40 percent go on to higher education, if we assume one-half of the 20 percent considered prepared for work are in the college group, this leaves 50 percent of the nation's youth finished with their schooling and not ready for work.

There is no need to pillory the school systems for this great head start toward poverty that is provided for half our nation's youth. Perhaps other institutions should be developed to prepare the young for work. But obviously something is wrong with our system of education and management of our children if half of them face the responsibility of earning a living "ill-equipped to enter the labor force."

The school system itself has responded to the challenge and has recently expressed interest in *career education*, a vague term but one which expresses a yearning for secondary schooling that will give the

[2]Jacob Mincer, *Youth, Education and Work*, National Bureau of Economic Research Report Supplement, January 1973, p. 6.
[3]"Vocational Education for the 70's," U.S. Office of Education, 1971, p. 3.

student better direction toward good jobs. At best, career education involves cooperation with local employers and schools that focus on vocational training to provide the student with educational tools, skill training, and some work experience. Then the student can enter the labor market successfully after high school graduation if he or she wishes to leave school then.

We should not criticize the tentative beginning of career education but can hope that budgetary stringencies will be relaxed to permit expansion of programs successfully begun. The current career education programs of the city of Milwaukee offer a microcosm of the beginning national movement.[4] In 1973, about 700, or 10 percent, of the city's high school seniors were enrolled in career development programs which prepared students for employment in distribution, office work, production jobs in industry, and in health occupations.[5] The students spend half their time in school and the other half at work, where they receive a training wage. They sometimes receive specific job training at their schools or at a vocational school, and their schoolwork itself is heavily laden with career education subjects—they will have some course work in labor relations, employee rights and benefits, work attitudes, and industrial safety.

The programs have a successful record of later job placement. But apart from their limited coverage of the population they could beneficially serve, they are criticized for tending to reach students who already show promise for solid employment futures. In keeping with the American tradition of free choice among a variety of schooling options, participation in the programs is voluntary, a procedure that screens out the less motivated. Futhermore, requirements of regular attendance and good academic standing, with the probability of graduation within a year, excludes the less able or the weaker school performers. Thus, adherence to the principle of voluntary participation and concern with a record of program success may greatly improve the work experience of those with a high potential for employment success but does little to cut into the core of the poverty problem. This requires special programming for the less motivated and less able, those least likely to profit from general instructional educational programs.

How different from the American schooling system—with its emphasis on voluntarism, sameness of educational content (if not quality of cov-

---

[4]Many school systems have developed various forms of career education programs. For a recent appraisal of their performance, see William Deegan, G. Theodore Elmgren, Milo Johnson, and Gordon Ray, "Career Education: Progress, Proposals and Problems," *Thrust for Educational Leadership,* November 1972.

[5]Career education in Milwaukee is discussed in Peter Kobrak and Richard Perlman, *Toward a Comprehensive Manpower Plan: Milwaukee Needs, Programs, and Strategies,* Milwaukee Urban Observatory, 1974.

erage), and passing interest in career preparation—is the European system of screening, selection, academic channeling, and career development. In Germany, for example, children are tested early, and those who score well in their national scholastic exams are channeled towards vigorous academic training for the rest of their school lives. Thus they become prepared for careers in government, diplomacy, business leadership, and the professions. The much more numerous others are directed toward careers in trades and office work, with preparation for those jobs begun in the middle childhood years.

Figure 3-1 shows the structure of the German school system, with its turns and channels all carefully designed to place the student into an employment niche that appears to suit the early indications of his or her aptitudes. The system practically prevents any student from escaping career preparation and falling into the labor market undirected and "ill-equipped." Note that while Figure 3-1 shows the detailed direction received by German children and youth, it also reveals barriers to opportunity for late choice for higher education. In theory, all children receive the same education until their eleventh year. But the chart obscures differences in basic school quality, or more specifically, in preparatory efforts for the exams taken by all (not shown on the chart) at the close of basic school, which determine their future school course.

Only about 25 percent are channeled from basic school into (academic) high school, and most of them make it on to college. But only a few of the 75 percent who do not score high enough on their eleventh-year exam to qualify for high school can get to university later. Thus the German educational system goes a long way toward saving its youth from aimless thrashing about in the labor market, and it reduces if it does not eliminate the possibility that sporadic employment and low earnings—unrelated to a business downturn—will contribute to poverty. But at the same time, it imposes career decisions based on educational attainment on children.

The antipoverty aspects of highly structured European educational systems do not recommend them as the best of all possible systems. Even Europeans have their doubts. The "eleven-plus" examination in Great Britain—which, like the German test, screens young children to channel their future schooling—has come under fire as being too arbitrary, too restrictive, and even unfair, since children whose families stress education have the advantage of examination preparation.

At what a tender age are competitive pressures imposed! As evidence of this pressure, in some countries the child's mother is permitted to sit in during the examination that everyone knows will determine his or her future career. That the Copenhagen telephone book reads like the yellow pages, with subscribers listed alphabetically by occupation, may serve as silent testimony of the success of the Danish educational sys-

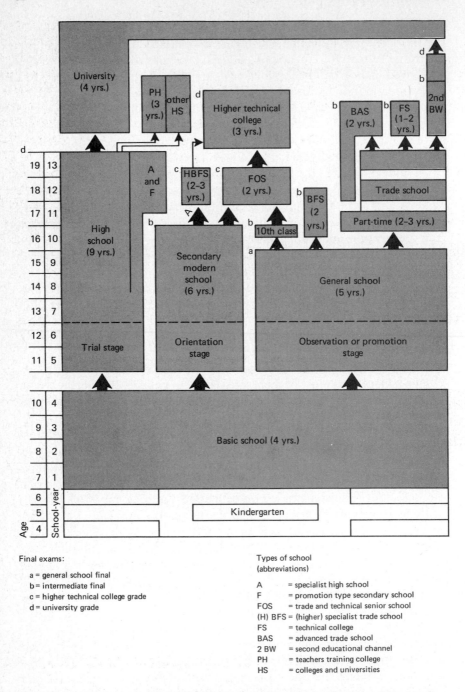

Figure 3-1 Educational channels in the Federal Republic of Germany. (*Source:* German Information Center, New York City.)

tem in employment preparation; but it also implies the crucial importance to self-esteem and public regard associated with one's place in the occupational hierarchy.

What is obviously needed is a compromise between the American and European systems. Grafted onto our principles of "the second chance" and free choice must be closer direction and guidance as well as curriculum emphasis on career development. While we might find a system that forecloses opportunities at an early age too restrictive, free choice becomes no choice but a hard life of employment uncertainty if we let our youth slide through the school years "ill-equipped for the labor force."

INEQUALITY IN EDUCATION

Knowledge, Education, and Earnings

Earnings in later life depend on a multitude of factors. There is first the child's background, his or her immediate culture of family and associates. Are the child's parents well off? Closely knit? Intelligent? Ambitious for his or her future? Does the child have few brothers and sisters competing for parental attention and resources? Are the child's friends and associates ambitious for success so that he or she is raised in an environment in which competition stimulates motivation? Is the child free from the handicaps of discrimination?

A yes answer to all these questions forecasts later success in work, especially if for our purposes we define *success* modestly, as earning enough through work to avoid poverty. Note these questions do not touch at all on the individual's mental capacity or mental development through education.

Economists have long puzzled over the skewness of the income distribution, which shows a bunching of the population toward the lower end of the scale and a tapering off toward higher income levels. Intelligence, on the other hand, is normally distributed. It would be attributing too much to schooling as a conditioner of intelligence affecting earnings to link the income distribution to the modern schooling distribution, which has also developed a pronounced positive skew, with most people attaining twelve years of education and the number going on for still more years gradually dwindling.

A much simpler explanation of the difference between income and intelligence distribution holds that income depends on many variables other than the ability to think—the easiest, if not clearest, definition of intelligence. Let psychologists, sociologists, and geneticists worry about the essential nature of intelligence and its development and transmission. For our limited purposes, we are searching for a word that expresses competency in the language arts, or communication through writing and speaking, and in basic mathematical calculations and problem solving.

Command of these skills as a minimum will enable their possessor to qualify for jobs such as selling or machine work, both yielding above poverty-level earnings, provided he or she acquires other techniques and knowledge more closely related to this work. These cognitive skills, or knowing through understanding, depend on the individual's native capacity to learn, and the amount that has been learned at school.

Psychologists have been trying heroically to develop a culture-free intelligence test that measures pure reasoning power. They probably have very good reasons to want to rank individuals by their capacity to think, but this ranking has little relevance to the economics of poverty. Even schoolwork requires or assumes outside knowledge for successful performance. An eighth grader may be a budding astronomical wizard but yet stumble on the question, "If it is noon in Paris, is it sunrise or sunset in New York?" because he or she is completely ignorant of geography and misguessed that Paris was west of New York.

The office or factory is much less interested in the worker's intellectual capacity compared with intellectual performance than is the classroom. An employer may want to know if a prospective worker can read a blueprint; but the employer is not concerned about the worker's reading grade level or the quickness with which he or she can cross-multiply. There is no denying the association between these aptitudes and blueprint reading, but this association determines how easily and how well the skill can be learned. Without the skill, though, the worker is not ready for employment in jobs that require reading of blueprints.

Expressed alternatively, the higher the individual's learning capacity, or intelligence, the better and quicker that person can acquire skills which require reasoning. Schools may not improve basic reasoning power, but they can develop skills that require reasoning. Without teaching skills specific to any occupation, they can add to the students' cognitive skills—in language and mathematics. "Drawing out," the literal meaning of *education*, indicates its role, which is to develop from a student's intelligence the learning of the three R's.

Schools often test their students' intelligence and the development of their cognitive skills. The former tests are often criticized for their culture-based content, and rightfully so if they aim to measure the students' "pure reasoning power." But tests of cognitive skills assume expanded knowledge of the student in their measurement of his or her capacity to apply reasoning to this knowledge.

Thus, it is obvious that if an ideal intelligence test were devised, schools would have no effect in raising that score; but the very purpose of the academic side of education is to develop cognitive skills. The success of this effort could be measured by ideal tests of this skill development. Some analysts argue that schools are unsuccessful in developing cognitive skills, and they offer test score results to support their claim. In the extreme, this view leads to the conclusion that schools do not teach anything. In disagreeing with the most well-known study supporting this view, the following argument abstracts from the possibility that the tests of cognitive skills are faulty in that their questions do not contain enough knowledge taught in the schools and are thus too close to intelligence tests of reasoning power alone.

The Coleman Report

Findings and Implications   The Civil Rights Act of 1964 commissioned the U.S. Office of Education to study the extent of inequality of educational opportunity in American public schools. Two years later, the study, familiarly known as the Coleman Report[6] after its principal researcher, reported its findings, which shocked not only professional educators and political leaders but the American public as well. What had been expected was a report detailing the sad story of sharp inequality in the quality of American schools, with this inequality, measured by students' test scores on national examinations in language and mathematical proficiency, contributing heavily to the pronounced disparity in cognitive skills among American children. What was actually reported was quite the opposite. The Coleman Report did find inequality in American schools (measured by financial resources allotted to schools) and in educational facilities, but a far greater inequality was found in student background factors that influence learning—parents' education, income, family size and stability, etc. What is more significant, the report concluded that the quality of schools was not a significant factor influencing learning; that is, given background factors and backgrounds and capacities of their schoolmates, next to nothing was contributed by differences in school resources, curricula, and facilities to variations in students' test scores. Students learned just as well if much or little was spent on their education, if class sizes were large or small, if the school library and laboratories were well or poorly stocked and equipped, etc.

The implications of these findings were not lost on those interested in and responsible for American educational financing and planning. If the Coleman Report is correct, the schools are powerless to affect children's cognitive skills. Put more bluntly, they do not teach anything that adds to understanding and perception that would not be learned just as easily outside of the classroom. Putting money into currently lightly financed

[6]James S. Coleman et al., *Equality of Educational Opportunity,* U.S. Office of Education, 1966.

schools would be a waste of public funds, since this money could do nothing to educate the attending children whose learning during school-age years would be determined by their background characteristics.

According to the Coleman Report, schools could add to a child's knowledge by rearranging enrollment composition. If equality of learning were the goal, a step in the right direction would involve randomizing school populations with regard to family background characteristics and student motivation and scholastic interest instead of continuing with the current pattern in which students of similar backgrounds and academic motivation cluster in individual schools.

But since schools do not teach anything worthwhile, we could devise other centers for concentrating children by age which might, by eliminating wasteful and often distasteful academic activities, be made more useful or at least pleasanter for the children forced to attend. We could, without loss, drastically reduce the minimum school-leaving age, and since the average fourteen-year-old has at least the stamina of a fifty-year-old, he might as well work if he is not learning anything at school. For earlier years, schools could serve as holding institutions which keep children out of mischief and care for them until they are physically developed enough to work, while their parents pursue more satisfying activities than child rearing. There would be no foolishness in racing intellectual engines, since schools would know that they could not contribute to mental development.

Carrying the Coleman Report argument to its ridiculous conclusions, if differences in resource input of schools do not explain variations in mental development, so that learning is unaffected whether little or much is spent on schooling, why strive to equalize school expenditures? Since this will not lead to greater equality of opportunity for success in later life, in fact, why put any money into schools at all? Christopher Jencks, whose widely circulated study[7] will receive closer examination in the following section, accepts the Coleman Report without reservation and consequently does not find this conclusion ridiculous. He does not come out and say that schools should be abandoned because they fail in their primary educational function, but he does state that if we must have schools, they should be as pleasant places as possible in which to spend one's childhood. Fairness, according to Jencks, dictates equal expenditures and facilities so that all may enjoy the same amenities.

We can only guess whether Jencks is serious in his justification for equality of expenditure or whether he is indulging in a little sarcasm, based on his confidence in the validity of the Coleman Report and his own extension of its findings as he really advocates the abolishment of the

---

[7]Christopher Jencks et al., *Inequality: A Reassessment of the Effect of Family and Schooling in America,* Basic Books, New York, 1972.

school system. For surely, if schools are nothing but glorified prework social and recreational centers, taxpayers would prefer the centers to be more like children's counterparts of Senior Citizen services than institutions that are fiscally wasteful which merely go through the motions of education.

Perhaps the most negative aspect of the Coleman Report is the pessimistic attitude it instills in those, including the poor and disadvantaged themselves, who strive to improve their future chances by improving their own mental development through an investment in schooling. The simple, bitter message to those at the bottom of the socioeconomic scale is clear: "Putting more resources into your education won't help. Go change your background."

Criticism of the Coleman Report   This report, with its dismal, fatalistic findings, has not gone unchallenged. Attacks on many fronts, many of them emotional, have been launched against the report, but this summary of the criticisms confines itself to those based on reason which expose its faulty methods.[8] In defense of the report, though, while the criticisms might damage the validity of its principal finding that schools do not develop cognitive skills, they do not prove that schools do contribute to learning skills. At best, we are left with nagging doubts about the effectiveness of formal education.

The main shortcoming of the Coleman Report is that it studies the wrong relationships for policy purposes. Even if its statistical methods were faultless, there is little surprise or substance to the finding that more of the variation in student test scores is attributable to background factors than to school quality (expenditure on facilities) differences, inasmuch as the differences in background were found to be much greater than those in school quality.

The information we want is not the contribution of each to test score differences but how changes in either would affect these scores. Specifically, we want to know how much scores will improve from an extra dollar spent on schooling. There is some interest in the finding that inequality in schools, measured by resources and facilities, was less than most people thought; but there would be much more interest in knowing the effect of reducing inequality in equalizing test scores.

Our interest in which variable subset—background or schooling—explains more of current test-score variation may be mainly academic. But we have a strong practical interest in knowing what the response in test

---

[8]Samuel Bowles and Henry M. Levin, "The Determinants of Scholastic Achievement—An Appraisal of Some Recent Evidence," *Journal of Human Resources,* Winter 1968; and Glen G. Cain and Harold W. Watts, "Problems in Making Policy Inferences from the Coleman Report," *American Sociological Review,* April 1970, pp. 228–241. Both of these present detailed criticism of the report.

scores will be to a change in the variables. How many points will be added per pupil from each additional school dollar spent on each? The Coleman Report does not tell us, and despite the cogency of its criticisms, we are still uncertain whether greater expenditures and curriculum innovation will improve the learning of those prime candidates for adult poverty with the lowest test scores. At least these changes are worth the try.

SCHOOLING AND EARNINGS

Schooling can lead to increased productivity either because education increases workers' productive capacity or because employers think it does. In the latter case, firms use the attainment of a certain number of years of schooling, usually to the completion of an educational level, as a screening device for hiring and to a lesser extent for on-the-job training. This use of a diploma as a surrogate for demonstrated skill is called "credentialism." This last section begins with a discussion of the relationship between credentialism and poverty. Then the Jencks study, which concludes that schooling quality and quantity do not contribute to earnings, is critically evaluated.

Credentialism and Poverty

In their search for workers quick to adapt to company work surroundings and conditions and who are likely candidates for successful training in new techniques and skills, firms use many predictive devices. They test their new job applicants, interview them, examine their past employment records, and even employ some individuals on a trial basis in order to screen out those applicants least likely to succeed and to hire only those the company wishes to retain and train even further. One screening device whose application has increased over the years is education, specifically the number of years of schooling attained or, even more usually, the achievement of a certain education level as evidenced by the holding of a degree, diploma, certificate, or other credential. A college diploma signifies the successful completion of a curriculum of courses, which may or may not be relevant to a firm's job tasks for a particular opening. But it does signify to the firm that the holder has demonstrated a capacity to learn, perseverance, discipline, and conformity—qualities held in high esteem by firms who plan long-term associations with their hired trainable applicants.

When the firm uses the latter implications of the degree as a screening device, it can be said to practice credentialism, a form of discrimination. For while the degree eases the way of its holder, it screens out from employment consideration job candidates who do not possess this symbol of proficiency and potentially good company citizenship who might be just as qualified to perform job tasks and as apt at learning new ones and who may show just as much work stability as the hired degree holder. From the company's point of view, its discrimination may save it money. As long as there is a probability that the college educated would be more suitable to the firm, the hiring costs—interviewing, testing, etc.—can be saved by considering college graduation as an entry pass to employment. Even though mistakes may be made by this bureaucratic procedure, with some better qualified lesser educated being screened out, the hiring cost savings may more than compensate for the losses associated with these hiring errors.

The following three chapters develop the concept of employment discrimination as it relates to poverty; but even at this early stage, we can see that discriminatory employment practices can quite easily serve the firm's self-interest. There is no question that credentialism involves discrimination against the less educated. Even if the odds are great that a random group of graduates will be better hiring risks than a similar group of nongraduates, each applicant must, if discrimination is to be avoided, be evaluated on characteristics more closely related to job performance than on symbols of achievement and stability.

There is no concrete evidence on the extent of credentialism, but one well-known study finds many instances when firms report no difference in performance among workers of different educational levels, even for occupations and jobs which typically demand advanced educational attainment.[9] So far, the discussion has been about credentialism applied to college graduation. This practice has little application to the issue of poverty, since—for jobs which arbitrarily demand college completion—the presumption can be made that those who are discriminated against would almost all be at least high school graduates, a group that has a low poverty rate in any case.

But credentialism does more than distort the labor market of the educational elite; it reaches down to lower levels of schooling and occupation. The higher unemployment and poverty rates of dropouts and the relatively high educational level reached by those doing semiskilled and even unskilled work all suggest that a high school diploma improves the employment opportunities of its holder and denies them to those who are less well endowed educationally. Credentialism at the high school completion level helps push those negatively affected below the poverty level.

While there may be some credentialism at the high school level, there is much room for doubt whether the simple policy of adapting measures to increase the flow of high school graduates will solve the problem. A study

[9]Ivar Berg, *Education and Jobs: The Great Training Robbery,* Praeger, New York, 1970, pp. 85–104.

of those whose scores were in the lowest quartile of the Armed Forces
Qualifying Test (a rough measure of cognitive skills) showed the absence
of a "sheepskin effect."[10] That is, there was no significant positive difference in earnings among those who were high school graduates compared to those who were not, and prior training had a much greater positive influence on earnings than years of schooling. This study was of
young men, so that possibly the positive earnings effects of credentialism
simply had not had time to work themselves out. Nevertheless, this and
other evidence indicate that the mere attainment of a diploma, or the
simple piling on of years of schooling, might not be the key to raising the
labor income of those who show the weakest level of cognitive skill development, those most likely to be poor.

In his denial of the link between schooling, cognitive skills, and earnings, Jencks correctly points out that calculated high rates of return on investment in schooling and high earnings of those with substantial
schooling only reflect actual or revealed relationships and do not necessarily indicate that more schooling for those who now receive less would
add to their earnings. In effect, simply adding to school years without al-
tering curricula to serve the needs of the potential dropout might simply
attack the result instead of the cause of little schooling. While this
argument against this easy solution to credentialism by accommodation is
well taken, the more provocative conclusions of Jencks's study are less
easily accepted.

The Jencks Study

Findings and Implications If the Coleman Report casts serious
doubts on the positive influence of schooling quality in the development
of cognitive skills, the Jencks study claims that the issue is irrelevant insofar as the effect on earnings is concerned. Jencks finds that hardly anything affects earnings. He writes that "Economic success seems to
depend on varieties of luck and on-the-job competence that are only
moderately related to family background, schooling, or scores on standardized tests. The definition of competence varies greatly from one job
to another, but it seems in most cases to depend more on personality than
on technical skills."[11]

Even the word "moderately" exaggerates Jencks's reported findings,
which show no statistically significant relationship between any popularly
acknowledged influential variable—family wealth and parental educational level, schooling expenditures and curriculum, etc.—and earnings. It
seems odd to base an explanation of the earnings distribution on random

---

[10]W. Lee Hansen, Burton A. Weisbrod, and William J. Scanlon, "Schooling and Earnings of Low Achievers," *American Economic Review,* June 1970, pp. 409–418.
[11]Jencks, op. cit., p. 8.

and immeasurable qualities such as luck and personality, but Jencks's negative findings for all the other measurable variables leave him no alternative but to rely on unmeasurable values and an untestable hypothesis. If Jencks is correct, we are left with a nineteenth-century explanation of poverty; people are poor because they have bad luck or unpleasant personalities.

Since we cannot conceive of measures to raise competence, based as it is mainly on personality, and since luck by its very definition defies structuring, we must, if we are fatalistic, accept the income distribution as it is, with all its inequality. But Jencks recommends that we move towards equality, with its implied reduction in poverty, by the only means possible—through a radical change in our economic system toward socialism or a massive income redistribution plan. Neither of these, in today's political climate, come under the heading of practical policy recommendations.

Criticism of the Jencks Study   As would be expected from a report that comes down so heavily against schooling and the educational system as contributors of anything worthwhile to their captive audience of students, Jencks's study generated a great deal of criticism, much of it even before the final report appeared. A group of leading educators submitted their rebuttal to Jencks's preliminary statement of findings.[12]

Among other things, these papers criticized Jencks's use of existing data collected in the early 1960s, before major school reforms were instituted; his unsubstantiated contradiction of many scholarly studies which showed high positive rates of return on investment in education and a close association between earnings and school attainment; and his appeal to socialism as the only remedy for poverty. There is much more than self-interest defended in these educators' counterattack against the Jencks study, but in the main they strike only at the periphery of the report.

The basic weakness of the report lies much deeper than in its use of stale data, unpopular policy prescription, and denial of the obvious documented by prior respected studies of the strong influence of schooling on earnings.[13] It lies in its very faulty statistical analysis, upon

[12]*Christopher Jencks in Perspective*, American Association of School Administrators, 1973. This collection was in response to Mary Jo Bane and Christopher Jencks, "The Schools and Equal Opportunity," *Saturday Review of Literature*, September 16, 1972. This article is reprinted in the collection.

[13]Contrary to Jencks's conclusion, Finis Welch, "Educational and Racial Discrimination," *Discrimination in Labor Markets* ed. Orley Ashenfelter and Albert Rees, Princeton University Press, 1973, pp. 43–81, found that returns from education for blacks rose relative to white returns as the quality of their schooling rose towards the white level, with quality based on the conventional measures of teacher-student ratio, expenditures per student, etc.

which its radical solutions and carelessly tossed out, shocking conclusions and style of subdued inconoclasm are based. One of the papers in the cited collection pinpoints the bad statistics of the report when it criticizes Jencks's measuring of inequality in terms of individual differences rather than group differences.[14]

As an example of this grave error, which is made repeatedly through the book, note Jencks's explanation of factors that affect earnings difference. Recall that Jencks credits only chance and personality as definite contributors to earnings. His report minimizes the relationship between IQ scores and earnings, because those in the top fifth of the IQ scale average only 35 to 40 percent higher earnings than those in the bottom fifth, while for workers as a whole the top fifth average 600 percent more income than the bottom fifth.

The same low rating is given to parental income and educational difference, which produces mean income differences similar to those resulting from grouping by IQ level. But what matters in evaluating the importance of any individual element is not the variations resulting from classification by this element compared to the large variation in the overall population, which may be partly due to the cumulative effects of these elements operating in the same direction. What matters is whether the differences in average results obtained by grouping individuals at different values of the element are dissimilar.

In this sense, Jencks's findings indicate that IQ, parental income, and education variations contribute significantly to differences in earnings. These actual results are quite opposite to the conclusions he arrived at by way of his faulty statistical analysis.

SUMMARY

The data of the previous chapter that showed a close inverse relationship between schooling level and poverty have been reinforced by associating occupation with these two variables. The tie among the three is very close; the jobs with highest educational requirements are those whose holders are least likely to be poor. Low educational attainment is associated not only with low-paying jobs but also with nonparticipation in the work force, another factor inducing poverty.

Average American educational attainment has continued to rise, so that presently close to three-quarters of the work force are high school graduates, with the likelihood that the ratio will continue to grow. Despite this advanced level of schooling, the incidence of poverty remains high.

[14]See the paper "As I See It ... " by Kenneth Clark, Laurence Plotkin, and Gordon I. Swanson.

American schools have been characteristically weak in specific job preparation. Unlike European schools, which channel their students towards career preparation at an early age, our schools allow students to drift aimlessly towards college or the job market, for which one study finds 80 percent of high school graduates are "ill-equipped." The obvious need is for more "career education," which, ideally, will improve the employment potential of graduates without abandoning the American principle of voluntarism and will open options for future schooling and work direction.

The main tasks of schools are in the development of cognitive skills in improving the students' ability to communicate in words and numbers. In doing this, schools raise students' employment opportunities and earning power, making education a human investment even if the schools' main purpose is not economic development of its students.

The Coleman Report, in effect, concludes that schools perform this task poorly. Specifically, the report finds that variations in test scores that measure cognitive skills are not related to differences in school quality, implying that schools do little and—what is more significant—*can* do little to raise the cognitive skill level. But no actual information is provided on the report's finding of the crucial question of how scores would be affected by changes in schooling variables. Furthermore, even the finding that student backgrounds count more than schooling in explaining existing test score variation is questionable because of the high correlation between these explanatory variables.

Even if schools did not add much to students' employability through development of cognitive skills, as long as employers thought they did or believed that they otherwise contributed to students' potential for successful job performance, employment opportunities for graduates would widen. While credentialism may be condemned as a discriminatory practice, it does add to the earning power of the educated.

Despite the obvious relationship between earnings and schooling, Jencks concludes that education does not contribute to earnings. In fact, his study exceeds the negativism of the Coleman Report by finding little or no relationship between cognitive skills and earnings, making the issue of what contributes most to cognitive skills irrelevant to the question of poverty. To make matters more extreme, Jencks finds that family background difference makes only a minor contribution to income variations.

But Jencks's findings are based on a preoccupation with individual earnings differences, which leads him to understate the significance of the effect on earnings of family background, peer association, IQ, and schooling elements that we have long accepted as greatly influential on earnings. He is left with the view that earnings depend mainly on luck and on-the-job competence, which in turn "seems in most cases to depend more on personality." Thus he would conclude that the high incidence of poverty among blacks, women, and old people—an incidence which the next three chapters relate to disadvantage and discrimination—arises because these groups have bad luck and unpleasant personalities. This conclusion could be most charitably described as preposterous.

Chapter 4

Racial Discrimination and Poverty

The economist has little or nothing to contribute to an explanation of the origins of prejudice. In fact, he can even claim that monetary gain plays no role in initiating discrimination against any demographic group when the characteristics discriminated against have nothing to do with work performance. If this were not the case, the economist would be able to point to attempts to oppress many other identifiable population groups besides blacks and women. At the same time he admits that once established, consequent economic gains from discrimination for favored groups may dampen their enthusiasm for its elimination.[1]

While psychologists, sociologists, political scientists, and historians can try to explain why prejudice and discrimination exist and persist and may thus perhaps contribute toward the eradication of this most pernicious social disease, the economist can only detail the economic cost of discrimination, a cost which obviously falls heaviest on the oppressed group but which spreads to the economy as a whole.

[1]Kenneth Arrow, "Models of Job Discrimination," in Anthony H. Pascal (ed.), *Racial Discrimination in Economic Life*, Heath, Boston, 1972, p. 100, makes this argument.

This and the following chapter examine the economic effects of racial and sexist discrimination respectively. Certainly the prejudicial attitudes on which discrimination is based differ greatly for the two groups, as do the intensity and range of their application. Nevertheless, there is a common thread running from prejudice through discrimination to economic loss that characterizes all types of group oppression. The first part of this chapter discusses this common thread. Then, the economic effects of racial discrimination are detailed insofar as they contribute to the high incidence of black poverty.

ECONOMIC ASPECTS OF DISCRIMINATION

Definitions and Their Application

Prejudice   Unfortunately, economists had no part in compiling the dictionary. When we look up the word *prejudice,* we get no help in disentangling the elements that contribute to lower incomes of oppressed groups but rather receive most of them in a confused heap. Let us examine the following three relevant entries under prejudice:

> **1**   Irrational suspicion or hatred of a particular group, race, or religion
> **2**   An adverse judgment or opinion formed beforehand or without knowledge or examination of the facts
> **3**   Detriment or injury caused to a person by the preconceived and unfavorable conviction of another or others

The first entry we will call prejudice, pure and simple—the attitudes springing from the evil side of the human spirit which defy economic analysis.

Screening   The second entry is more complicated. Consider the following hypothetical but realistic examples of employment requirements: "Male applicants for the police force must be over 5 feet 4 inches and must weigh more than 125 pounds." "Applicants for dock work must be males under forty-five years of age."

Only slight prejudice seems involved in these cases. Both jobs require strength and vigor. Considering the physical nature of much police work, it is unlikely that many small and slight men could perform all police tasks satisfactorily, and it might even be argued that the size barrier to job entry actually protects those who show more bravery than wisdom in applying. Similarly, despite recent technology that has lightened the load of dock work, there are not many sixty-three-year-old women who could qualify as stevedores.

In fact, an erroneous but understandable argument might conclude that there is no prejudice involved here at all. The judgment against the excluded applicants is certainly adverse, but it is made with knowledge and examination of the facts; those who do not meet the age-sex-size qualifications are unlikely to satisfy job requirements. But these barriers are only proxies for *screening* out those with the unacceptable characteristic of inadequate strength.

A nonprejudiced policy would require that the employer review all applicants and strive to measure expected job performance by objective testing and, if necessary, through trial on actual job tasks before deciding whether the applicant does not meet the physical requirements. The firm may engage in screening without any prejudicial intent simply because it is cheaper to play the percentages that the savings on testing and evaluation costs would more than compensate for the loss of services of those few screened who would qualify for the jobs.

Nevertheless, the workers do suffer from a mild form of *overt discrimination* in that there is use of a characteristic other than job qualification in employment decisions. They are barred as women or as older or slightly built individuals. The discrimination is not mild for those few with these characteristics who meet the strength qualifications. But *mildness* describes the purpose of the discrimination, which is not to satisfy attitudinal bias against a group but to save money. Discrimination of this type is closely related to that aspect of education credentialism which screens out nongraduates who actually have a low probability of adequate job performance. In the case of dock workers, there is not an actual credential or certificate involved; but we can stretch the definition of credentialism to include use of any attitude or characteristic as a positive or negative measure of potential job performance.

An obvious problem in removing this form of discrimination is that its elimination would go against the economic interests of the discriminator. Profits would be reduced if screening were prohibited. Here we have a case in which economic factors cause discrimination because the characteristics discriminated against are negatively correlated to work performance. The discrimination is real, even though it is not based on negative attitudes.

Obviously, though, screening has no application to racial prejudice. Blacks do not have unusual characteristics that affect their probability for successful job performance. Nevertheless, the effects of screening often weigh heavily against particular ethnic groups. Even though the screening is not specifically directed against given groups, police force height requirements exclude many Latin Americans and educational credential prerequisites bar many capable blacks from jobs they could adequately fill.

Overt Discrimination   The ugliest economic manifestation of prejudice is *overt discrimination,* the application of prejudice to aspects of economic life in which the discriminator makes an economic decision based on noneconomic factors such as race, sex, national origin, or religion. Overt discrimination can occur in production and consumption. As an example of the latter, a landlord may not rent to black tenants even though they are able to pay. This chapter will not discuss (overt) discrimination in consumption, not because it is unimportant or rare but because poverty statistics which serve as the basis of the exposition unfortunately do not take into account differential costs, even if they do try to include differences in expenses in their adjustment for family size, etc., in their illogical preoccupation with income as the unique measure of spending power inadequacy.

In production, overt discrimination may be practiced by employers who indulge their racial prejudices by discriminating against qualified blacks in the various aspects of employment—hiring, promotion, layoff, and wages. Overt discrimination is the one economic expression of prejudice that the law prohibits. Since the passage of the Civil Rights Act of 1964, it is illegal to practice overt discrimination. Relevant to this chapter, race cannot be used as a criterion for employment decisions. But there is some doubt that obvious forms of this prejudice were widely practiced even before the act.

In a study conducted almost a quarter of a century ago, Donald Dewey found no evidence of racial wage discrimination in the South.[2] That is, he found similar wages for blacks and whites doing the same work in the same setting. He did find, though, much evidence of segregation in that blacks were excluded from certain jobs and that blacks and whites rarely worked together at the same job level. Thus, while the most blatant form of racial employment discrimination—the payment of different wages for equal work—has long been a part of past history, the more subtle forms of discrimination—such as placing qualified blacks in inferior jobs and the frequent failure to promote blacks to supervisory positions—have been practiced and are undoubtedly still practiced against the law, which is often difficult to administer and which is not always rigorously applied in these cases.

Institutionalized Racism—The Vicious Circle of Discrimination   In any case, overt discrimination is not the most serious economic handicap facing blacks. In fact, up to this point, we have not noted very serious racial barriers to adequate earnings. Prejudice, as defined here, is just an attitude which needs translation into behavior before it has eco-

[2]Donald Dewey, "Negro Employment in Southern Industries," *Journal of Political Economy,* June 1952, pp. 279–293.

nomic implication. Screening, when it is not specifically racial, might have a greater impact on blacks than on whites when education is the characteristic used. But insofar as racial discrimination is not involved, the negative effects on blacks from this form of screening will continue to weaken if black educational attainment keeps advancing. The crudest forms of overt discrimination had fallen into disuse even before they were made illegal, and only the more difficult-to-spot forms remain in defiance of the law. There is no need to minimize the harmful effects of these last practices on black earnings, but their existence cannot begin to explain the wide and persistent imbalance in racial earnings.

What does explain this disparity is *institutionalized racism,* the maintenance of racial (economic) barriers established by past discrimination which do not depend on current overt discrimination for their continuation. Thus, institutionalized racism can be and very often is practiced by those who have no racial prejudice and who abhor the immorality of overt discrimination.

Let us trace through a hypothetical but realistic example of the effect of institutionalized racism in the absence of overt discrimination. A department store recruits management trainees among recent graduates of a college business administration curriculum. It loudly and proudly announces that race, creed, etc., will play no part in its employment decisions. There is no overt discrimination here; it is not the store's fault that there are few blacks who can meet its minimum hiring standard of business degree attainment. The college, in turn, accepts all qualified applicants. The college is not practicing overt discrimination if it receives few such black applicants. Is it to be blamed because weak prior schooling and insufficient financial resources foreclose college to blacks? Early schooling was inadequate because the public schools that blacks attend are weakly financed and are thus often poorly staffed and equipped. Their education is further handicapped by a home environment preoccupied with the problems of economic survival and a neighborhood in which all are beset with the basic monetary problems of maintaining life rather than in preparing for a livelihood—a way of life in keeping with the old proverb that man must eat before he can philosophize.

Again, these circumstances need not result from current overt discrimination. Blacks may theoretically, be free to move to liberally funded school districts and to benefit from well-paid and prepared teachers and well-equipped schools and to live in neighborhoods whose residents can afford the luxury of cultural pursuits. Residents of many wealthy suburbs, seemingly unaware of their sanctimony and hypocrisy, feel they have contributed their last measure to the cause of equity when they pass open housing ordinances assuring free access to all those—again, regardless of race, creed, etc.—who choose to buy houses in their communities—houses whose average selling price is $60,000. This policy is about as relevant to equity as the observation of a sardonic and wise Frenchman, who noted that true democracy prevailed because rich Parisians had the same right as the poor to sleep under the bridges of the Seine.

This example describes the full vicious circle of discrimination implied in institutionalized racism. Most blacks do not qualify for management training opportunities because they do not have business degrees, because they cannot afford to obtain them and have been unprepared for college by poor prior schooling, because of their unfavorable environment for successful schooling and the sparse funding on their schooling, because they lived in poor districts, because they (in this case their families) did not hold high-paying jobs since they did not qualify for them—but we are now on another lap of the track of institutionalized racism.

Figure 4-1 offers a diagramatic presentation of the circular pattern of institutionalized racism in which the black is trapped. Although blacks suffer mainly from institutionalized racism, this is not to deny that overt

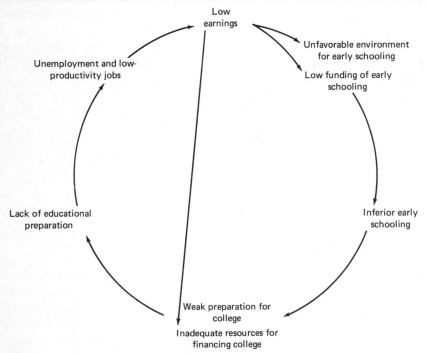

Figure 4-1 The vicious circle of institutionalized racism.

discrimination might exacerbate their diffculties in avoiding poverty. Thurow categorizes seven types of racial discrimination:

1   Employment (concentration of unemployment among blacks)
2   Wages (blacks paid less than whites for the same type of work)
3   Occupation (concentration of blacks in lower-level jobs and restrictive entry to better jobs)
4   Human capital (lower investment in human capital—mainly in education and health for blacks)
5   Capital (higher interest rates or restricted credit to black borrowers)
6   Monopoly power (low black participation in monopolistic organizations, e.g., unions which benefit members)
7   Price (black buyers pay higher prices and black sellers receive lower prices)[3]

Thurow does not attempt to differentiate between overt discrimination and institutionalized racism in his catalog of economic discrimination, but it is interesting to note that except for types 2 and 7, which can only reflect overt discrimination, blacks may suffer from either class of applied prejudice.

In type 1, blacks may be concentrated in jobs which are unemployment-prone; in type 3, their lack of adequate preparation may keep them from better jobs; in type 4, their lower earnings and weaker financial resources limit their human capital investment; in type 5, their uncertain employment and weak collateral make them credit risks; in type 6, their jobs tend to be in areas of low union concentration, for example, service jobs. Thus, while overt discrimination may appear in all these categories, institutionalized racism suffices to explain their presence. Moving from type 4 to the other four categories not necessarily associated with overt discrimination explains the lower earnings of blacks. This results in type 4 discrimination, and thus the vicious circle of institutionalized racism is described once again.

Differentiating between the two types of discrimination entails more than mere semantic exercise. It can lead to sensible evaluation of the data and suggest appropriate policies for corrective action against economic discrimination. For example, black unemployment rates have been chronically about twice the white level. A statistician might note that blacks are heavily concentrated in occupations which have high unemployment rates and might find that—after standardizing for occupa-

[3]Lester Thurow, *Poverty and Racial Discrimination,* Brookings, Washington, 1969, pp. 117–126.

tion—there is little if any racial difference in unemployment occupation by occupation.

While this finding may be of some interest in that it would deny the presence of overt discrimination in layoff and discharge practices, it would be incorrect to conclude from it that blackness was not a factor in explaining unemployment. Why are blacks concentrated in jobs susceptible to unemployment? The answer lies in institutionalized racism, a term of conceptual simplicity but a pressing social problem often misunderstood or neglected and always difficult to attack. After all, in the absence of overt discrimination, who is the culprit responsible for institutionalized racism? The answer can be "no one at this time," if only its existence is considered, or "everyone who practices it," if the more important aspect of its perpetuation is at issue.

In the unemployment example, the question of how much each discriminatory factor contributes to the higher unemployment rates of blacks has policy importance. In all cases, overt discrimination should be eliminated simply because it is immoral, to say nothing of its illegality. If there is little evidence of this because of the finding of similar unemployment rates by race for individual occupational classifications, then steps must be taken to break the circle at this point of institutionalized racial employment discrimination. What needs to be stressed is that regardless of the weight of the two types of discrimination as causes of higher unemployment rates for blacks, the higher rates themselves are evidence enough of racial discrimination.

Economic Effects of Discrimination

This section deals with the economic impact of discrimination. Obviously, losses are incurred by the discriminated group, so that the only uncertainty is over the gains and losses to discriminators and others and to society as a whole.

At the outset it must be emphasized that the purpose of this analysis is not to study a cost-benefit relationship which would conclude that if the financial benefits to discriminators exceeded the losses of those discriminated against, then discrimination would be economically beneficial and should be continued. This might be the goal of customary cost-benefit studies, but the analysis of "benefits" of discrimination has quite the contrary purpose of evaluating the gains and losses as an indicator of the ease or difficulty with which economic discrimination can be eliminated. It is presumed that those who gain from discrimination will be reluctant to support its removal and that, in general, efforts to eradicate the practice from our economic life must face the possible opposition of those who profit from its continuation.

Overt Discrimination It might seem strange to study the economic impact of overt discrimination, since its practice has been illegal for many years. But a realistic view of legal compliance or lack of it, as reflected by the weighty evidence of its continued existence in more subtle forms than wage discrimination, makes the study relevant to current behavior. The most widely known analysis of these economic effects is that of Gary Becker.[4] A careful study of Becker's analysis yields the unhappy result that there are no real losers among discriminators. This result is described as unhappy for those who would like to see an easy end to discrimination—an end that could result when people's sense of morality coincided with their economic self-interest.

Take the case of a discriminating employer, one who is prejudiced against blacks and is therefore reluctant to hire them. Becker says that he has a "taste" for discrimination. Perhaps the word "taste" has a conciliatory ring to the noneconomist in that it implies that one's wish to satisfy his prejudices should be considered just as legitimate or ethical as one's taste in automobiles, shoes, or vacation trips. But all Becker is doing here is describing an economic demand by the employer, in this case of a service rather than a good, for making his product without black employees.

The conventional theory considers employers as profit maximizers. Becker's analysis shows that discriminators are utility maximizers instead. That is, in production, along with earning profits, they also indulge their taste for discriminating against black workers. While profits become lower because of this taste satisfaction, total utility for the discriminator is no less than for the nondiscriminator. In effect, then, the labor cost to him of hiring a black worker equals the wage he must pay plus what Becker calls the "coefficient of discrimination," an additional fraction of the wage that represents his disutility in employing a black. Thus he would like to pay black workers less than equally productive white workers and will make lower offers to blacks and even higher offers to preferred whites than the labor market demands.

Other firms that did not discriminate would tend to pay the same wage for both. But to the extent that the discriminatory firm was an important (monopsonistic) buyer of labor, the other firms would improve their relative profit position by hiring more blacks than whites, which they would do by moving the black wage closer to the white.

Thus, under imperfect labor market conditions, the discriminating firm would be in a weaker profit position since its white workers would be paid a higher wage, above the value of their productivity, indicating the need to have fewer of them to raise profits. Black workers would be

---

[4]Gary Becker, *Economics of Discrimination*, University of Chicago Press, Chicago. 1957.

paid less than their productivity, indicating the need to hire more blacks to raise profits.[5] The nondiscriminating firms take advantage of these profit opportunities.

Under competitive labor market conditions, racial wage differences would disappear, and the discriminator would hire a completely white labor force. Thus the manifestation of prejudice in overt discrimination, in the form of differential wages or inferior jobs for qualified blacks, requires the presence of imperfection in the labor market. Otherwise, while the discriminator may satisfy his tastes costlessly, blacks would not suffer lower wages or jobs below their qualifications; they would be hired by nondiscriminating firms along with whites.

Despite this market imperfection requirement, there is much obvious evidence of widespread overt discrimination in the marketplace. Take the example of professional sports, an area which seems made to order for racial fairness in employment, if for no other reason than the costs of indulging taste for discrimination are extremely high. Any team that fails to recruit the best players regardless of color will find itself losing out to other teams that do not discriminate.

In fact, the data suggest little wage or employment discrimination in general in baseball.[6] But there are few blacks in supervisory jobs and, at this writing, despite the hundreds of blacks who have finished their playing careers, there is but one black manager. In the key player leadership positions of pitcher and shortstop, blacks are substantially under-represented. Moving to professional football, the number of blacks in the crucial leadership positions of middle linebacker on defense, and quarterback on offense, can be counted on one hand.

We are now in a position to summarize the economic impact of discrimination on the various groups affected, using the discriminating employer as a model.

1 Effect on the *discriminating employer* is neutral. He "pays"in lower profits, for satisfying his taste for discrimination.

2 Effect on the *black worker* is negative. This needs no further explanation.

3 Effect on the *white worker* is favorable. Note that in this case he

---

[5]If black applicants are less qualified on balance—because of inferior prior training and education, reflecting institutionalized racism—then the overtly discriminating employer may actually gain monetarily from screening out blacks. In this case the motivation behind screening may be prejudice transferred to overt discrimination, but an economic gain results nevertheless.

[6]Anthony H. Pascal and Leonard A. Rapping, "The Economics of Racial Discrimination in Organized Baseball," in Anthony H. Pascal (ed.), *Racial Discrimination in Economic Life,* pp. 119–156.

is not a discriminator, but he profits from the discrimination of others; here, the white employer.

But this last conclusion needs modification. Only whites who qualify for the better jobs gain. Less qualified whites face increasing job market competition in fields crowded with the addition of suppressed blacks.[7] Sports is not the only field in which blacks are easily accepted in production as opposed to supervisory jobs; but applying this crowding phenomenon into baseball, white outfielders face stiffer competition than white shortstops.

We see the same pattern in housing. Discrimination against affluent blacks keeps rents lower for whites in expensive neighborhoods and raises them in slums, where blacks are confined. The slum landlord will not win any popularity contests, but he can rightly claim that in charging high rates to blacks (and whites), he is serving a housing need while taking advantage of the discrimination of others, not his own. He sees himself as no different from a nondiscriminatory employer who hires qualified black labor at a discount and who is often praised as a fair-minded businessman.

In brief, economics being the dismal science that it is, the dreary results are predictable. The discriminator only pays for satisfying his tastes—the way he would for any consumer good. Nondiscriminating, highly skilled, and affluent whites gain; all blacks and the poor of both races suffer. Society as a whole is the loser in the misallocation of its human resources.

In theory, overt discrimination should be easy to eliminate. The culprit is the discriminator, and he should be discouraged from translating his prejudice into economic behavior. In the absence of a sudden shift toward unbiased attitudes, the discriminator must be made to pay a higher price for satisfying his tastes in this area. We do have antidiscrimination laws, but they must be made stronger and be more rigorously enforced. Discrimination cannot continue as a normal consumption good but should be treated the same as traffic in hard drugs and other illegal goods—as socially destructive and demanding harsh penalties. You cannot legislate brotherhood, but you can make discrimination prohibitively expensive.

Institutionalized Racism In the case of institutionalized racism, there is no prime moving discriminator that generates economic effects felt by the rest of society. Nevertheless, gains and losses do occur. Again,

---

[7]Barbara R. Bergman, in "The Effect on White Income of Discrimination in Employment," *Journal of Political Economy,* March/April 1971, pp. 294–313, finds the effects of crowding greatest for job levels held by the least educated groups, where favored whites would suffer about a 10 percent loss in income if the elimination of discrimination increased black employment in the better jobs at these levels.

society is the big loser in that the full potential of blacks remains underdeveloped. Once again blacks are crowded into inferior jobs and poor neighborhoods, to their loss and to that of others who face artificially strong competition for scarce, unsatisfying jobs and housing. At the same time, whites fortunate enough to have received much human investment are insulated from the competition of the developed black potential.

Since overt discrimination is a more obvious practice, it can be dealt with more easily than institutionalized racism. The Civil Rights Act and other antidiscriminatory measures cannot reach institutionalized racism, but the circle can be broken.

Efforts must be made to counteract the forces that have eroded the black's competitive position. Compensatory efforts must be made against all links of the chain. This does not mean that reverse discrimination is the appropriate policy, though shortsighted analysts may see this as the only way to overcome institutionalized racism. Since (white) society as a whole has been responsible for the establishment and perpetuation of institutionalized racism, it should pay the price for its removal, and the full cost should not fall on any single subgroup.

Beginning in the period of preparation, more money should be spent on the education of black children to compensate for the unfavorable background factors resulting from their low-income family and neighborhood environment. (How opposite this policy is to the current tendency, whereby little money and effort are expended on black children.) But white children need not pay for this compensatory education by having their educational resources equivalently reduced—the total education budget must be raised.

Similarly, blacks must be allowed admittance to higher education and to better jobs even when their qualifications, limited by past discrimination, do not meet conventional requirements. But it must be emphasized that the current thinking that such a policy must prejudice the opportunities for whites is wrong. There is no need for this if the circle of institutionalized racism is to be broken at many places. For example, the admission of more blacks to law schools, even if their Law School Admission Test scores are not quite up to admission standards, need not push out qualified whites. A simple adjustment would increase the number of admissions to law schools. At first view, the fundamental scarcity principle of economics seems violated by this suggestion. Would the result not simply be a surplus of lawyers, both black and white? Admittedly, this would be the result if there were no other breaks in the circle, but the simultaneous breaks in other parts of the circle would raise black incomes all along the line and create a demand for additional lawyers. There is no implication here that black lawyers would serve only black clients, but the demand for legal services in general would rise with the increase in total production that would result from the elimination of institutionalized racism. In keeping with the principle of sharing of the costs of eliminating institutionalized racism, extra public funding for expanding law school facilities may be required, at least in the short run, before the rise in demand for more lawyers is felt.

Rationing available places by race in the better jobs and in advanced training and education may reduce the racial imbalance in income, but it will do nothing to improve the national economy. Expansion of facilities to accommodate disadvantaged blacks would allow for economic growth and remove the economic circle of institutionalized racism. Furthermore, from a practical point of view, if the short-run costs of compensatory practices are shared by all of society rather than by those whites facing the new competition, then current, sometimes highly emotional opposition to these practices may be dissipated and their chances for acceptance and implementation greatly increased.

Unfortunately the economy is not currently in the best state to adopt compensatory practices or what has come to be called affirmative action in employment. While we can argue that there need not be white losses from their adoption in a growing economy, during deep recessions like the current one, it is questionable whether black gains can be maintained without reverse discrimination. Our argument has more validity in an expanding economy, but it should be emphasized that a complete rupture of the circle of institutionalized racism would itself lead to growth from economic development of blacks.

THE EVIDENCE ON RACIAL
ECONOMIC DISCRIMINATION

The popular view holds that despite lingering overt discrimination and continued institutionalized racism, the relative black economic position is steadily improving and approaching the white level. Reports of gains in income for many blacks and improved job status encourage this view, but the data do not indicate any pronounced move toward equality. What is sometimes overlooked in this wishful thinking on the disappearance of the economic basis to our racial unrest is that while blacks have been gaining steadily both in income and employment conditions, so have whites, and to such a degree as to leave the prospect of equality in the still unforeseeable future. Moreover, just as with poverty itself, the comparisons relative to social attitudes are not intertemporal within a population subgroup but cross-sectional within the larger mass at a particular time.

In this section we will look at data on income and poverty and labor force experience to substantiate the position that overt discrimination and more prevalent institutionalized racism have made black progress towards economic equality slow and uncertain.

Racial Income and Poverty Differences

Income From 1950 to 1973, a period which extends from post-World War II through the vast social, political, and judicial changes directed at reducing racial inequality, black median family income rose only 4 percentage points from 54 to 58 percent of the white level. At this trend rate we would reach equality in about another hundred years. Complacency over this pattern reflects gradualism with a vengeance. Moreover, as Table 4-1 indicates, the trend has not been a steady one but has been composed of three currents: a period of stability from 1950 to 1965, a period of narrowing from 1965 to 1969, and a downward drift for the last three years of the time span. It is always difficult to assign causes to economic effects, but the gain in the relative income position of blacks occurred during the brief period of strong governmental anti-poverty policies and actions and of the most open manifestations of black discontent during the nationwide demonstrations of the late 1960s.

In other words, there is really no trend in the data but just one brief period of improvement. The table presents strong support for the

Table 4-1 Median Family Income by Race of Head, Selected Years 1950–1973

Year	White	Black	Ratio of blacks and other races to whites, percent
1950	3,445	1,869	54
1955	4,605	2,549	55
1960	5,835	3,233	55
1965	6,251	3,994	55
1969	9,794	5,999	.61
1970	10,236	6,279	.61
1971	10,672	6,440	.60
1972	11,549	6,864	.59
1973	12,595	7,269	.58

*As was the case for poverty, the black income experience was close to that of all minority groups. In 1971, for example, Puerto Rican family income was 58 percent of the white total. See Paul M. Ryscavage and Earl F. Mellor, "The Economic Situation of Spanish Americans," *Monthly Labor Review*, April 1973, pp. 3–9. But the black rate is slightly less than that when combined with the rates of other races. In 1971, for example, it was 61 percent. The designation "black and other races" is kept to allow for an extended period of comparison; the black rate was not disaggregated earlier.

Source: U.S. Census, *Current Population Report*, Series P-60/97, January 1975.

argument that "natural" forces will not lead toward income equality but that conscious effort must be made in that direction.

Certain subgroups within the black population do approach the white level. For example, in 1971, when black family incomes were 61 percent of the white median, for husband-wife families in which the husband was the only earner, the ratio was 68 percent; for families in which both worked, the ratio was 80 percent. For these last households in which the family head (husband) was under thirty-five, the ratio was 90 percent.

But we should not read too much into these figures. Only a minority of families have husband and wife earners. Thirty-nine percent of white families and 35 percent of black ones had both husband and wife working. That a great deal of the lower income of blacks can be explained by the high percentage of black famillies headed by women, (35 percent for blacks and 10 percent for whites in 1972) and families in which the head is a nonearner (24 percent for blacks to 14 percent for whites) reflects the effect of institutionalized racism on family structure and work opportunities.

Poverty   Chapter 2 presented data on the racial distribution of poverty. Table 2-6 told the story of the persistently high ratio of black to white poverty, which—if anything—has risen over the years, while poverty rates for both groups has been in a steady decline. Furthermore, Table 2-3 gave the facts on the greater incidence of black poverty for every educational level, with emphasis on the serious income problems facing the black dropout.

No matter how hard you look, you cannot find one instance in which blacks do not have a worse poverty experience; the incidence of poverty among blacks is higher everywhere—in households headed by men or women, among unrelated individuals, for each age group, etc. Even for families in which both the husband and wife work—the families for which black incomes are closest to white—the poverty rate for black families was 7.9 percent, as compared to 2.1 percent for white ones.

But apart from all these effects of institutionalized racism, the poverty data also reflect overt discrimination. Table 4-2 presents the poverty incidence by race and occupational classification.

It is not surprising to find the concentration of blacks increasing as we move down the occupational ladder. But the incidence of black poverty is significantly greater than for whites for each occupational classification. Despite the fact that the broad classes undoubtedly obscure the concentration of blacks in the lower-paying jobs in each group, it is hard to believe, considering the disparity in poverty rates, that there is not a distinct difference in poverty incidence, to the blacks' disadvantage, among households whose heads have similar jobs.

Table 4-2   Family Poverty Rates with Working Head by Race and Selected Occupations, 1973

Occupation of head	Number of families (thousands)		Percentage of families with working head		Percentage in poverty	
	White	Black	White	Black	White	Black
Professional and technical	5,996	266	16.2	7.4	1.5	7.8
Managers and administrators (nonfarm)	6,433	151	17.4	4.2	2.1	10.8
Clerical and sales	5,690	498	15.4	13.8	3.9	11.2
Craftsmen	9,088	538	24.6	14.9	2.7	8.7
Operatives	4,587	748	12.4	20.7	4.6	16.3
Private household workers	75	180	0.2	4.9	36.6	54.6
Other service workers	2,831	711	7.6	19.6	8.5	24.3
Laborers, nonfarm	1,849	430	4.9	11.9	7.4	20.7
Farm laborers	503	95	1.3	2.6	24.6	59.5
Total	37,032	3,617	100.0	100.0	4.7	19.1

Source: U.S. Census, *Current Population Reports,* Series P-60/98, January 1975.

Labor Force Experience

Since poverty is closely associated with low earnings, we should look to the black work experience for the proximate causes of low black incomes and high poverty incidence. Three important aspects of black-white labor force comparisons are reviewed—unemployment, labor force participation, and occupational status.

Unemployment   As is to be expected, black unemployment rates are relatively high. In fact, Table 4-3 shows that the situation has recently deteriorated with the black/white ratio, which was characteristically about 2.0 and more or less stable over the entire 1948–1972 period, rising above this level in 1973 and 1974. This disturbing trend raises the possibility that perhaps there has been a trade-off of slightly higher relative black earnings and income instead of lower unemployment rates.[8] Certainly such a pattern describes negligible improvement in the relative black economic situation.

The last column of Table 4-3 gives the ratio of the black to white rate. This is the correct measure of their relative experience over time for rates with no apparent long-term trend, but it gives a misleading picture of

[8]In a study of regional racial unemployment ("Economic Discrimination and Unemployment," *American Economic Review,* December 1965, pp. 1077–1091), Harry J. Gilman finds greater variability in northern than southern relative rates, with the south having greater racial wage differences and more employment segregation.

**Table 4-3　Black-White Unemployment Rates,
Selected Years 1948–1974**

Year	Unemployment rate		Black/white ratio
	Black and other races	White	
1948	5.9	3.5	1.7
1950	9.0	4.9	1.8
1952	5.4	2.8	1.9
1954	9.9	5.0	2.0
1956	8.3	3.6	2.3
1958	12.6	6.1	2.1
1960	10.2	4.9	2.2
1962	10.9	4.9	2.1
1964	9.6	4.6	2.1
1966	7.3	3.3	2.2
1968	6.7	3.2	2.1
1969	6.4	3.1	2.1
1970	8.2	4.5	1.8
1971	9.9	5.4	1.8
1972	10.0	5.0	2.0
1973	8.9	3.7	2.4
1974	9.9	4.3	2.3

Source: *Manpower Report of the President*, 1975, Table A-18.

cyclical changes in relative unemployment. For example, from 1964 to 1966 the ratio widened slightly, from 2.1 to 2.2, suggesting a worsening of the black position during a cyclical rise in the economy; but in fact there was a whole percentage point greater drop in black unemployment (2.3 points to 1.3 points for white). There was, in fact, a reduction in black unemployment of 18 blacks for every 10 whites $[(9.6 - 7.3)/(4.6 - 3.3)]$, a relationship which reveals an improvement for blacks. This should be expected during prosperity, as overt discrimination becomes more expensive and labor demand reaches the less qualified worker and the lower job classification.[9] Similarly, in the slump between 1969 and 1970, the drop in the ratio from 2.1 to 1.8 gives a spurious measure of black improvement, when in reality there were 13 more blacks added to unemployment for every 10 whites.

The breakdown of employment by age shows the particularly severe problems of black youth, especially young women. Young people of all races have relatively high unemployment rates, but the impact is much

[9]Curtis L. Gilroy, in "Black and White Unemployment: The Dynamics of the Differential," *Monthly Labor Review*, February 1974, pp. 38–41 explains the relevancy of this ratio, $\Delta B/\Delta W$, which he calls the *incremental ratio* to the measurement of cyclical changes in unemployment status.

greater for blacks. In 1972, when the overall unemployment rate was 5.6 percent, for white eighteen-and nineteen-year-old males the rate was 12.4 percent and for blacks it was 26.2 percent or 2.1 times as high. For females, however, the rates were 12.3 percent and 38.7 percent, respectively, putting the black rate 3.2 times as high.

For all men and women, the black rates are slightly below twice the white level, although the overall ratio was exactly 2.0 in 1972. This peculiarity in the rate is explained by the relatively larger black female and smaller black male labor force, with unemployment rates being higher for women of both races.

Labor Force Participation   Racial labor force participation rates are quite similar, but the rate for black men is lower (73.3 percent in 1974 compared to 79.4 percent for whites) and for black women it is higher (49.1 percent to 45.2 percent for whites).

The age-sex breakdown of the data, presented in Table 4-4, shows some clear disparities.

For males, the comparatively low participation of prime age (twenty-five to forty-four) blacks is especially disturbing. Five or six percentage points might not seem large, but these are the ages of maximum employment potential. It is interesting to note that in these age groups, total black participation is actually greater than that of whites; but this result comes from the large percentage of (lower earning) women in the black work force population at these ages.

The youth figures underscore the terribly weak economic position of young blacks. Even for women, the black participation rates for those in the sixteen to twenty-four age brackets is lower than for whites, this de-

Table 4-4 Racial Labor Force Participation Rates by Age and Sex, 1974

	Males		Females	
Age group	White	Black	White	Black
16 years and over	79.4	73.3	45.2	49.1
16–17	53.3	34.6	43.3	24.2
18–19	73.6	62.4	60.4	44.6
20–24	86.5	82.1	63.8	58.2
25–34	96.3	92.3	51.1	60.8
35–44	96.7	90.9	53.7	61.5
45–54	93.0	84.7	54.3	56.9
55–64	78.1	70.2	40.4	43.5
65 and over	22.5	21.7	8.0	10.0

Source: Manpower Report of the President, 1975, Table A-4.

spite the higher overall black female rate. Combining these labor force figures with those on unemployment points a dismal picture of employment opportunities for young blacks. Relative unemployment rates for young blacks are very high, but they would be even higher if the young black labor force participation were as high relative to whites as it is for older workers. This relationship between unemployment and labor force participation suggests that many young blacks drop out of the labor force in discouragement as they no longer seek jobs, an action which may keep their unemployment rate from rising even higher but which does nothing to relieve their economic plight.

School leavers of both races have serious employment problems, but again these are more severe for young blacks. In 1971, of white high school graduates sixteen to twenty-four years old who did not go on to college, 79.3 percent were in the work force and 15.1 percent were unemployed. For blacks, the figures were 73.3 percent and 35.5 percent respectively. For dropouts, 68.4 percent of whites were in the work force and 23.2 percent were unemployed; for blacks, only 57.1 percent were in the labor force while 31.2 percent were unemployed. These figures certainly deny that blacks quit school because of the lure of work opportunities. Less than 30 percent of them are employed, a percentage even smaller than that for those who remain at school.

Occupational Status   In his study of discrimination, Becker, using an index comprising the racial composition of the skilled, semiskilled, and unskilled work force, found no change in occupational status of blacks over the 40-year period 1910–1950. Elaborating on Becker's analysis and extending it to 1960, Hiestand found some slight improvement in the later years, with the overall index moving from about 81 to 83 over the decade of the 1950s.[10] There have been particular gains among black women, who have moved in large numbers from service to clerical jobs.

But the changes in this group give us some clue to an important source of the persistence of low black incomes. In 1968, although the percentage black in clerical jobs was 7.3 percent, the percentage of black stenographers, typists, and secretaries—the highest echelon in the clerical category—was only 5.1 percent. Since almost all in these jobs were female and black women make up about 13 percent of the total female labor force, black women had only 40 percent of full representation in the subgroup.

Nevertheless, the recent data on broad occupational classifications do suggest some improvement in black relative economic status. Table

[10]Dale Hiestand, *Economic Growth and Employment Opportunities for Minorities,* Columbia University Press, 1964.

4-5 presents the data on changes in occupational composition of the work force by race. The occupations, as listed by the Bureau of Labor Statistics, might conform roughly to a sociological concept of occupational status even if there are some inconsistencies as far as earnings and poverty tendencies are concerned—certainly craftsmen earn more than clerical workers. But still the table does suggest some relative movement of blacks to the better-paying occupations.

An optimist would look at the figures and note substantial movement of blacks toward occupational equality. A pessimist would emphasize the large gap that still remains; for example, the drop in black employment percentage in private household work (domestic service) from 15.4 to 6.8 percent is a positive change, but there is no comfort in the fact that about 15 percent of all employed black females work in this menial field.

SUMMARY

Racial prejudice leads to overt discrimination and institutionalized racism, basic causes of low black incomes and the high incidence of poverty among blacks. The former manifestation of prejudice has been illegal since passage of the Civil Rights Act of 1964, but there is much evidence of the continued prejudicial use of race as a negative factor in economic decisions. But more detrimental to the movement toward racial economic equality is the persistence of institutionalized racism, the vicious circle of discrimination, whose continuation does not depend on overt discrimination or even prejudicial attitudes.

The results of either practice obviously have their greatest impact in limiting black economic potential. The discriminating employer may earn lower profits, but he accepts this loss in exchange for indulging his taste for discrimination. In cases where black applicants have weaker qualifications, screening out blacks through discrimination may actually raise profits. Favored whites gain from the absence of black competition, but whites with less human investment and in less demanding occupations experience additional competition from the crowding of suppressed blacks into inferior jobs.

If efforts to eliminate discrimination are undertaken with purpose and persistence, it would probably be easier to attack overt discrimination. This could be done by making the "consumption good" of discrimination more expensive through applying stronger penalties for violation of existing civil rights legislation and through rigorous application of the law.

Institutionalized racism is a more stubborn if less emotion-arousing evil. Its removal requires efforts to compensate for the weaker position in which past discrimination has placed blacks. Efforts to break the circle need not require reverse discrimination against whites but can be success-

Table 4-5 Percentage Distribution of Employed Persons Sixteen Years of Age and Over by Occupation Group, 1958 and 1974

Occupations	Percentage of white employed		Percentage of black employed	
	1958	1974	1958	1974
White-collar workers	45.8	50.6	13.8	32.0
Professional and technical	11.8	14.8	4.1	10.4
Managers and administration	11.7	11.2	2.4	4.1
Sales workers	6.9	6.8	1.2	2.3
Clerical workers	15.4	17.8	6.1	15.2
Blue-collar workers	36.6	33.9	40.7	40.2
Craftsmen	14.3	13.8	5.9	9.4
Operatives	17.9	15.5	20.1	21.9
Nonfarm laborers	4.5	4.6	14.7	8.9
Service workers	9.5	12.0	33.0	25.1
Private household workers	1.7	1.2*	15.4*	6.8*
Other service workers	7.7	10.6*	17.7*	20.5*
Farm workers	8.0	3.6	12.5	2.7
Farmers and farm managers	5.0	2.2*	3.7*	.6*
Farm laborers and foremen	3.0	1.6*	8.8*	2.4*

*1972 figures. Breakdowns are not available for 1974.
Source: Manpower Report of the President, 1975, p. 35, Table 8.

fully undertaken through expansion of the facilities and opportunities that will be needed as increased black purchasing power raises total demand. Reverse discrimination, though, may be temporarily necessary in a stagnant and especially in a declining economic period. In the short run, (white) society as a whole will have to pay the costs for repairing the social and economic damage inflicted in the past. Ultimately, society as a whole will be a large gainer if all forms of racial discrimination are eliminated, thus bringing about the improved and increased utilization of all our human resources.

Despite improvements in black economic conditions, there has been little change in relative racial economic status, the sociologically important comparison. Over a recent generation, the ratio of black to white income rose only from 54 to 58 percent, a growth rate that would lead to equality in about a century. Moreover, there has been no steady trend in this growth, slight though it is; it represents but one brief period of mild improvement during the late 1960s. The black poverty rate has fallen sharply and steadily over the years, but the ratio of black to white poverty has even increased over time.

The relatively high black poverty rate is closely related to unfavorable work experience. Relative black unemployment rates have been steady for many years at about twice the white level. The situation is particularly bad for black youths, who have very high unemployment rates and low labor force participation rates. That is, their unemployment rates, high as they are, understate their lack of employment opportunities, with many leaving the labor force in discouragement. In addition, the large young black population in the employment void—out of school and not in the labor force—reflects the most damaging effects of discrimination.

There has been some improvement in relative occupational status for blacks in recent years, but the racial gap remains large. The failure of the racial income differential to narrow despite the increasing concentration of blacks in better-paying occupations results partially from the tendency of blacks to hold lower-rated jobs within each classification. It could also signal greater dispersion in the black income distribution,[11] with a widening gulf between middle-class and poor blacks, having little effect on median incomes and on the incidence of black poverty and doing little to solve the most pressing socioeconomic problems of racial discrimination.

[11]Albert Wohlsetter and Sinclair Coleman, in "Race Differences in Income," *Racial Discrimination in Economic Life,* pp. 3–81, found only slight differences between black and white income distribution up to the late 1950s.

Chapter 5

Female Poverty

Certainly the discrimination women face is less pervasive and oppressive than that which blacks encounter. For one thing, women must contend with very little personal animus and social ostracism. Quite the countrary, whether they regard women as sex objects, life partners, or means of satisfying an old-fashioned sense of chivalry, the discriminating group (men) is kindly disposed toward women. Such a patronizing basis for favorable attitudes may do nothing for female ego satisfaction,[1] but relevant to economic matters, it might be expected to forestall female poverty.

Then, too, regardless of the translation of sex discrimination into a lower earnings potential, many women can and do avoid poverty by the simple expedient of having the good luck (or good sense) to marry men with a high enough income to keep themselves, their wives, and their other dependents above the poverty level.

[1]A typical male student's (chauvinistic) response to the question of whether women should be considered a minority group was "You know we love the girls. We'll take care of them." Quoted in Juanita Kreps, *Sex in the Marketplace,* Johns Hopkins, Baltimore, 1971, p. viii.

Finally, the background factors for women equal those of men in their quest for good-paying jobs. Girls receive more or less the same home treatment as boys, they get the same degree of education—measured in school years completed—and consequently test out as well in measurements of their intellectual development.

Considering all these favorable factors on their side, the wonder is that women suffer the same economic disadvantages as blacks and experience a similar high incidence of poverty. Of course, qualification must be made to the description to exclude those many women shielded from the harmful effects of sex discrimination on earnings by marriage to men who earn enough to support two and more adequately. Thus, the relationship between discrimination and female poverty refers to three groups of women: those unable to earn enough to help pull their male-headed households above the poverty level, those who themselves head households, and those who live alone.

SEX DISCRIMINATION IN THE LABOR MARKET

As noted above, most of the elements of prejudice do not apply to women, nor is there a vicious circle of institutionalized sexism similar to that of racism discussed in the previous chapter and depicted in Figure 4-1. All the economic discrimination faced by women centers on the labor market, and it is testimony to the power of these forces that they suffice to create so much financial misery and poverty among a large segment of our population. Women are not poor because of low earnings that are attributable to weak investment in human capital—in their schooling and in their health—which disqualifies them from better jobs. Their earnings are low simply because in many instances they are denied access to the better jobs for which their training and/or aptitudes qualify them. In brief, while the structure of discrimination is much less complex for sex than race, the negative effect on earnings and push toward poverty is very much the same. Overt discrimination and institutionalized sexism in the labor market can do all the damage without the aid of other discriminatory disadvantages.

While the crudeness of overt discrimination—in the form of using sex as a standard for wages, hiring, promotion, etc.—needs no further elaboration, institutionalized sexism requires explanation, since it differs from the structure of institutionalized racism. Unlike racism, sexism does not refer to a connected circle of labor market disadvantages but the accepted traditions, myths, and encrusted habits which assign women to roles and status which retard their labor force participation, channel them into a narrow range of occupations, and consequently keep their earnings low.

Female Labor Force Participation

One of the most striking socioeconomic features of the past generation has been the expansion of the female labor force. The female participation rate has increased from 31.8 percent in 1947 to 45.7 percent in 1974. Table 5-1 shows that the trend has been rather constant, with no noticeable tendency for the upward movement to slacken.

Thus, the first impression of the change in female labor force activity is a favorable one as far as poverty reduction is concerned. There is no better way to raise income levels than through work earnings, and women have been coming into the labor market in increasing numbers. What is more, they are finding jobs too; while the female unemployment rate has been characteristically above the male level in recent years, the difference is rarely more than a percentage point or so.

But close examination of the structure of female labor force participation leads to pessimism about the positive effect of work force participation or employment on poverty reduction. Columns 3, 4, and 5 of Table 5-1 show that the increase in work force activity over the years has been confined mainly to married women. A decline in participation of single women occurred during 1947—1974 with a little recovery in recent years.

Table 5-1   Female Labor Force Participation Rates by Marital Status and Race, Selected Years 1947–1974

Years	All	Married	Single	Widowed, divorced, separated	White	Black
1947	31.8	20.0	51.2	37.4		
1948	32.7	22.0	51.1	38.7	31.3	45.6
1951	34.7	25.2	49.6	39.2	33.4	46.3
1954	39.6	26.6	49.0	39.4	33.3	46.1
1957	36.9	29.6	46.8	40.0	35.7	47.2
1960	37.8	30.5	44.1	40.0	36.5	40.2
1963	38.3	33.7	41.0	38.9	37.2	48.1
1966	40.5	35.4	40.8	39.5	39.2	49.3
1967*	41.2	36.8	41.3	39.4	40.1	49.5
1969	42.7	39.6	41.7	39.2	41.8	49.8
1972	43.9	41.5	44.7	40.1	43.2	48.7
1973	44.7	42.2	45.5	39.6	44.1	49.1
1974	45.7	44.3	46.5	40.9	45.2	49.1

*Prior to 1967, reported values are for women fourteen years of age and over; from 1967 on, they are for women sixteen years of age and over. These values have been adjusted in the last three entries to include women of fourteen and over to make the data comparable throughout. The significant (downward) adjustment was, of course, needed only for the *single* category.

Source: *Manpower Report of the President,* 1973

Formerly married women have experienced only slight growth in participation.

Certainly, women who work add to household income and raise many families above the poverty level who would otherwise lie below it were they dependent solely on the earnings of a male head. But the center of the female poverty problem lies among unattached women, and even more emphatically among families headed by women. These last two groups combined have demonstrated a stagnant labor force participation.

A further breakdown of the female work force, this time by race, shows the same tendency of the increase being centered in the group least susceptible to poverty (white women), with little change in labor market participation by the group most in need of income increases to avoid poverty (black women). White female participation rose from 31.3 percent to 45.2 percent over the 1948–1974 period, a gain of over 40 per-

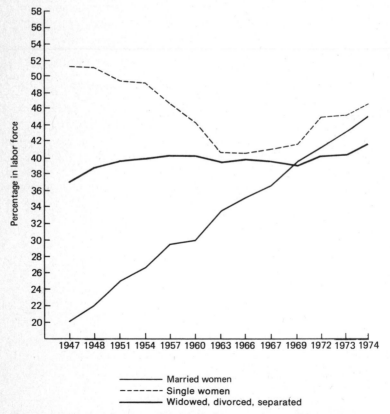

Figure 5-1 Labor force participation of women by marital status.

cent, while the rate for black women rose by only about 8 percent, from 45.6 percent to 49.1 percent (See Table 5-1).

Figures 5-1 and 5-2 show the trend in female labor activity according to marital status and race, respectively. They clearly reveal the stagnation in participation of the groups most likely to suffer poverty, with the rapid growth concentrated in those least susceptible to low incomes.

Analysts of the growth in the female work force point to explanatory factors that favor labor market effort by middle- and upper-class women. They cite improved technology in the home, translated into economic terms to mean that machines and processes, such as electrical appliances and frozen foods, have fallen in price relative to the wages housewives can earn at work to pay for these home work substitutes.

Higher educational attainment of women is also cited as a factor leading to greater labor force participation. As their job preparation has

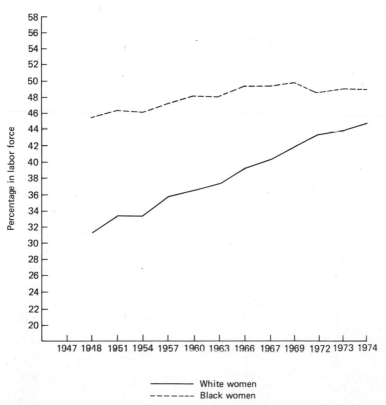

Figure 5-2 Labor force participation of women by race.

become more developed, women are sought for a wider variety of challenging and responsible jobs, which ease the way for them to make the important family decision to leave the home for work.

Then, higher family consumption aspirations have driven the house-wife into the labor market to satisfy these expanded wants that turn into needs. A close look at these three factors—rising wages for women, making use of still expensive housework substitutes economically sensible; higher education levels (meaning some college completion), opening up interesting job opportunities; and compelling socioeconomic status aspirations—reveals forces that have driven middle-class women into the labor force but which have little impact on the work participation of women in poverty, and particularly poor black[2] and unmarried women.

The relatively high labor force participation of unmarried women has not kept them off the poverty roles. The poverty rates for both single women and those who head households are among the highest for population subgroups. The point is that the female groups most active in the work force still have a great many nonparticipants, enough to make their group poverty rates high.

So far the discussion has been of factors that have induced growth of female labor force activity. Kreps in her *Sex in the Marketplace* notes these factors as the usual focus of labor market analysts, who feel the need to study the reasons why women have shaken loose from the confines of their homes in increasing numbers. She says, "whereas we go to some pains to explain the *absence* from the labor force of any significant number of males, it is the *presence* of females we feel must be analyzed."[3]

But in reality, nonparticipation of women is easy to explain, at least superficially. It stems from the fact that so many women feel that household duties prevent them from holding jobs. At least, this is their response to the census question of why they are nonparticipants in the labor force.

Table 5-2 lists the reasons given for nonparticipation by men and women. The similarity in number of responses for most explanations for nonparticipation is just as striking as the sex difference in the one item on household responsibilities. Just a figurative handful of men report they cannot work because they must keep house, but almost 80 percent of the women cite this reason for their nonparticipation.

Only retirement as a reason also shows a sex difference in response, but the larger number of men in this category simply reflects the fact that

---

[2]Glen Cain, in *Married Women in the Labor Force,* University of Chicago Press, Chicago, 1966, explains the racial difference in labor force trends of wives with reference to these factors.
[3]Kreps, op. cit., p. 18. Italics in the original.

Table 5-2   Persons Not in the Labor Force by Reason of Nonparticipation, 1973

(Numbers in Thousands)

Reason for Nonparticipation	Men	Women	Percentage of men	Percentage of women
In school	3,762	3,582	26.0	8.2
Ill health, disability	2,675	2,516	18.4	5.6
Home responsibilities	226	32,962	1.6	78.3
Retirement, old age	5,927	1,238	40.7	2.6
Think cannot get work	225	454	1.6	1.1
All other reasons	1,725	1,928	11.8	4.3
Totals	14,540	42,681	100.0	100.0

Source: Manpower Report of the President, 1974.

retirement depends on prior work participation, a status attained by many more men than women.

If we accept the conventional roles assigned to men and women, the data offer no surprises and merely substantiate "traditional values"; men work and women stay home to "keep house" and "mind the children." If married families want to follow these rules, and the recent labor force data show an increasing number breaking them, there is little effect on the poverty count. But who is going to provide for nonworking single women, and especially the female heads-of-household who must face the added financial burden of children while trying to combat custom, which still does not easily accept the concept of working mothers?

Unfortunately, the data do not separate out women by marital status, but the 33.0 million women in 1973 who were out of the labor force because of household responsibilities exceeds the 27.1 million married women not in the work force for all reasons. Thus, more than 5.9 million of the 15.7 million not married—which include 6.0 million single and 9.7 million widowed, divorced, separated women—do not work because of housework duties.

But in truth, those in the last group without husbands but with children might have the most demands for their housekeeping services while their need for labor market earnings are the most pressing, a combination of factors with a strong pull toward poverty.

In any case, the number of married women who work at home instead of in the labor market forms a substantial population. For among all women, there are slightly more who do not work for the one reason of household duties than work for pay. If this statistic does not suffice to measure the strength of the custom that woman's role (place?) is still in the home, there is the figure of only 226 thousand men who report that home responsibilities keep them from market work.[4] This value represents only 1.6 percent of male nonparticipants and 3.0 percent of the male labor force, while it is only 0.7 percent of the number of females for whom housework prevents market work. Perhaps women's rights have expanded and their status has improved over the years, and certainly their entry into the work force has increased. But these figures reveal a still powerful social force keeping them at home.

For surely "home responsibilities" offered as an ostensible reason for nonparticipation can cover a multitude of other real reasons. At least some adult or parent is required at home when small children are present, and we can assume that, in the present state of society, it will be the woman. We are not here making the stronger argument for true sexual equality in employment opportunity, which could make the choice of home parent dependent on earning capability, skills in housework, etc., instead of making the duties of homemaker fall on the woman as a matter of course. But still there must be many women who, while reporting that they do not seek work because of home responsibilities, in reality stay out of the labor force because they accept their roles as nonparticipants—they may even like it. They may stay home because they feel they would be breaking tradition by working for pay; because they comply with their husbands' wishes not to work; and because, for various other reasons, they wish to continue playing the role of homemaker.

The acceptability and even prestige of their role may lead many women, when they feel they cannot get jobs, to report home responsibilities as the cause of nonparticipation to support their pride. For males the counterpart is retirement, which is often a euphemism to obscure the inability of older workers to get jobs.

There is a relatively small population (4.5 million) who are not counted in the labor force because they do not seek work but who would take jobs if they became available. The data on this group reveal only a slight expressed yearning of women to break out of the binds of household duties. Of the 3.1 million women in this labor force limbo, almost one-third report that household duties prevent their active search for work. But this percentage only represents 1.0 million women at the edge of the labor force, a small percentage of the 33.0 million who are prevented from work force activity because of home responsibilities. Thus, if we take the data literally, there are still 32.0 million women who would not work for

---

[4]This figure includes men who head households without wives, a small classification which the census ignores, probably because of its insignificant size, but perhaps also, consistent with its sexist reporting, because the census does not consider the absent wife a socioeconomically important family characteristic.

pay under any conditions because, as they report, their work at home prevents them from doing so.

Occupations of Women

If following the role of homemaker keeps many women out of the work force, role playing determines the jobs they hold when they do work. Women are experienced at the menial tasks of housework, so they form the bulk of the food service work force except for the more prestigious, higher paying, and administrative jobs such as head waiter or chief cook; and they hold exclusive rights to all household servant jobs. Women are experienced in raising children, so they hold all the child-care jobs and most of the early education jobs, no matter that many of these child-care workers and schoolteachers are childless.

"Women are handy, dexterous, nimble with their fingers," thus they run all the office machinery. Since so many men make good violinists, one wonders why so few can type a letter.

"Behind every man there is a woman," thus women fill jobs that, in effect, provide auxiliary services to men in responsible jobs. How many male nurses assist women surgeons? Do we still see want ads for that literary contradiction, the "girl Friday"? How many male all-purpose office factotums serve female bosses?

"Women have no head for business." The labor market seems to agree, seeing the handful of women in important managerial positions. Without continuing this one-by-one listing of jobs that match female roles, examination of the entire occupational structure and trends for particular jobs reveals the tendency for women to concentrate in work closely related to their conventional roles.

Overall industry and occupational data obscure the details of the crowding of women into a few particular fields. In 1970 as in 1940, the service industry ranked first in female employment.[5] In both years most women in this industry were in the same three occupational groups: professional and technical; service occupations in educational, personal, and technical services; and the clerical-sales area. Concentrations of women workers are also found in government and retail trade. The sex breakdown of occupations within industry presented in Table 5-3 only begins to tell the story of the crowding of women in inferior jobs, those with less prestige, less responsibility, and—what is most important for the issue of poverty—lower pay. Looking into the narrower job classifications within

[5]For data and trends in female employment by broad industrial and occupational classification, see Elizabeth Waldman and Beverly J. McEady, "Where Women Work: An Analysis by Industry and Occupation," *Monthly Labor Review*, May 1974, pp. 1–13.

Table 5-3   Occupational Groups of Employees in Nonagricultural Industries, 1970
(Percentage of Each Sex)

Occupation in industry	Men 100.0	Women 100.0
Professional, technical, etc.	14.6	16.6
Managers and administra-tors	10.5	3.2
Sales work	6.9	7.4
Clerical work	8.6	37.5
Craft workers	22.2	1.8
Operatives	21.6	15.5
Laborers except farm	7.0	0.9
Service workers*	8.8	17.1

*Private household workers are not included in this breakdown, which is on an industrial basis.
Source: Waldheim and McEady, op. cit.

each broad occupational group yields closer insight into these characteristics of the jobs women hold.

For example, Table 5-3 shows that the percentage of women in the professional-technical group, the highest-paid job category, actually exceeded that of men (16.6 percent to 14.6 percent) in 1970. But of the 4.2 million women in this group, over 2 million, or about half, are schoolteachers.

Women also dominate the fields of nursing, social work, library work, dietetics, and dental hygiene. In the teaching profession itself, it is interesting to note that about 70 percent of college and university teachers are men and that the same percentage of grade school and high school teachers are women.

The prevalence of women in the lower-paying professional jobs has little to do with the issue of female poverty, because almost all workers in this occupational category have incomes well above the poverty level. But the increased membership of women in the once exclusively male, better-paid professions is looked upon as symptomatic of the occupational advancement of women. In reality, though, the growth in the female share of these occupations has not been so dramatic as to suggest an early achievement of equal representation of both sexes.

A study of the long-term trend of the sex distribution of professional occupations finds that the female percentage rose from 1870 (27.5 percent) to 1930 (44.4 percent) but has actually fallen since that time (40.8 percent in 1970).[6] This surprising drop results from a relative decline in labor demand for those professional jobs that are dominated by women

[6]Rudolph G. Blitz, "Women in Professions, 1870–1970," *Monthly Labor Review*, May 1974, pp. 34–35.

(mainly elementary schoolteachers), and growth in professional jobs dominated by men (such as engineers).

The trend is upward for some of the most sexually imbalanced fields—since 1870, female architects have risen from 1 to 4 percent of the total and lawyers from 1 to 6 percent, but the overall percentages are still small.

Indications of future growth of female employment in male-dominated professions appear in the number of female students enrolled in specific educational programs. In the legal profession in 1970, for example, 5.9 percent of the new law school graduates were women; but women represented 9 percent of law school enrollments and 10 percent of the first-year class.[7] In medicine, the comparable figures for 1972 were 9 percent, 13 percent, and 17 percent, respectively.[8] But for engineering these figures were only 1 percent, 3 percent, and 3 percent, and the situation in dentistry was exactly the same. The winds of change in these professions are a gentle breeze.

It is interesting to note the manner in which no less a women's advocate than the Labor Department's Women's Bureau offers advice to women on future career opportunities. It notes that there will be a large demand for jobs in environmental protection and unemotionally mentions "that the evolving fields of environmental law, environmental engineering, and environmental journalism are expected to offer numerous opportunities." But when the bureau discusses the expected high demand for physician's assistants, "who perform many of the routine duties usually carried out [now] only by the physician," it becomes enthusiastic in its advice that "women should certainly consider this field when looking at future job prospects as part of the professional health service team."[9]

The *absolute* job status of women has improved slightly as the whole work force has enjoyed upward mobility. The percentage of women workers in the low-paid, low-prestige household service field has fallen from 17.6 percent in 1940 to 10.5 percent in 1950 and 5.5 percent in 1969. But—greatly counteracting this trend—the percentage of women workers in other service jobs has risen from 11.3 percent to 12.6 percent to 16.1 percent over the 30-year period. (Table 5-4 shows the percentage of jobs held by women in major occupational groups.)

Concentration figures for 1960 for specific jobs—babysitters (98 percent); attendants in hospitals, etc. (74 percent); waitresses (87 percent); kitchen workers (50 percent); chambermaids (98 percent)—though out of

[7]John B. Parrish, "Women in Professional Training," *Monthly Labor Review,* May 1974, p. 41.

[8]The future growth trend in law and medicine for women appears stronger when it is noted that in 1970 only 4 percent of lawyers and 7 percent of doctors were women.

[9]*Careers for Women in the '70's,* Women's Bureau, U.S. Department of Labor, 1973, p. 7.

Table 5-4 Female Percentages in Major Occupational Groups 1940–1969

Occupation	1940	1950	1969
White-collar workers			
Professional and technical	45.4	41.8	37.3
Managers, officials, etc.	11.7	14.8	15.8
Clerical workers	52.6	59.3	74.5
Sales workers	27.9	39.0	43.0
Blue-collar workers			
Craftsmen, foremen	2.1	2.4	3.3
Operatives	25.7	26.9	31.2
Nonfarm laborers	3.2	2.2	4.0
Service workers			
Private household workers	93.8	92.1	97.6
Other service workers	40.1	45.4	59.3
Farm workers			
Farmers, farm managers	n.a.	5.5	4.3
Farm laborers, foremen	n.a.	27.4	33.8
Total	25.9	29.3	37.3

Source: Lise Vogel, *Women Workers—Some Basic Statistics*, Conference for Working Women, 1970, p. 9.

date, undoubtedly reflect current concentrations. Such figures point to the existence of a high proportion of females among the working poor.

Female Earnings, Role Playing, and Sex Discrimination in the Labor Market

Having detailed the pattern of female participation or lack of it in the labor market and the types of jobs women hold, which are generally low-paying, we have disclosed the two sources of high female poverty: (1) the fact that many women are not gainfully employed and that (2) those women who do work earn relatively little.

Earnings trends for women, as compared to those for men, are certainly discouraging. Relative pay rates for women declined over the 1949–1969 period. These rates indicate earnings potential even if they do not measure the degree of low earnings resulting from less than full-time labor, which we know is much more characteristic of female labor than male. The female/male ratio of average hourly earnings fell from 0.75 in 1949 to 0.61 in 1959, and it recovered only to 0.64 in 1969.[10]

[10]Data are from Henry Sanborn, "Pay Differences between Men and Women," *Industrial and Labor Relations Review,* July 1964, pp. 534–550; Victor R. Fuchs, "Differences in Hourly Earnings between Men and Women," *Monthly Labor Review,* May 1971, pp. 9–15; and Fuchs, "Women's Earnings, Recent Trends and Long-Run Prospects," *Monthly Labor Review,* May 1974, pp. 23–26.

Whether they are explaining the downward movement and later stability of the ratio or the low ratio at a moment in time, analysts imply the presence of institutionalized sexism if not outright overt discrimination in the labor market. The two decades from 1949 to 1969 witnessed a great influx of women, especially married women, into the labor force, and these new entrants had less experience and education than the average women worker. This can explain some of the weakness in the female earnings ratio on the purely economic grounds of lower female productivity without evoking a suggestion of increased sex discrimination.

Fuchs finds an understatement of the improving earning trend for women in the slight increase in the earnings ratio over the decade of the 1960s. He supports this view with the statement that "if during a period of rapid increase in supply [of women workers], earnings of women were more than able to hold their own . . . , the long-run prospects for women must be viewed as favorable." But in saying this he is implying that the labor market is sexually dichotomized.

Unfortunately, there is nothing incorrect about this implication; the fact that there are "women's jobs" explains why growth in their labor force participation weakens their earnings position. Otherwise, as women entrants replaced older and younger men in the labor market, there would not be negative pressure on women's wages and women would simply constitute a larger share of a more or less stable overall supply.

Since women do, however, collect in or are crowded into particular fields, an increase in their numbers creates the negative pressure on wages inferred by Fuchs.[11]

The same suggestion of role playing or institutionalized sexism exists in the analysis of the causes for lower wages for women at a moment in time. In his summary of the factors that lead to low wages for women, Fuchs assigns the major causes to the different roles assigned to women that lead them to a looser work force attachment in jobs close to their homes, requiring comparatively less prior training and postschool investment. When corrections are made for these factors—that is, when the comparison is between wages of women and men in jobs requiring the same skill and training with both having the same continuous work experience—much of the differential evaporates. In fact, when the job classification becomes narrower—that is, when wages by sex are compared for the

---

[11]Economists have long been aware of the negative effect of crowding on women's wages and its evidence of labor market discrimination against them. Thus, over 50 years ago, F. Y. Edgeworth (in "Equal Pay to Men and Women for Equal Work," *Economic Journal,* 1921), wrote about "that crowding of women into a comparatively few occupations, which is universally recognized as a main factor in the depression of their wages. Such crowding is *prima facie* a flagrant violation of that free competition which results in maximum production and in distribution of the kind here defined as equal pay for equal work," p. 439.

same specific job such as payroll clerk or office boy (girl)—the sex differential narrows further, which leads Fuchs to conclude that "if one pushes occupational classifications far enough, one could 'explain' nearly all of the differential."

But he then astutely points out that "in doing so, however, one merely changes the form of the problem. We would then have to explain why occupational distributions differ so much." The answer, of course, lies in role playing, the sexual counterpart to racism as a form of institutionalized discrimination.

That the average hourly wage differential between the sexes is sharply reduced by comparison of wages for men and women performing the same type of work supports the view that overt sex discrimination contributes little to the differential. A 1970 study of 10 office occupations yields data consistent with this hypothesis.[12] The simple wage differential by sex for those occupations favored men by 18 percent. But the differential was wider, 22 percent, among establishments that employed only one sex in an occupation; and it was narrower, 11 percent, among establishments employing both sexes.

These findings show that women tend to receive much lower pay than men when they alone work for low-wage employers, but they come closer to the male level when the sexes work together. Under these latter conditions, the entire differential is explained by the preponderance of women in low-wage establishments, those that pay little to men and women indiscriminately. Data collected on an establishment basis revealed no wage difference between men and women doing the same work within the same plant.

Further proof that low wages for women result from institutionalized sexism rather than overt discrimination can be found in the relatively few settlements under the Equal Pay Act of 1963. This act provides that where men and women perform equal work on jobs that require equal skill, effort, and responsibility in the same establishment, they must receive equal pay, under penalty of fines and retroactive pay for noncompliance. In the first seven years of the act's implementation, $17 million in underpayments were assigned to 50,000 women.[13] This retribution was certainly welcome to these women, but considering that the size of the female labor force is over 30 million, that the basis of most of the cases involved less pay for women in different occupations but which were judged equal to those held by higher-paid males (nurse's aide and

[12]John E. Buckley, "Pay Differences between Men and Women in the Same Job," *Monthly Labor Review,* November 1971, pp. 36–40.

[13]Robert D. Moran, "Reducing Discrimination: Role of the Equal Pay Act," *Monthly Labor Review,* June 1970, pp. 30–34.

orderly for example), and the vigor with which the new law was applied, the dollar and population figures do not uncover much evidence of overt sex discrimination in the marketplace.

POVERTY AMONG HOUSEHOLDS HEADED BY WOMEN

So far we have studied the three sources of low (labor) earnings of women: their nonparticipation in the work force, their employment in low-paying jobs, and the low rates of pay they receive on their jobs. In this section we examine two aspects of the incidence of poverty among female-headed households, those in which the lower earning power of women affects family income the most. First we look at the overall trend in poverty incidence among those households, their degree of poverty, and their family and racial composition—in short, the socioeconomic background of these families. Then we observe the relationship between the work experience of these women and the incidence of poverty among them.

Socioeconomic Aspects of Poverty in Households Headed by Women

Not only is the incidence of poverty high among persons in female-headed households but, what is even more disturbing, this incidence relative to that for male-headed households is worsening. As Table 5-5 shows, the poverty rate has declined for both sexes, but the ratio of female to male incidence has increased steadily. A more dramatic expression of the tendency toward poverty among persons living in female-headed households is shown by the fact that in 1972 the 11.5 million poor in these households were not much fewer than the 12.8 million in male-headed households. They thus represented over 45 percent of the poverty popu-

Table 5-5 Percentage of Persons in Female- and Male-headed Households in Poverty, Selected Years 1959–1973

Year	Female-headed household	Male-headed household	Female/male
1959	50.2	18.7	2.7
1962	50.5	16.9	3.0
1965	46.0	13.2	3.5
1968	38.9	8.8	4.4
1970	38.2	8.2	4.7
1971	38.0	8.1	4.7
1972	36.9	7.4	5.0
1973	34.9	6.6	5.3

Source: Current Population Reports, Characteristics of the Low-Income Population: 1973, Series P-60/94, July 1974.

Table 5-6 Poverty Incidence in 1969 among Families Headed by Women, by Number of Children and by Race
(Numbers in Hundreds of Thousands)

Number of children under 18	White			Black		
	Number poor	Percentage poor	Average income deficit	Number poor	Percentage poor	Average income deficit
No children under 18	2.3	12	700	0.8	29	700
One child	2.3	25	1,100	1.3	43	1,100
Two children	2.6	37	1,300	1.3	50	1,100
Three children	1.6	46	1,700	1.2	61	1,500
Four children	1.0	60	1,700	1.1	75	1,600
Five children or more	0.9	66	2,400	1.7	81	2,400
Total	10.6	25	$1,200	7.4	53	$1,400

Source: Robert L. Stein, "The Economic Status of Families Headed by Women," *Monthly Labor Review,* December 1970.

lation but only 15 percent of the overall population. The income deficit was greater for families with female heads, $1,616, compared to $1,416 for male-headed families.

Most women who headed families had dependent children. Those who did not were generally older and had a lower poverty probability because they often had children over eighteen or other potential labor force members in their households. But for those with children, over two-thirds of the total, the task of maintaining an adequate income is handicapped both by a rise in needs as the number of family members increases and by the difficulty of partaking in continuous employment because of pressing demand for the mother's services at home.

The probability and intensity of poverty increase with the number of children. As we see in Table 5-6, the rates become astronomical for families with large numbers of children, especially black families.

Despite the fact that there are three times as many white as black families headed by women, the number of such poor black families is 70 percent the number of white ones. Furthermore, the number of black and poor black families is highest for the largest-family category, so that there are twice as many poverty stricken black as white families headed by women with five or more children. What a tale of desperation lies behind these simple numbers. That the income deficit is not even larger for the big families obviously reflects the receipt of (insufficient) welfare supplements, since incomes for those with five or more children average twice the level of one-child families. This differential certainly does not result from higher earnings of these women encumbered with half a dozen children. Equally obvious, from the upward movement of the deficit as the number of children increases, is the increased depth of poverty to which these families sink as each child adds less to (transfer) income than he or she adds to family costs, as measured by the grudging rise in the poverty line in response to increased family size.

Work Experience

Table 2-7 showed the strong effect of part-time employment on poverty among female-headed families. But the weaker economic condition of these families, compared to those headed by males, applies to every type of work force status. Table 5-7 presents the data for the broad categories of work force participation. Not only is the percentage unemployed slightly higher and the percentage out of the labor force three times higher—relationships noted earlier between women and men in general—but the female poverty rates shown in the table systematically surpass the male by overwhelming margins for each labor force category. As usual, the black poverty incidence is higher for every class.

Table 5-7   Employment Status of Head, 1974—Families in Poverty in 1973
(Percentage in Classification Poor)

	White		Black	
	Male head	Female head	Male head	Female head
Employed	3.6	13.2	10.4	31.6
Unemployed	13.3	40.3	30.9	64.2
Not in labor force	13.8	37.1	33.1	70.2
Total	5.5	24.5	15.4	52.7

Source: Current Population Reports, Series P-60/98, January 1975.

SUMMARY

For married women, sex discrimination in the labor market does little to push their families into poverty. Of course, if they could realize the full potential of their earning power, they would, in many cases, be able to lift total family income above the poverty level. But the brunt of market disadvantages that lead to poverty falls heavily on women who head families.

Four labor market factors inhibit the attainment of adequate income by these women: (1) low labor market participation, (2) prevalence of part-time and sporadic work effort, (3) concentration in low-paying jobs, (4) lower pay than men receive in the jobs they do hold.

The first three factors are a consequence of the family role women play either by choice, custom, or coercion. While the labor force participation of women has been increasing steadily, it is still only about half the male rate, and the significant gains have been made by married women, those least susceptible to poverty. Over half the women without husbands do not work. With children under their care, they usually have the greatest impediments to gainful employment and the greatest need for work income.

Thus, the factors that retard the earnings of all women expose women without husbands to poverty. Household responsibilities make it difficult for them to work. Often these duties limit their working effort to part-time and temporary employment.

Even if their education equals that of men, they are channeled into "women's work." Despite the widely reported and often exaggerated gains in female occupational status, they still remain concentrated in low-paid sales, office, and service work.

The little evidence of differential pay for equal work only indicates that women, like blacks, do not face much of the crudest form of market handicaps—overt discrimination. Role playing, voluntary or forced, creates a fabric of institutionalized sexism with threads that form a clear design of poverty. But it would be incorrect to attribute all the poverty among female-headed households to discrimination. The need to work at home, in housekeeping and child care, prevents many women from earning a living. This work is vital to the family and important to the nation, but unfortunately it is unpaid.

Chapter 6

Age and Poverty

INTRODUCTION:
THE LIFETIME STRUCTURE OF POVERTY

The highest incidence of poverty occurs at the ends of the life span. The poverty rates for children under eighteen and the aged over sixty-five are much above the rate for those in the middle phases of the life cycle.

Despite the obvious differences between childhood and old age, these two ends of the life span share one common poverty-inducing characteristic—they are both nonworking periods. Some (older) children do work, and many of the aged, especially those just past the traditional sixty-five-year retirement age, are also gainfully employed; but it is only a slight exaggeration to claim that the spending power of the young and old is derived from income transfers backward and forward in time from the earning years (from eighteen to sixty-five). It is the inadequacy of these transfers—or, expressed differently, the insufficiency of income in these productive years—that prevents adequate financing of the first and last years of life. This explains the high incidence of poverty among the young and the old.

These transfers, apart from public programs, occur intergenerationally within the family unit. A child's consumption needs, at least as his or her parents see these needs, are financed by these parents, whose income covers their own plus their children's living costs. But enough must also be earned during these productive years to meet the consumption requirements in the Golden Years, which for so many may be better described as leaden. This latter financing may be made directly through visible savings and/or indirectly through deferred wages later received as social security or private pension benefits.

This pattern of private intertemporal income transfers can account for the high incidence of poverty in the nonearning years and the perpetuation of poverty in particular families through lifetimes and generations. Children born in poor families will be disadvantaged in developing their adult earning power by inferior schooling, oppressive financial environment, poor health, etc. Then, when they have children themselves, they too will grow up in a poverty setting. For many whose incomes are high enough to keep themselves and their children out of poverty during their economically productive years, thus arresting the generational transfer of poverty, these incomes will not suffice to finance their last, nonearning years. This pattern describes a life span of childhood poverty, adequate earnings during the work years, and then the reappearance of poverty at the end of life.

At first view, if it is assumed that children born of parents with adequate earnings themselves will escape poverty during their working years, this pattern may seem unrealistic. Will not the children, in turn, generously support the old age of their parents? For one thing, their incomes may not suffice for this purpose, their earnings being barely high enough to keep themselves and their children out of poverty. For another, they might not feel the obligation or desire to give generational balance to the life cycle of support and dependency, lending credence to that bitter lament of the aged, "a parent can raise eight children, but eight children cannot take care of one old parent." In any case, whichever of the two reasons applies, the fact that only 2 percent of the income of the aged comes from family contributions to their support makes all too realistic the pattern of childhood poverty, income adequacy during the working years, and poverty again in old age—notwithstanding the presence of non-poor and perhaps even affluent children.

The life sequence described above is but one of five lifetime income adequacy patterns. Table 6-1 presents these five; it includes all the possibilities under the assumptions that all those whose childhood years are in families with adequate incomes (above poverty level) will have adequate incomes during their working years, and that those who are poor as work-age adults will remain poor in their old age. The first assumption is based

Table 6-1 Income Adequacy Patterns during Preearning, Earning, and Postearning Life Periods

Childhood	Work years	Old age
Poor	Poor	Poor
Poor	Adequate	Poor
Poor	Adequate	Adequate
Adequate	Adequate	Poor
Adequate	Adequate	Adequate

on the tendency for children in families with adequate parental income to receive enough human investment to lift their earning power above poverty; the second assumption is based on the realistic view that if an individual has too little income during the work years to keep out of poverty, his or her chances of doing so in old age, in the absence of work, are very slim.

Note that there are three poverty cases in both the childhood and old age periods and only one for the working years stage. This is not surprising considering the very high poverty incidence at both ends of the life span.

While Table 6-1 may appear descriptive of the poverty situation at a moment of time, at first view it seems to suggest a generational pattern contrary to the actual process. With the sound assumption that those of adequate income will have children who will not be poor, and with these children becoming adults with adequate income, the four adequate income cells in the work years suggest a sharper generational reduction in poverty than has actually occurred over the years. But while the adequate income designation outscores the poor cells four to one for the work years, it is the weight in each cell that counts; and many more poor children become poor adults than attain adequate incomes. Moreover, poor adults have many more children than those with higher incomes, thus keeping up the poverty count over the generations.

Before leaving this general discussion of childhood and aged poverty and going to the specifics of the poverty count and categorical approaches to meet this particular problem, two important public policy differences between the groups are worth noting.

The first concerns the pervading issue over different approaches to poverty relief: whether improvement should occur through increased earning power or expanded income transfers. For the young, the former route is practical and even probably preferred as a long-run solution. But it is highly impractical to expect manpower development to contribute much to increasing the income of the aged, who must rely mainly on the provision of more generous income transfers if they are to lower their poverty count.

The second policy decision closed to the aged relates to population control. One controversial way to approach the problem of childhood poverty is through a positive population policy, a euphemism for keeping down the number of births in poor families. Obviously, no such counterpart population policy option exists for the aged; that is, up to now no pondering bureaucrat has come up with the imaginative idea that aged poverty is best treated by liquidating the aged poor.

Thus the fundamental difference between childhood poverty and poverty in old age is that the former is susceptible to correction through remedial policies, which would reduce the need for transfers in later life. The latter can only be treated through injection of money, a method which has merit for the alleviation of poverty wherever it exists.

POVERTY AMONG CHILDREN

The Data

Children have no control over their parental heritage. If they did and exercised rational economic choice, fewer of them would have chosen poor parents. The 1973 poverty rate for children under eighteen in families exceeds that for the population as a whole by a substantial margin, 14.2 to 11.1 percent. But since the overall rate includes childhood poverty, a more relevant comparison lies between the rate for children and their family head. This leads to a wider differential, 14.2 to 8.8 percent. It is this last comparison which indicates the tendency of poorer families to have more children.

The detailed data on childhood poverty will be examined for two purposes: (1) to note the presence or absence of trend and uniformity in the pattern and (2) to lead to an answer to the important question of whether children are clustered in poor families because of the tendency for low-income families to have more children or because the presence of numerous children drags family income below the poverty standard—a trend which is, of course, greater among large families. Both aspects have important policy implications.

Trends and Patterns of Childhood Poverty The dominant feature of the distribution of childhood poverty is its constancy and uniformity among many demographic family types. Table 6-2 shows the incidence of poverty for children and family head for all family groups and for both white and black families during 1959 and 1973. During the period between these two years, the poverty rate for all people in families fell over 50 percent.

**Table 6-2   Poverty Percentages for Children and Family Heads
of All Families, White and Black, 1959 and 1973**

	1959	1973	1973 as percentage of 1959
All persons in families	20.8	9.7	46.6
All families			
Head	18.5	8.8	47.5
Children under 18	26.9	14.2	52.7
Children as percentage of head	145	161	
White families			
Head	15.2	6.9	45.4
Children under 18	20.6	9.7	47.1
Children as percentage of head	136	140	
Black families			
Head	50.4	28.8	57.1
Children under 18	66.7	38.3	57.4
Children as percentage of head	132	133	

Source: "Characteristics of the Low-Income Population," 1973.

The striking feature of Table 6-2 is the similar downward drift in the poverty subgroups. The last column reveals the greater relative improvement among whites. But considering the strong movement in the poverty rate throughout society, the overall racial difference in reduction is not substantial.

For all subgroups the relative position of children worsened; but again the difference was slight considering the sharp changes in poverty rates involved. That there is a persistent higher poverty rate among black children is not surprising, but of key significance is the racial similarity in the ratio of poverty among children to that of the heads of their household. In both 1959 and 1973 this ratio was slightly higher for whites than for blacks; the rise in the ratio for each rate reflects the worsening relative position for children of both races.[1]

These ratios show that while there is a tendency for black children to be congregated in poor families—the meaning of a high poverty incidence for children—this pattern is no stronger for blacks than for whites. Expressed differently, the association between large families with many children as a factor inducing poverty is not stronger for blacks than for

[1]It might seem contradictory that the overall ratio—in 1972, for example—of childhood to family head poverty is, at 160, greater than for either of the racial components: 142 for whites and 149 for blacks. But the ratio of black to white children, 18 percent, is much higher than the ratio of black to white family heads, 11 percent, which gives heavier weight to total childhood poverty.

whites. This racial similarity between family size and poverty is obscured and often mistakenly denied because of preoccupation with the abnormally high poverty rate among black children, 38.3 percent in 1973. This rate is four times higher than the rate for white children, but this ratio is not much different from that for black and white family heads.

The policy implications of these figures do contain suggestions that special attention should be paid to children in categorical antipoverty programs. They also suggest that future adult poverty could be controlled by putting special effort into human capital investment for poor children; however, any childhood poverty data would support this policy. But of paramount importance, they do not indicate that special population control programs should be geared toward blacks or other minorities. There is no denying that they have more children, and many more poor children, but the presence of children in their families creates no special poverty problems that large white families do not face. In short, programs and policies for reducing poverty insofar as they relate to population control need not and should not have a racial focus. There is much black childhood poverty, but not more than the high level of black poverty in general would suggest. Attack the latter successfully, and black childhood poverty will be reduced to white dimensions.

But for both races, the higher percentage of childhood than family-head poverty indicates an association between poverty and children in the family, with poorer families having more children. Breaking the data down by sex of head shows the particular problems faced by female-headed families with children. For male-headed families in 1972, the respective poverty rates for heads and children are 6.1 and 8.6 percent, a children-head ratio of 141. For female-headed families, the comparable values are 32.7 percent, 53.1 percent, and 162.

Thus, the data show a pronounced income disadvantage for female-headed families with children. In fact, the sex differential in the effect of children on income status is even sharper with respect to the influence of number of children. For male-headed (husband-wife) families, the pattern is somewhat similar to that of the all-family category, with poverty incidence becoming stronger only when several children are present. For all families, the 1972 poverty rate was 10.7 percent. The rate for those with no children was 10.0 percent; with one child, 8.1 percent; with two children, 8.4 percent; and with three or more children, 16.5 percent. That is, the poverty rate actually declined with one or two children and only rose, sharply, with more children to support.

For families headed by males, age thirty-five to forty-four, for example, the overall rate was 5.9 percent. The poverty rate for families with no children was 3.7 percent; with one child, 3.0 percent; with two children, 3.4 percent; three children, 4.8 percent; with more than three,

11.5 percent.[2] The point that poverty is induced only by the presence of large numbers of children—at least more than three—does not need exaggeration.

For female-headed households, though, the situation is entirely different. The very first child imposes a financial burden such that the poverty incidence jumps above the no-children level. For example, for two-member families headed by a woman under thirty-five, the poverty rate for those with no children is only 14.7 percent. With one child, the rate rises to 40.0 percent. Of course, the second member in those families that had no children could have been a wage earner; but in many cases it was an aged mother or some other nonearner. The important difference between an adult and child nonearner as far as family income goes is that the latter requires care which can prevent the mother from working.

The data are less ambiguous for three and four or more family members. For the former with no children under eighteen, the 1970 poverty rate was 12.3 percent; with one child, it was 24.6 percent. For the latter, the comparable rates were 21.4 and 32.1 percent. These figures show that in female-headed households with at least two and often more adults, the presence of even one child sharply increased the poverty incidence. For all these families, the poverty rate rose rapidly with an increase in the number of children.

These figures on female-headed households simply substantiate our earlier findings that the presence of children in families women head is the basis of high poverty rates among women. They do emphasize, though, that while the number of children does affect the poverty level, the problem is a threshold one, arising with the first child. The only policy implication of this pattern is for a redoubling of efforts by social services and other agencies to keep families together. Insofar as financial pressures lead to divorce and separation, certainly raising earnings for those at the bottom of the income distribution would help. This policy is not as circular as it sounds—since rising incomes would lift people out of poverty in any case—because the strengthening of family stability with rising income would be an additive factor in lowering the poverty count by reducing the number of female-headed families with children.

Poverty as a Cause or Result of Large Families?

The data point clearly to the conclusion that the poverty rate rises as low-income families have numerous children but that there is no tendency for low-income families to have more children than those higher up the income scale. To be more precise, as Table 6-3 shows, there is even a slight

[2]To be precise, the data are for family size. That is, the one-child value is for three-person families, the two-child value for four-person families. The omission of families with additional adults does not distort the argument of the text; by far the bulk of family membership is made up of parents and children under eighteen.

tendency for family size to rise with income level or average income to rise for families with more children. (Table 6-3 is on page 114.)

These figures will receive closer reference in the following discussion of population control as antipoverty policy, but at this stage it can be seen that there is little source of poverty alleviation from feasible population limitation among the poor. If all low-income families—those with annual incomes below $4,000—had been childless and assuming those with children followed the pattern of the childless group, the poverty rate would have dropped only from 10.7 to 10.0 percent.

The values of Table 6-3 suggest that most improvement in the poverty rate would have occurred if all low-income families had one child, a 2.6 point drop to 8.1 percent. This is a most unrealistic calculation since it involves, among other things, the addition of a child to childless families. Torturing the data once more to focus on the families with highest poverty incidence, those with three or more children, if they had had only one child, the overall poverty level would have fallen only by 1.7 points to 9.0 percent.[3]

Population Control as Antipoverty Policy

The main approaches to poverty alleviation among children are obvious. For the long run there is career development and improvement in employment preparation in the schools, steps much needed but yet inadequately provided. For the short run, there are income transfer programs aimed at raising the purchasing power of poor children. Aid to Families with Dependent Children (AFDC) gives support to these children through transfers to their parents. This program has not been very successful in its goal of pulling children out of poverty by raising the earnings potential of their parents, but at least its transfer mechanism does move in the right direction of alleviating the pangs of childhood poverty.

The one controversial area of childhood antipoverty policy that receives our attention at this point is that of population control, family planning, or whatever term applies to the policy of reducing poverty among children by reducing the number of them that are born into poor families. At the outset it should be acknowledged that a reduction in the number of children in poor families would obviously reduce the poverty count. The data of Table 6-3 are for families, not individuals, so that while we could note that if all poor families were childless the decline in the family poverty rate would be estimated at only 0.7 points, from 10.7 percent to 10.0 percent, there would be substantially fewer people poor.

[3]The value was derived by substituting the 1.7 million in the three-or-more-children poverty cell by 0.8 million, an estimate calculated by adding all (0.5) in the under $2,000 income group to $0.3/0.7 \times 0.7$, the ratio of the number poor with one child in the $2,000 to $4,999 income group multiplied by the actual number in that group with three or more children.

Table 6-3 Family Income in 1969 by Size of Family and Number of Children under 18 Years Old, 1970 (Numbers in Millions)

| | All families | | | Family income in 1969 | | | | | | | | Median income (thousands of dollars) |
| | Total | Less than poverty level | | Less than $2,000 | $2,000 to $3,999 | $4,000 to $5,999 | $6,000 to $7,999 | $8,000 to $9,999 | $10,000 to $14,999 | $15,000 to $24,999 | $25,000 or more | |
		Number	Percentage									
All families	51.1	5.5	10.7	3.0	4.7	5.5	6.6	7.1	13.6	8.2	2.4	9.7
No children under 18	22.9	2.3	10.0	1.7	2.9	2.8	2.9	2.8	5.3	3.6	1.1	8.9
One under 18	9.2	0.7	8.1	0.5	0.7	1.0	1.3	1.4	2.6	1.5	0.4	9.9
Two under 18	8.7	0.7	8.4	0.4	0.5	0.7	1.1	1.4	2.7	1.5	0.4	10.5
Three or more under 18	10.3	1.7	16.5	0.5	0.7	1.0	1.3	1.6	3.0	1.6	0.5	10.0
Mean number under 18	1.30	1.76	...	1.12	0.97	1.17	1.33	1.42	1.43	1.30	1.25	...

Source: 1970 Census of Population, Subject Reports—Family Composition.

Thus each family with several children that falls into poverty has a stronger effect on poor population than on the family poverty count. The key to the high average size of poor families (1.76 children per family) compared to any income subgroup lies in analysis of the $2,000-to-$3,999 income group's contribution to the family poverty count. All those in the lower-income group having less than $2,000 per year are poor regardless of family size. But note that the number of poor families is much lower than the sum of the total of families in the first two income groups for those with no children or one child and that the figure is slightly lower for families with two children. For large families, the total number poor exceeds the sum of the two lower-income groups and even cuts into the next highest. That is, some very large families which earn over $4,000 are poor by our classification, which relates the poverty line to basic family consumption needs.

Thus, fewer children in families in the lowest-income group would reduce the number of poor people even if it did little or nothing to reduce the number of poor families. Fewer in the next two income groups would sharply lower both the family and the population poverty count.

But that poor people therefore have large families should not, as is often the case, be mistakenly taken to mean that low-income families have many children. In fact, this is absolutely false. As Table 6-3 shows, the three lowest-income groups have the fewest children per family.[4] This demographic fact may run counter to popular intuition, but there is no denying the data. Economic analysis has been applied to the tendency for family size to increase slightly with rising incomes. Gary Becker analyzes children as a consumer durable good for parents who increase their expenditure substantially on each child as family income increases, leading to "higher-quality" children. The latter is an unfortunate term loaded with possibly incorrect normative implications of the human worth of these children, but Becker means simply to refer to the greater investment in time, attention, and consumption goods and services that parents lavish on them. This higher expenditure per child acts to reduce the number of children per family, but Becker concludes that this force is more than counteracted by the tendency for families to treat children as an income-sensitive consumer good, increasing their total expenditure on them enough to increase their number as well as increasing outlay per child as income rises.[5]

---

[4]For blacks, the family size for the lowest-income groups is at about the average for all black families; but, of course, family size for poor black families is also much above the black average, for the same reasons as apply to the all-family case.

[5]Gary Becker, "An Economic Analysis of Fertility," *Demographic and Economic Change in Developing Countries,* National Bureau of Economic Research, 1960, p. 212. More recent studies in effect support Becker's thesis. See papers in "New Economic Approaches to Fertility," *Journal of Political Economy,* March, April 1973, and "Marriage, Family Human Capital, and Fertility," the same journal, March, April 1974.

Putting perspective to these facts, the basic problem is not one of large families but of low incomes. While fewer children per low-income family would reduce the poverty count, striving for tighter population control among these families seems a questionable if not pessimistic and even unfair policy, especially when these families at present are smaller than average. A seemingly fairer and more productive national policy would involve measures to raise the earnings of low-income families.

Those who think that a deliberate, selective birth control program aimed at the poor would kill two birds with one stone—by alleviating poverty and striking at the heart of the population growth–environmental decay problem—are taking dead aim at only one bird, and a beneficial one at that. Low-income families actually contribute less to overall population growth than those with higher incomes. Furthermore, while the problem of technical poverty can be eased by a reduction in family size among the poor, we must stress that the changes in income adequacy from fewer children among low-income families would be minimal. Many families would be pulled above the poverty line, but only because, with no change in family income, this line would be lowered slightly for each less child. This marginal pull might cause a substantial improvement in the official poverty data but would do very little to lead these low-income families toward comfortable living standards.

The relationship between demand for children and income does strongly suggest that raising income through increased earnings potential for the poor would be more consistent with a policy of population limitation than a system of income transfers. The latter would raise income without increasing the cost of the time devoted to raising children; the former would increase these costs equally if earnings were generated by an increase of women's (especially wives') work effort.[6] Of course, the provision of subsidized day-care services would to some degree counteract the negative effect on population of increased time costs of child raising for these wives, who could work instead of caring for young children.[7] But removal of these services would be a great price for poor families to pay in the cause of population control, while their provision would do so much to raise their living standards.

There is nothing inconsistent with the finding of increasing family size with rising income and the fact that population growth is weaker in economically advanced countries than in poor ones. Along with develop-

[6]Glenn Cain and Adriana Weininger, "Economic Determinants of Fertility Results from Cross-Sectional Aggregate Data," *Demography*, May 1973, pp. 205–223. Note that an increase in wages of the wife acts as a deterrent to family size.

[7]Cain, "Issues in the Economics of a Population Policy for the United States," *American Economic Review*, May 1971, pp. 408–417, agrees that subsidized day care poses a problem for population limitation but argues that it is not an important issue.

ment and a general rise in family incomes, the more affluent families spend more on goods and services in education, health care, better clothes and food, entertainment, and amusements, etc., for their children, thus expressing a demand for "high-quality" children. Hence, while there might at any time be more children per family at higher levels of family income, the entire child-cost schedule shifts upward as national income rises, and in this way population growth is retarded.

Harold Sheppard argues that since, in recent years, the developing countries with the greatest improvement in living standard have been those with the slowest population growth, a domestic analogy should be applied which would encourage population control among the "developing" poor.[8] Thus the potential gains in living standard from higher family incomes would not be dissipated by the basic consumption needs of larger families. But population growth in developing countries is only a short-run phenomenon. In every country that has gone through the development process, population has tended to level off as affluence was approached and the cost of child services rose with increased demand.

Third World countries are aware of this process, even if developing countries seem to lose sight of these stages in their anxiety to see world population stabilize. At population conferences, Third World representatives point out—not always unemotionally—that population control at their current economic level would be a negative approach to their problem of income inadequacy. If this problem were solved through economic growth, they say, this growth process itself would generate forces to limit population. So, too, the poorer people in a richer country such as ours could argue with equally compelling logic that their paramount current need is for more income and not fewer children. Over time, as their incomes rise and demand for "higher-quality" children rises, raising the cost of these children for themselves and others, a dampening long-run effect on national population will replace any short-run stimulating effects from their higher incomes.

AGED POVERTY

Poverty and Income Data

Many forces determining income have been favorable toward the reduction of the relative incidence of aged poverty. For one thing, as noted in Chapter 2, the educational level of those over sixty-five has increased strongly and steadily over the years and—while aged poverty rates are higher for each educational level—certainly the increase in average

---

[8]Harold Sheppard, *Effects of Family Planning on Poverty in the United States,* Upjohn Institute for Employment Research, 1967, Battle Creek, Mich., pp. 9–10.

Table 6-4 Aged Poverty Related to and as a Share of Total Poverty, 1959–1973

Year*	Percentage of 65-years-old and over population poor	Percentage of total population poor	Aged poor percentage ÷ total poor percentage	Percentage of poor 65 and over
1959	35.2	22.0	1.60	14.1
1966	38.5	14.7	1.94	17.9
1967	29.5	14.2	2.07	19.4
1968	25.0	12.8	1.95	18.3
1969	25.3	12.2	2.07	19.7
1970	24.6	12.6	1.95	18.9
1971	21.6	12.5	1.72	16.7
1972	18.6	11.9	1.56	15.3
1973	16.3	11.1	1.47	14.6

Source: *Current Population Reports*, Series P-60/98
*Census data on aged poverty rates are not available for the 1960–1965 period.

schooling attained would operate favorably on earnings potential for the aged. Then, too, the long-run rise in average earnings during work years should provide a softer financial cushion for the retirement years. Finally, more generous social security benefits, reinforced by expanding private pension plan receipts, should greatly reduce the incidence of aged poverty.

The data, though, do not entirely agree with these positive elements and do not give us an unambiguous picture of continuous improvement. If we break up the poverty data into two periods—the long stretch from 1959 to 1970 and the most recent years, 1970–1973—we do note a sharply favorable recent trend in the pattern of aged poverty. The aged position worsened over the earlier period but improved over the latter, so that, as noted in Table 6-4, the 1973 relative poverty position for the aged was very close to that of 1959. An optimist would look at the most recent trend and see its continuation toward early age equality; a pessimist would see only a long-term waving trend and either look toward cyclical movement or emphasize the stability of high relative aged poverty between two rather distant terminal years.

The contrary long-term results of the last two columns of Table 6-4, with the relative aged share of total poverty rising slightly, reflects the aging of the population. With the recent and probably continuing decline in the birthrate, we should expect those over sixty-five to increase their percentage of the total population, 10.8 percent in 1974, compared with 9.1 percent in 1960 and 4.1 percent at the turn of the century. Thus demographic factors are working in the direction of making aged poverty an expanding component of the overall poverty problem.

When we look at income data, we find more pointed information on the stability of the low economic status of the aged. The proverbial "man in the street," who accepts myths over facts either because of good intentions or wishful thinking to avoid problems, believes that the economic status of women and blacks is on a sharp rise. Just so would he also probably guess that the income disparity between age levels has been narrowing toward equality. Unfortunately, the hard facts do not jibe with egalitarian sentiment. Actually, the relative income position of the aged, as Table 6-5 reveals, did not change over the decade of the 1960s.

Note the parallelism between poverty and income data. As with relative poverty, relative family income for the aged weakened during the early part of the decade and then strengthened at the end, with the most recent years perhaps suggesting a strongly improved trend.

For unrelated individuals, though, who form their largest grouping among the aged, the narrowing trend at the end of the decade failed to appear. In fact, the relative position of the unattached aged shows signs of

Table 6-5 Median Money Income of Families and Unrelated Individuals by Age, 1960–1971

| Year | Family income | | Income of aged as percentage of income of those under 65 | Income of aged individuals as a percentage of income of those under 65 |
	Head under 65	Head 65 and over		
1960	$ 5,905	$ 2,897	49.1	41.0
1961	6,099	3,026	49.6	42.7
1962	6,336	3,204	50.6	47.2
1963	6,644	3,332	50.4	49.3
1964	6,981	3,376	48.4	41.9
1965	7,413	3,514	47.4	41.2
1966	7,922	3,645	46.0	41.9
1967	8,504	3,928	46.2	40.5
1970	10,152	5,053	49.7	38.8
1971 (est.)	10,500	5,400	51.2	n.a.

Source: Statistical Abstract of the United States, 1974.

worsening in the most recent years, after a period of slight improvement during the middle years of the decade.

The parallelism between income and poverty data is not surprising. While the rise in average aged incomes can explain the drop in the aged poverty rate, the relative stability of the relative low-income status of those over sixty-five accounts for the failure of the relative aged poverty rate to decline.

The weakness of income as the sole measure of poverty does tend to lead to overstatement of the economic inferiority of the aged. As was noted in the earlier discussion of poverty definitions (see Chapter 1), income is used as a proxy measure for spending power adequacy—and an imperfect substitute it often is, especially in the presence of large asset holdings. When there are earning assets, the measurement problem is less serious. But most of the assets of the aged are in home ownership, which yields implicit (free rent) but not explicit measured income.

The 1968 Survey of the Demographic and Economic Characteristics of the Aged (DECA), the last such comprehensive study, reports that 77 percent of the families with heads over sixty-five owned their own homes—compared with 63 percent for all families—and four-fifths of the elderly who owned homes hold them free of mortgage.[9] Although asset holdings including home equity, as expected, were related to income, the percentage of poor aged homeowners, 71 percent, was not much less than that for the aged as a whole, but of course the equity in their homes was substantially less.

Although homes do not represent a liquid asset that is easily transferable into purchasing power, certainly some correction for this and other assets should be made in estimating the extent of poverty for any particular group. In a novel approach to the problem of combining both income and wealth (assets) into current purchasing power, Weisbrod and Hansen translate assets into potential income by calculating the annuity value of assets over the expected lifetime of the holder.[10] This annual value is added to income to find adjusted income, or annual purchasing power.

This adjusted income is then used to correct poverty rates for different age groups. Because of their greater net worth at all income levels, even the lowest, the corrected reduction in poverty is greatest for the aged. For 1962 data, using a 10 percent interest rate for calculating annuity values of assets, the poverty rate for the aged is reduced from 47 per-

---

[9]Janet Murray, "Homeownership and Financial Assets: Findings from the 1968 Survey of the Aged," *Social Security Bulletin,* August 1972, pp. 3–23.

[10]Burton A. Weisbrod and W. Lee Hansen," "An Income-Net Worth Approach to Measuring Economic Welfare," *American Economic Review,* December 1968, pp. 1315–1329.

cent based on income alone to 32 percent based on income-plus-annui-tized net worth. The same adjustment for the age group from fifty-five to sixty-four results in a reduction from only 19 percent to 15 percent.

Of course, these figures are old and the poverty rates for the aged remain relatively high even when adjusted for asset holdings; but the argument retains validity. Differential asset holdings lead to overstate-ment of relative purchasing power weakness among the poor when this power is measured by income alone. But let us not overstate the adjust-ment. By any measure, the poverty incidence among the aged remains relatively high.

Labor Force Participation

The long-run stability of (low) relative earnings of the aged and their related more or less constant relative poverty incidence result from the balancing of two conflicting forces on total income: a relative decline in earnings and a rise in transfer receipts from social security and private pension plans.

The drop in the earnings share of aged income results from a decline in labor market activity. The labor force participation rate for men over 65 has been in steady decline, with no end to this downward trend in sight; the 1974 rate of 22.4 percent was slightly less than half the 47.8 percent rate of 1947. As Figure 6-1 shows, the decline has been steady and continuous.

The labor force participation rate for older women workers has been propped up by the upward trend in female labor that has affected all women. Nevertheless, in recent years this force has not been strong enough to counteract the downward pressure of reduced participation by older workers of either sex. While Figure 6-1 shows that the older female rate in 1974 lies at almost exactly the 1947 rate, there has been a dis-tinct downward movement since the mid-1960s.

All this decline in work effort has not resulted in a reduction in aged income because it has been offset by an increase in nonwork income, par-ticularly in the receipt of social security benefits, supplemented, albeit to a lesser degree than probably generally believed, by private pension plan receipts.

Table 6-6 shows the growth in Old Age Survivors, Disability, and Health Insurance (OASDHI) retirement receipts over the years. While the social security program has expanded to include disability, health, and other benefits, by far the greatest share of receipts still takes the form of retirement benefits. Note that for the period of the data, retirement receipts have more than kept pace with the price level and have recently caught up with the rate of change in average labor earnings. The latter

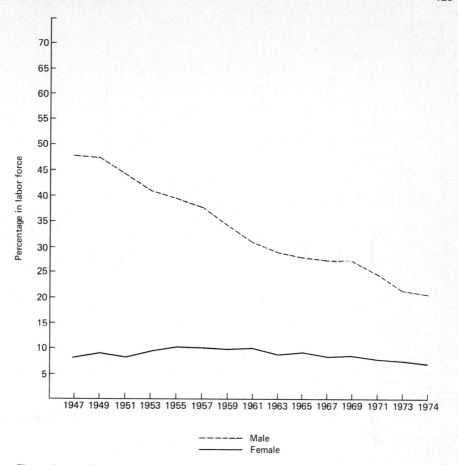

Figure 6-1 Labor force participation rates of males and females aged sixty-five years and over. (*Source: Manpower Report of the President,* 1975.)

relationship is consistent with the time pattern of relative income of the aged, noted above.

Reinforcing the growing level in average benefits as a prop to aged income has been the expansion in the number of recipients. Some growth is explained by the greater size of the older population, but the increase in number of beneficiaries has far outrun the aged population growth. The 1960 to 1972 population over sixty-five increased by 25.2 percent, from 16.7 to 20.9 million, while the number of OASDHI retirement beneficiaries expanded 71.7 percent, from 10.6 to 18.2 million.

We can only speculate on the future pattern, whether benefits will rise enough to keep the relative aged income rate from falling and the poverty rate from rising. On balance, though, the signs appear favorable

Table 6-6   Retirement Benefits under Social Security Compared with Price Level and Average Wages, 1960–1974

Year	Average monthly benefits for retired workers under OASDHI	Consumer Price Index (1967 = 100)	Real monthly value of benefits (benefits/CPI)	Average hourly index, nonfarm workers (1967 = 100)	Monthly benefits as percentage of wage index
1960	$ 74.04	88.7	$ 83.43	73.9	100.2
1961	75.65	89.6	84.43	76.3	99.1
1962	76.19	90.6	84.09	79.3	96.9
1963	76.88	91.7	83.84	82.2	93.5
1964	77.57	92.9	83.50	86.1	90.1
1965	83.92	94.5	88.80	89.2	94.1
1966	84.35	97.2	86.78	94.6	89.2
1967	85.37	100.0	85.37	100.0	85.3
1968	98.86	104.2	94.88	107.5	91.9
1969	100.40	109.8	91.44	114.6	87.6
1970	118.10	116.3	101.55	122.6	96.3
1971	132.17	121.3	108.96	130.6	101.2
1972	162.35	125.3	129.56	138.7	117.0
1973	166.42	133.1	125.03	149.0	111.7
1974	187.29	147.0	127.40	162.0	115.6

Source: Social Security Bulletin and Manpower Reports of the President.

for the aged. Concern has recently been expressed in the press and in Congress about the future capacity of Social Security to maintain an adequate benefit schedule. A serious long-term financing problem is posed by the combination of what seems unstoppable inflation and unfavorable demographic changes, with the aged population rising and the population contributing to the fund relatively shrinking because of declining birthrates.

But the prevailing sentiment seems to favor the maintenance at all costs of benefit adequacy, especially to those at the lower end of the income scale—those whose contributions to the fund during a low-earning work life were minimal—whether these costs take the form of a sharp rise in the maximum taxable earnings base or, in the extreme, of dipping into the general treasury tax receipts. These measures may violate the insurance principle of the fund, but their redistributional aspects augur well for a relative rise in the economic status of the low-income aged.

Social security benefits will most likely increase, augmented by private pension income. From 1950 to 1968 the number of workers covered by private plans rose from 6.4 to 28.6 million, or to almost half of all private wage and salary workers. In 1968 there were 3.7 million beneficiaries under these funds, and the number is projected to rise to 6.6 million by 1980. While the average benefit from private plans of $1,500 in 1970[11] is comparable to that from social security, the coverage is much narrower, at about half the number receiving public pensions. Furthermore, eligibility for coverage and benefit schedules in these plans are much more closely related to work period earnings levels, with less redistributional effects in aid of the potential poor evident in social security.

The opposite movement of labor force participation (downward) and public and private pension income (upward) is more than coincidental. For one thing, the receipt of nonwork income dampens the enthusiasm for work. Another and probably more important factor is that receipt of social security benefits is tied to a reduction in labor earnings. Unlike the receipt of private pension benefits, which requires only cessation from work in the covering firm, beneficiaries of social security must pass a so-called "retirement test" which reduces their benefits by 50 cents for each $1 earned from work after a certain earnings level and imposes an effective 100 percent tax on benefits by reducing them $1 for each $1 earned above a higher level. These cutoff levels have been raised over the years in step with rising earnings rates, but they still act as a deterrent to work for many over sixty-five.

[11]Robert Taggart, *The Labor Market Impact of the Private Retirement System,* Joint Economic Committee, U.S. Congress, 1973, p. 1. This report discusses the scope and limitation of private pension plans.

The retirement test was imposed, in fact, as an antidepression measure aimed at reducing unemployment by siphoning off part of the labor force into nonparticipation. With the recent jump in unemployment rates, the test is less susceptible to current criticism, but it does make uncertain whether the decline in the aged work force and growth in number retired reflects the undirected choice of older workers or conformity to requirements for the receipt of pension income.

Welfare Considerations

In any case, regardless of income level, and even for the poor, if an individual receives the same income from less work and more retirement benefits than he received previously from work alone, his welfare has improved. Since work involves effort, the individual is better off because he has the same income from less effort; he has more leisure at his disposal. Added leisure is particularly important to the aged, for whom long hours of work would be particularly arduous.

But even if an older individual is better off with a given low income if that income is comprised more of retirement benefits than of labor earnings, the issue of whether aged poverty is much less a social problem because of this added welfare is not settled. The issue depends on the degree of choice involved in the retirement decision. Have older workers *chosen* retirement, "buying" leisure at the cost of less work income, or have they been forced into retirement by lack of work opportunities?

For the poor, logic would seem to argue for the latter description of aged retirement. The very word "retirement" suggests a conscious, comfortable choice among alternatives, with adequate income allowing a selection of leisure over still more purchasing power earned through work effort. Given the low poverty thresholds established, it is difficult to accept the notion that many older people "choose to be poor," which would have to be the case if their retirement were truly voluntary.

In short, a voluntary retirement decision implies a background of nonlabor income adequacy. As Raymond Munts says so forcefully, "We can even define retirement for the poor as a poverty of choices. If the modern meaning of retirement is a range of choices in income and work opportunities, then by definition the poor cannot make a retirement decision. A narrow economic logic to the contrary can produce much mischief for public policy."[12] How much is leisure enjoyed in a tattered old age?

[12]Raymond Munts, "Minimum Income as a Retirement Policy Objective," Joint Economic Committee Subcommittee on Fiscal Policy, *Old Age Income Assurance*, part II, 1967, p. 292.

Nevertheless, Lowell Gallaway argues that the evidence suggests that expanded retirement represents a conscious choice, even for the poor.[13] Gallaway is correct in arguing that if the decision were involuntary, the reduction in the aged work force must be explained by a decline in demand for older workers. Using Becker's discrimination model, which would require a worsening of aged unemployment rates and/or a worsening of their relative wages to explain lower market demand for older workers, Gallaway finds no changes in these variables. The first test of stronger discrimination is somewhat circular in that older workers can keep their unemployment rates low by leaving the labor force and entering (involuntary) retirement.

The second test may be valid, and the low but steady relative earnings level of the aged—with the 1970 average for full-time workers over sixty-five at 68 percent of the earnings level of thirty-five to forty-four-year olds at close to its long-run value—indicates constant discrimination.[14] But this is just a test of discrimination and not of declining demand for older workers based on market forces associated with changing industrial labor requirements.

It is true that there is no indication of a deterioration in the productivity of older workers. In fact, improved health and education levels of the aged would suggest the contrary. In any case, productivity studies of older workers, who often show no weakening of efficiency with age, are themselves poor measures of employer demand since they obviously include only the most productive of the aged, those who have retained their jobs.

But modern industry has increased the demand for tooled and retooled human capital. The new technology demands on-the-job training and retraining. A study of training by age finds a slight inferiority in results for older workers, an inferiority that is more pronounced in tasks requiring speed and dexterity.[15] But again, the study includes only those relatively few older workers selected for retraining. Furthermore, the "older worker" population for this study includes workers over forty-five, not those over sixty-five.

There is no need to press the point of weak adaptability for retraining to argue for limited opportunities for older workers to prepare for the new

[13]Lowell Gallaway, "The Economic Impact of OASDHI on the Aged," Joint Economic Committee, 1967, and "The Extent of Poverty in the United States," *Southern Economic Journal*, October 1966.

[14]*The Employment Problems of Older Workers*, U.S. Bureau of Labor Statistics Bulletin 1721, November 1971.

[15]*Industrial Retraining Programs for Technological Change; A Study of the Performance of Older Workers*, U.S. Bureau of Labor Statistics Bulletin 1368, 1963, p. 5.

technology. On-the-job training costs are incurred by firms, which assume these costs not out of altruism but because they see financial returns from the increased productive capacity of the trained workers. It would rarely be an economically wise decision to train at company expense a worker in his sixties, considering the short time available for the firm to recoup its costs through the increased productivity of the worker during his few remaining work years. A sounder economic decision would have the firm retire him, on pension. It is interesting to note that the Age Discrimination in Employment Act (ADEA) of 1967 allows the firm this decision by permitting compulsory retirement provisions in private pension plans.

The growing industrial need for trained and retrained workers and the reluctance of firms to give older workers this training can explain both the decline in demand for older workers and the involuntary nature of the sharp growth in retirement. Pension income has filled the gap created by lower earnings, but those who remain poor have not *chosen* to do so; for many, retirement represents an involuntary response to declining market demand for their services. Writing in 1967, Gallaway predicted a rise in the relative income and reduction in poverty of the aged as the labor force participation rate of males aged over sixty-five bottomed out at about 25 percent. This might have occurred if retirement was voluntary and increased public and private pension benefits constituted a net addition to income rather than an offset to reduced earnings. But the relevant 1973 participation rate was 22.8 percent, down 1.6 points from the previous year. Where is the bottom? Does anyone still suggest that increased benefits meet a stubborn desire of a large segment of the older population to remain poor?

SUMMARY

Poverty rates are particularly high at both ends of the life span. Rates for children are high because poor families contain many children. Popular myth translates this fact into the belief that low-income families are larger than average. Such is simply not the case. Low-income families slip into poverty—the poverty line being measured by minimum consumption needs—when they are large; but average family size is no larger for low- than for higher-income families.

Of course, poverty could be reduced and the threat to the environment of overpopulation could be weakened if low-income families had fewer children. But since these families are not particularly large, a policy of income generation for them, either through improved earnings opportunities and/or transfers, seems more appropriate than one of emphasis on population limitation. Furthermore, it would be unfair to focus an environment-strengthening population-control policy on a group that has no particular tendency toward large families.

The poverty rates for the aged, those over sixty-five, have declined no more rapidly than those for the population as a whole, leaving them with a steady but high relative poverty incidence. Their relative income has also remained at a (low) constant level. Over the long run, steady increases in public and private retirement benefits have been offset by a decline in labor earnings to stabilize their low relative economic status.

The welfare of older retired individuals is undoubtedly improved when they receive the same real income with less work. But the social problem of aged poverty remains because the movement from labor force participation into retirement has not usually been voluntary but rather has been forced by a relative decline in demand for older labor. In view of this continuing reduction in demand for their services, improved social security transfers seem to be the answer to the poverty problem of the aged. Furthermore, in the case of the aged, there would be little taxpayer criticism of "supporting idleness" and less loss of production from consequent reduction in work participation than would arise from an expanded transfer program for younger groups.

Chapter 7

Unemployment, Underemployment, and Poverty

In previous chapters we studied the factors—such as the disadvantages of lack of education, race, sex, and age—that led to low earnings. Here we examine the proximate cause of poverty induced by these factors: inadequate earnings.

That earnings inadequacy arises from incomplete work effort associated with lack of participation in the labor force, unemployment, part-year, or part-time work is to be expected. Even well-paying jobs cannot yield annual incomes above poverty level if they are not held steadily, and they certainly cannot do so if they are not held at all. But it is surprising—perhaps shocking is a better word—that there are so many poor households whose heads work full time, full year. Income inadequacy associated with this complete labor effort deserves special attention.

The first section of this chapter examines the degree of income inadequacy related to labor force status. Then, the next section studies the factors that result in low-paying work and insufficient income regardless of the intensity of labor effort. This latter component of low earnings complicates the task of poverty elimination. Getting the poor into the mainstream of the labor market in steady, full-time jobs would certainly reduce the poverty rate, but it would still leave substantial poverty concentrated in high-incidence subgroups.

POVERTY COUNT AND LABOR FORCE STATUS

The Unemployed

The unemployed are the most frustrated members of the work force. By Labor Department definition, they are not only out of work but are actively seeking work. Although liberal interpretation of "job search" may not require rigorous pursuit of every possible job opening to comply with eligibility requirements for unemployment insurance, still the unemployed worker is one who has tried, to some extent and failed to find a job. This individual's income goals are accordingly thwarted and his or her spending power is reduced below its desired level. When unemployment strikes the family's principal breadwinner, the economic loss is particularly severe and the potential for an inadequate (poverty) income level is high.

Not all the unemployed, though, are in desperate economic straits. They include secondary family workers, family members whose principal breadwinner may be and usually is earning good wages. Unemployed married women, youths, and older family members are unhappy at not finding work, but their unhappiness does not usually reflect family financial misery. Nevertheless, the Labor Department adds them to the unemployment count just as it does unemployed family heads. As the Department reports, "The statistics on unemployment are not intended to be a count of all persons who are suffering a hardship but rather a count of unutilized available manpower resources."[1]

1974 was a time of relatively high unemployment, although the annual rate of 5.6 percent seems low compared to the 7 to 9 percent of late 1974 and afterward. But except for the 5.9 percent of 1971, it was the highest rate after 1963 until 1974. This overall rate is just an average of many diverse components. As Table 7-1 shows, of various rates, the lowest is for male breadwinners, the bulk of family heads. Females without husbands, roughly comprising the female household heads, had higher rates than did male household heads, but their rate was also significantly lower than that for single men and women, and it was only a small fraction of the rate for teenagers, those who rarely have major household responsibilities.

Table 2-8 showed the small contribution of the unemployed family heads to the poverty total. In 1973, when the overall unemployment rate

[1]*How the Government Measures Unemployment,* U.S. Department of Labor Statistics, Report 418, 1973, p. 7.

Table 7-1 1974 Unemployment Rates for Selected Population Subgroups

Group	Unemployment rate, percent
Total	5.6
Married men, wife present	2.8
Wives	4.7
Widowed, divorced, and separated women	6.1
Widowed, divorced, and separated men	5.8
Single women	9.1
Single men	10.9
18- and 19-year-old males	13.3
18- and 19-year-old females	15.4
16- and 17-year-old males	18.5
16- and 17-year-old females	18.2

Source: *Manpower Report of the President*, 1975, Tables A-20, B-1.

fell to 4.9 percent, the rate for family heads was a low 2.5 percent (1.345 million out of 55.0 million families). More significantly, there were only 263,000 poor families with unemployed heads, representing only 5.5 percent of poor families, although the incidence of poverty among these families was a high 19.5 percent.

But the raw figures of unemployment, centered on the experience of family heads, tend to understate the effect of unemployment on poverty. The rate itself is a rough measure of average unemployment during the year, being simply an average of the estimated monthly rates. As such, it does not measure the percentage who suffer from unemployment during the year nor the full effect of unemployment on poverty.

To demonstrate this by a hypothetical distribution of the data of Table 2-8, if the 2.5 percent family heads unemployed on average for the year were a different group each month, there would be a total of 30 percent unemployed for one month during the year. The number in poverty, measured by annual income inadequacy, would be influenced by the loss of one month's earnings for this larger group for the year. In fact, something like this sharing of unemployment must have occurred. Note that the poverty rate among the unemployed was a high 19.5 percent compared to the 5.5 percent rate for the employed; but considering the meager level of unemployment benefits, we should wonder why the rate was not much higher. The answer lies in the fact that many of the unemployed were out of work only part of the year. If the 1.3 million family-head jobless had been unemployed the entire year, almost all would have been poor.

On the other hand, this means that many of the so-called working poor entered poverty not because of low wages but because of partial unemployment. Moving to actual (1972) data, 15.4 percent of the work force was out of work at some time during the year. This percentage, as expected, varies with the average unemployment rate and was at a comparatively low 12.4 percent in 1968, when the overall rate was down to 3.6 percent. As for the poverty figure, while 53.5 percent of poor family heads worked during 1972, only 23.4 percent worked full-year, 50- to 52-week schedules, and the heads of 11.1 percent of poor families worked less than full schedules because they were unemployed at some time during the year. The other 19 percent who worked less than full schedules were not in the labor force during their nonwork periods.

Regarding poverty incidence, the rate was only 2.9 percent among families whose heads worked full schedules, but it was 14.5 percent for those who worked less than full schedules because of unemployment during the year. The figure reaches a high 25 percent for those who worked at full-time jobs for only 26 weeks or less.

The Working Poor

No matter how much we adjust the data to capture the broader effects of unemployment on poverty, the fact remains that there were over a million families in poverty whose heads work full-year, full-time schedules. Although the poverty incidence for these families was a very low 2.9 percent, at 1.0 million they constituted in 1972 19.8 percent of all poor families.

This measure of the *working poor,* to include only those who worked full schedules, is more conservative than the conventional grouping under this category, which includes all those who worked during the year, whether full or part year or full or part time. There are 2.7 million family heads, or 53.5 percent of all poor families, who fit this broader category. If we simply wish to measure the inadequacy of *earnings rates,* to emphasize the inability of many families to avoid poverty through full work effort, then our conservative (lower) count of the working poor offers a better guide to the limits of poverty elimination through complete work effort. It also has more relevance to the policy issue of whether poverty can be successfully attacked through programs that emphasize job creation at current skill levels rather than the more tedious and expensive process of job upgrading and human capital development among the current and potential poor.

Before examining this issue more closely, we must acknowledge that many people work less than full schedules out of choice and not because of inability to find steady work. Of the 9.5 million family heads who worked full time but less than a full year, many more (5.6 million) worked less than full schedules for reasons other than unemployment—such as illness or household duties—than because they were unemployed part of the year (3.9 million). As for the 12.4 million part-time workers, 10.0 million were on voluntary part time and only 2.5 million worked part time because of economic reasons, mainly because of slack business conditions.

But while most who worked less than full schedules did so because of reasons other than total or partial unemployment, it strains logic to argue that they all did so out of choice. It is true that they were not frustrated in an actual search for more work. But considering that 22.4 percent of families whose heads worked part time for whatever reason were poor and the percentage poor in families whose heads worked full time but less than full year for reasons other than unemployment during the year was 17.4 percent, this adds to a very large number who, according to official statistics, "choose to be poor" rather than attain adequate earnings through greater work effort. In short, we should conclude that official unemployment figures constitute a faulty measure of the contribution of insufficient work to a family's poverty status.

Our purpose here, though, is to study the extent to which the "working poor," defined as those whose income inadequacy stems from low earnings rates and consequent low full-schedule earnings rather than from incomplete work effort, form a part of the poverty problem. To repeat, while this group of family heads made up 19.8 percent of the total of poor family heads, their poverty incidence was only 2.9 percent. Certainly, if this were the prevailing overall rate, we could safely say that poverty would no longer be a pressing social problem. Thus the question at issue here is whether, if lack of work were no longer a contributor to poverty, the overall rate would fall at least close to, if not actually all the way to, this low value for the full-schedule work force.

This would be the case if the unemployed and part-time employed were distributed throughout the occupational classifications in proportion to their numbers attached to each. There are no data on part-time work by occupation, but the unemployed are spread out unevenly throughout the job spectrum, with concentration in low-wage poverty-susceptible fields. In 1972, when the overall unemployment rate stood at 5.6 percent (the same as in 1974), those occupations which suffered above-average unemployment were in the weak earnings areas of operatives, except workers in transportation (7.6 percent), nonfarm laborers (10.3 percent), and service workers (6.6 percent). On the other hand, unemployed rates in the well-paying fields were very low—professional and technical workers (2.2 percent), managers (1.4 percent), craftsmen (3.7 percent). If part-time work was similarly distributed throughout the occupational range, then the lower limit to poverty among our narrowly defined working poor would lie somewhat above 2.9 percent, since the fuller employment attained would be weighted more with low-earnings workers, those with high poverty rates.

Nevertheless, despite this limitation to the downward movement of the poverty rate that would result from full work effort, there is a tendency to overestimate the magnitude of the "working poor" component of the poverty problem. While there is no denying that 53.5 percent of all poor households in 1972 had a head who worked during the year, this group had a poverty rate of only 6.0 percent, compared to the overall 9.3 percent family rate. But what is most relevant to the issue of poverty among the working poor, this 6.0 percent rate must lie well above the true potential rate for a fully employed full-schedule work force. This follows since the 6.0 percent poverty rate includes all those who are only partially employed as well as those fully employed; recall the high part-year (17.4 percent) and part-time (22.4 percent) unemployment rates. If we allowed an upward adjustment of about 1 percent to the 2.9 percent poverty rate of the current "full-effort" work force because of the concentration of part-time and part-year workers among the lower-paid occupations, we would obtain an overall "working poor" poverty rate of about 4.0 percent. This is of some significance but not an indication of a major socioeconomic problem.

This section warrants a final defense of our narrow definition of "working poor," which, of course, leads to the low estimated poverty rate for this group. Conventionally, this group includes all poor households whose heads work during the year, regardless of their shortfall from "full effort" employment. But put briefly and directly, does not the poverty resulting from less than full effort at adequate wage rates measure the effect of not working rather than of low earnings from work?

The Hidden Unemployed

If the greatest share of poverty results from not working, by far the greatest number of those not working is represented by those who are out of the work force. Over 50 percent of the women and about 30 percent of the men claim no attachment to the world of work. Or have they all really disassociated themselves from the labor market? According to official Labor Department definitions and procedures, the answer is clear; since they are not employed or *actually seeking* work, they are out of the labor force. The assumption is that if they are poor—and many of the households they head will certainly fall into the poverty count since they will be missing that important income source, earnings of head—social policy cannot be directed toward their employment as a means of reducing the poverty population.

But for practical purposes, the Labor Department definition of the labor force is too narrow to include all those who might work and thus be practical targets for an antipoverty policy of job creation and career development. Recall that only those are counted in the labor force who are either working or are unemployed, with the latter condition requiring active job search.

But there are those not counted in the labor force who would like to work but have given up looking for jobs because they do not think they would be able to find them. These are the "discouraged workers," a term coined during the Great Depression of the 1930s which described those who left the labor force in frustration. This group exists at any time in the business cycle, but it becomes larger in bad times. Thus the discouraged workers form a more numerous group as the official unemployment rate rises.

This volatile labor force group therefore serves to dampen the swings in the official unemployment rate. By leaving the work force when the unemployment rate increases, they keep this rate from rising to the level that would have been reached had they kept looking, fruitlessly, for work.[2] For purposes of relating poverty alleviation to increased work effort, though, "discouraged workers" should be counted among those who could possibly escape poverty through measures to strengthen the labor market. They should not be counted among those outside the world of work, those best reached by antipoverty income transfer programs.

More modern terminology calls discouraged workers the *hidden unemployed*. This term focuses the complaint of those who claim that the official unemployment rates should be corrected to include those whose only reason for exclusion is that they do not seek (nonexistent) jobs. Certainly they are unhappy about their labor force status; they would really prefer to work and they do not consider themselves detached from the labor market.

There is some question, though, about the degree of economic misery their households suffer or the extent to which their idleness contributes to family poverty. For one thing, most *hidden unemployment* occurs among secondary family workers—wives of working husbands, older children, older household members; necessity keeps the principal breadwinner from becoming easily discouraged.[3] For another factor reducing the im-

---

[2] Many studies have noted the inverse relationship between (official) labor force participation and unemployment rates. See, for example, Alfred Tella, "The Relation of Labor Force to Employment," *Industrial and Labor Relations Review,* April 1964, pp. 454–469; and Kenneth Strand and Thomas Dernburg, "Cyclical Variation in Civilian Labor Force," *Review of Economics and Statistics,* November 1964, pp. 378–391.

[3] The studies cited in footnote 2 find swings in labor force activity opposite to those in the unemployment rate to be confined to secondary workers. Glen Cain, in "Unemployment in the Labor-Force Participation of Secondary Workers," *Industrial and Labor Relations Review,* January 1967, pp. 275–297, notes exceptions to this pattern in the stable participation of nonwhite wives and female family heads. But are these women truly secondary workers?

pact of the "hidden unemployed" on poverty, they do not form a large population. Table 7-2 shows the small share of the hidden unemployed ("Think cannot get job" category in Labor Department terminology) among those not in the labor force. Furthermore, the table shows that the percentage of the hidden unemployed is in a declining trend in relation to official unemployment, falling from 24.3 percent of the total in 1967 to 15.8 percent in 1973.

The table also presents the change in the unemployment rate that would occur if all the hidden unemployment were counted in the labor force. It depends on one's viewpoint whether the approximately 1 percent rise in the rate should be considered significant or not. A few years ago this adjustment would have been important for policy, since our full employment, or at least our minimum unemployment goal, was at a set 4 to 5 percent level. But now, with much higher unemployment rates prevailing, we have lost sight of this goal, and the policy minimum is much more flexible.

As far as the impact of the hidden unemployed on antipoverty policy is concerned, their presence poses an added but not substantial potential to the group that may have their incomes increased by earnings from employment in a stronger labor market. The hidden unemployed may thus be expected to respond to improved job opportunities by working.

There is still a larger group out of the labor force in which the hidden unemployed form a small element, a group that might be considered susceptible to income increases through work effort. This is the group that gives the work status response that they "want a job now," even though they are not actively seeking work. In 1972, this group numbered 4.5 million people age sixteen and over, or about 8 percent of the 56.5 million this age who were not in the work force.

Reasons cited for nonparticipation among this population, apart from the 0.8 million who thought they would not find a job, were as follows: in school (1.2 million); ill health, disability (0.6 million); home responsibilities (1.1 million); and the catch-all, "all other reasons" (0.8 million).

Certainly, this group's interest in work is less intense than that of members of the hidden unemployment component who lack only active job search to be counted in the (unemployed) work force. But still some wish to work is expressed. How much this wish represents a vague yearning to work and earn and how much represents tentative planning to overcome the barriers to work cannot be measured by the data.

While about 33 million women—almost 60 percent of the 56.5 million out of the work force—claim that home responsibilities prevent their labor market participation, only 1.0 million report that they "want a job now." Although only a comparatively small number of people are in-

Table 7-2 Hidden Unemployment as a Component of Official Unemployment, 1967–1973

Year	Total not in labor force (millions)	Not in labor force because "think cannot get job"* (millions)	Number unem- ployed* (millions)	Hidden unemployed as percentage of number unemployed	Official unemploy- ment rates (percent)	Unemployment rates adjusted for hidden unemployment (percent)†
1967	52.5	0.73	3.0	24.3	3.8	4.7
1968	53.3	0.67	2.8	23.9	3.6	4.5
1969	53.6	0.57	2.8	20.4	3.5	4.2
1970	54.3	0.64	4.1	15.6	4.9	5.7
1971	55.7	0.77	4.9	15.7	5.9	6.8
1972	56.5	0.72	4.8	16.0	5.6	6.5
1973	57.2	0.68	4.3	15.8	4.9	5.7

*Note rough confirmation by these figures of the statistical studies which show that changes in the hidden unemployment move in the same direction as the unemployment rate. If this pattern holds, 1974 and 1975 recession data should show increases in the hidden unemployed.

†This adustment adds all the hidden unemployment to the official unemployment count.

Source: Manpower Report of the President, 1974.

volved, might we not conclude that these women would be the first to seek work if child-care arrangements were developed or other household obstacles to work were removed? Similarly, with those who are in ill health and disabled who would like to work (about one in eight), would not a slight improvement in their condition move them into the job market?

Public day-care programs, improved public health facilities, and special job market information programs for students might move a few million more out of nonparticipation status into the job market.

One might question the wisdom of such policies to expand the labor force during current weak economic conditions. But if we are focusing on antipoverty measures, changes toward active work force status help. Many would enjoy high income through work. At worst, many new entrants would be unemployed, but would their income then be any lower than it was when they were out of the work force?

In any case, the numbers involved would be small compared to the size of the poverty population. No matter how we stretch the figures of the potential work force, still about half the poor families would not be included and would be more easily reached by income maintenance transfer programs than by job development and placement as means of alleviating their poverty.

Underemployment

So far we have been attempting to measure the association of poverty to working and nonworking periods of labor force activity. The separation is not artificial in that the isolation of the two groups or time periods—for those who work part year or part time—allows for close evaluation of the effectiveness of policies that will promote full-effort employment in eliminating poverty. But the conventional approach simply examines the labor force factors which relate to poverty without separating low earnings potential from insufficiency of employment (other than unemployment). That is, according to conventional enumeration, the working poor include all those who work, no matter how much their effort falls short of full-year, full-time work.

Nevertheless, the concept of *underemployment* has been developed to complement unemployment as an adverse labor force status that induces poverty. The underemployed include all those not totally unemployed who would prefer to work more than they do. Thus they are the involuntary part-timers and those who work only part of the year not out of choice but because of lack of opportunity to complete full-year schedules. These groups are also excluded from our narrow grouping of the working poor.

But the *underemployed* also include those working at full effort who earn less than a poverty-level income—our working-poor group. Finally, those working at jobs below their capabilities, training, and potential earnings rates are also counted among the underemployed.

We cannot fault this taxonomy of the underemployed because it does not conform to our separation of the influence on poverty of inadequate earnings potential from that of incomplete work effort. The purpose of its enumeration is different. While our measure of the working poor is designed to show the gains in poverty relief that could be achieved by full-effort employment, underemployment together with unemployment attempts to lump together the effects of both labor market weakness and low earnings potential in creating income inadequacy. This melding of poverty factors measures the combined need for a stronger labor market and manpower development; our method of separating out the working poor from those who are poor because of below full-effort labor allows weighing the importance of each need. Both methods imply that other measures such as income transfers are needed for treating the poverty of those outside the labor force.

Perhaps the most thorough attempt to measure the relationship of labor force pathology to poverty has been undertaken by Levitan and Taggart,[4] who follow the combined unemployment-underemployment method of accounting. Their Employment and Earnings Inadequacy Index (EEII) is the total of those in the labor force—including the hidden unemployed—with inadequate employment and earnings expressed as a percentage of the labor force.

There can be little criticism of their exclusion of full-time young students and those over sixty-five from Levitan and Taggart's count of the universe of need for more financially successful work experience. Both have weak attachment to the labor force. The former often live at home, so that their parents' earnings and income levels are the major determinant of their purchasing power adequacy; in any case, their full-time commitment to school suggests an absence of pressing financial need, even if they are in search of work. Levitan and Taggart agree with our conclusion that older people's poverty problems will probably be best treated through income transfer rather than by expanded labor market opportunities.

To arrive at the 9.9 million who comprise the universe of need, the EEII total, the writers include the unemployed, the discouraged workers, fully employed workers earning less than poverty-level incomes, part-

---

[4]Sar Levitan and Robert Taggart, *Employment and Earnings Inadequacy*, Johns Hopkins, Baltimore, 1974, pp. 31–47.

year workers with earnings that place them below the poverty line, and the involuntary part-timers. Each group is adjusted downward by the number whose total household income lies above the national average, despite their employment and earnings disabilities. The presumption is that these households have substantial alternative sources of income that obviate the need for successful work experience to avoid poverty.

In 1972, these 9.9 million in the universe of need for manpower development and for employment stability were 11.5 percent of the adjusted 86.1 million labor force. The EEII, which the writers calculated back to 1968, moves in the same direction as the unemployment rate but with much less oscillation, moving only within a 1.5 percentage point range for the five-year period 1968–1972.

Certainly the EEII provides a better measure of labor force policy need in alleviating poverty than any single variable, such as the unemployment rate. But Levitan and Taggart's calculations do not alter our conclusion that incomplete employment is a more severe contributor to poverty than inadequate earnings potential. They write that "Low earnings are clearly as much or more of a problem than unemployment, discouragement, and involuntary part-time work." Their conclusion is based on their finding that these three groups make up only 44.2 percent of the total universe of need, while families with full-effort heads and those who worked part-year or worked voluntarily on a part-time basis formed the other 55.8 percent of this universe.

We still maintain that the measure of employment inadequacy should include not only the three groups incorporated by Levitan and Taggart to arrive at the 44.2 percent universe share, but the part-year workers and many of the voluntary part-timers as well. The presumption is that upgrading of skills would turn many of these part-timers into full-year workers. We can give a little ground, though, and agree that some who work less than full time, full-year voluntarily would be best reached by supplementary income transfers than any form of labor force policy. These would be workers whose effort was limited by home responsibilities, age, and health. But in any case, the groups for whom low earnings is certainly the problem and not incomplete work, which should be attacked by manpower development, include only the full-effort workers. Those comprise only 20.9 percent of the Levitan and Taggart EEII, and their poverty rate is only 2.6 percent. Our more conservative approach in not minimizing the extent of poverty among the working poor, which includes those work force families whose heads are over 65 and which allows for the concentration of unemployment and underemployment among groups with low full-effort earnings potential, raises the rate for a full-effort household-head work force to a still low 4 percent.

In short, a great deal of the poverty which Levitan and Taggart attribute to low earnings our analysis assigns to insufficient employment. There is more than a difference in emphasis involved here. Our method allows for measurement, at least qualitatively, of the relative needs for manpower development (occupational upgrading of the work force) and for policies to achieve fuller work effort in combating poverty.

THE DUAL LABOR MARKET

In discussing appropriate manpower policy for alleviating poverty, we have been stressing the relative importance of improving the quality of jobs and reducing total and partial unemployment to allow for full work. The data might seem to lead us to the conclusion that underutilization of labor offered is the more serious problem, which should thus receive a higher priority for improvement through government antipoverty policy. But just because the data show low poverty rates for full-effort workers, this does not mean that full-employment policies will easily solve the major part of the poverty problem. We have already conceded that there is some concentration of unemployment among low-wage workers, so that a move to full employment would raise the poverty rate above the current level for full-effort workers.

This low-wage concentration also exists among part-time and part-year workers, a factor that would raise the poverty rate of the hypothetical full-effort work-force still higher. But by far the most serious criticism leveled against emphasis on full-employment policies to attack labor force poverty is that the approach is unrealistic. It ignores the facts of labor market life. Literally millions of workers hold jobs which, by their very nature, regardless of the state of the economy, are not only low-wage—and permanently so—but transitory, unsteady, and unattractive. Thus, without occupational upgrading away from these jobs, there would be no way for making them full-effort activities. Neither steady employer demand nor total supply effort exist in these fields. In short, this view holds that a full-employment policy without occupational upgrading would fruitlessly attack the effect of sporadic work experience that resulted from the cause of inferior jobs.

The Dual Labor Market—Theory and Practice

The hypothesis that the labor market is segmented into two distinct parts, the *primary* and *secondary* markets, with the latter containing jobs that make their holders prone to poverty, is called the *dual labor market* theory. This theory has received its best-known exposition from Doeringer and Piore,[5] although earlier writers hinted at the existence of such a dual market.[6]

According to the theory, all that is best for the worker exists in the primary market and all that is worst is in the secondary market. In the former, jobs are well-paying, pleasant, steady, and, what is most important, they lead to training and advancement. The secondary labor market has dead-end jobs that are low-paying, unpleasant, arduous, and impermanent, and those holding them receive no additional company training to allow for advancement.

The novel part of the theory lies in its labor market segmentation aspect. Orthodox labor economics certainly does not dispute the obvious fact that there are good jobs and bad jobs. But what it cannot explain is why the wage mechanism in the labor market does not operate, as classical economists would argue, to induce labor mobility toward the better jobs, with a consequent rise in wages in those unpleasant jobs which could have no other attraction than that which higher wages would provide. There would be an accompanying relative decline in wages in the now more crowded primary job fields.

Obviously what is needed and what the theory provides is an explanation of the barrier to mobility which keeps the labor market segmented. A combination of demand and supply factors are thought to keep a large part of the work force suppressed and unable to rise into the primary market.

Demand Forces Radical economists who have adopted the dual labor market theory see a sinister collusion among employers to take advantage of opportunities to create a large labor market reserve which provides firms with a ready, cheap source of necessary common labor. Unions, sometimes not unwittingly, play their part in fostering this system through their seniority provisions for training and advancement which work against temporary job holders, if not currently or legally, then

---

[5]Peter Doeringer and Michael Piore, *Internal Labor Markets and Manpower Analysis,* Heath, Boston, 1971.

[6]Clark Kerr, in "The Balkanization of Labor Markets," *Labor Mobility and Economic Opportunity,* Wiley, New York, 1954, pp. 92–110, discusses the differences in employment opportunity between the "internal" labor market for higher jobs within the company and the "external" market for dead-end jobs. Dean Morse, in "The Peripheral Worker in the Affluent Society," *Industrial Relations Research Association Proceedings,* 1967, pp. 129–136, likens the low-status holders of low-status jobs to the compartmentalization of immigrant labor in the earlier days of our industrial history.

through their discriminatory membership policies.[7] At the same time, employers abet racial and sexist discrimination among workers in order to divide the work force and assure themselves of a steady, handy supply of cheap labor.

Stripped of its conspirational view of economic history, the radical view has a point in arguing that the economic system itself, with its motivating force of profit maximization, generates a dual labor market pattern. Many firms, and practically the entire service industry, operate at the margin of profitability. These firms—restaurants, hotels, warehouses, car-wash establishments, hospitals, and laundries, for example—have their preponderance of labor demand in low-wage, dead-end jobs. There are no competitive forces operating to make the firms pay their workers higher wages. If they paid more, they would get more ambitious workers whose ambition would be frustrated by lack of promotion opportunities. They would get more punctual, loyal, dedicated, hard-working employees when all these firms want is someone to fill a slot temporarily, with minimum efficiency. In short, higher wages would draw better workers, but they would not be worth the price; the returns to higher productivity from them are low.

These jobs, according to Reder's terminology, lack *responsibility* and *sensitivity*.[8] That is, they entail little or no control over workers and machinery, and whether the productivity of their holders is high or low makes very little difference in terms of company output. Even in competition, such firms find no inducement to bid for more efficient labor effort.

The secondary labor force often works in the same firm with primary workers. For example, in a department store, secondary workers will be sales clerks, wrappers, material handlers, etc. Primary workers will be in managerial training programs and, of course, will hold jobs throughout the decision-making and supervisory hierarchy. Firms seek primary workers for *entry jobs* at the lower echelons of their occupational structure. But with the prevalence of internal labor markets as the mechanism for filling higher jobs through on-the-job training, these entry jobs, while at a low level, hold out the promise of advancement. The company thus seeks

[7]This view of unions' role in the internal labor market, without radical economic overtones, is expressed by Kerr, op. cit., and Doeringer and Piore, op. cit. The unions are given a less innocent role by Michael Reich, David Gordon, and Richard Edwards in "Theory of Labor Market Segmentation," *American Economic Review*, May 1973, pp. 329–365, and by Gordon in *Theories of Poverty and Underemployment*, Heath, Boston, 1972.

[8]Melvin Reder, "A Partial Survey of the Theory of Income Size Distribution," in Lee Soltow (ed.), *Six Papers on the Size Distribution of Wealth and Income*, National Bureau of Economic Research, New York, 1969, pp. 205–253.

primary workers whom it considers trainable and capable of promotion.[9] They will often consider education as being a credential that promises this productive potential as well as being an indicator of perseverance, reliability, trust, and ambition—all attributes which the firm seeks in workers it hopes to tie more or less permanently to the firm and in whom it will place much investment in occupational development. How much some employers read into a college diploma!

Not all those who fill the primary entry jobs are lucky or capable enough to climb to positions of status, authority, and, at issue here, high salaries. While firms seek only promotable and trainable workers for their primary jobs, the occupational structure forms a pyramid, with only a few rising to the top. Those who climb only part way through entry jobs upward fill *subordinate* primary jobs.[10] These require performance of routine tasks but still demand dependability, "responsiveness to rules and authority, and acceptance of a firm's goals." While only a modest degree of responsibility and sensitivity appear in these jobs—as in low-level plant supervision and higher clerical positions—they are, of course, closed to members of the secondary labor force.

Supply of Secondary Labor   Whenever possible, firms that hire a great deal of secondary labor locate in the poorest neighborhoods, where the supply is abundant. The city's slums, ghettos, central cities, inner cities, or whatever terminology is used to describe the areas in which the oppressed, the suppressed, those with meager human capital investments and limited employment and upgrading opportunities reside, are the places where you will find most of the laundries, warehouses, etc.

Of course nearness to the pool of secondary labor cannot be the only determinant of business location. Restaurants and motels must establish themselves where the customers are, and consequently they often have operational difficulty because of inability to maintain an adequate (secondary) work force of shifting personnel which may be located far away. Thus they tend to employ teenagers, married women, and secondary family workers rather than family heads.

In any case, for our purposes of relating poverty to labor force status, we are interested in family-head membership in the secondary labor

---

[9]For a study showing the negative attitudes of employers toward the potential for promotion of the disadvantaged and the consequent reluctance to hire them for entry jobs, see John Iacobelli, "A Survey of Employers' Attitudes toward Training the Disadvantaged," *Monthly Labor Review*, June 1970, pp. 51–55.

[10]This term is suggested by Reich et al., op. cit.

market, and these heads can be found mainly in the poverty areas. There many workers display characteristics typical of the secondary market. They have little schooling, career motivation, or job attachment and show negative employment tendencies such as lateness and frequent job quitting which, though undesired by the employer, are acceptable for secondary market work.

Taking an unfortunate earlier quote of Piore that "insofar as secondary workers are barred from primary jobs by a real qualification, it is generally their inability to show up for work regularly and on time," a critic of the dual labor market theory argues that the case for segmentation hangs on negative work characteristics and that those "who are motivated to work and display regular work habits can be assimilated in the primary labor market."[11] A strong defender of the theory rebuts this attack by claiming it "ignores that motivation in particular and worker behavior in general are formed in response to confinement [to the secondary labor force]." Furthermore, "embedded in the dual labor market theory is the hypothesis that productivity and stability increase as wages increase."[12]

Does it really matter who said what? The fact remains, analogous to the conclusion in Chapter 1, that poverty was responsible for attitudes and behavior that foster its continuation. We cannot expect much labor market motivation from those who suffer overt and institutionalized discrimination and weak human capital investment and who reside near firms that put no premium on efficiency or firm attachment—or what some self-serving employers like to call "good industrial citizenship." These workers have their vitality drained, their ambition stunted, and their spirits smothered by their poverty and their low employment opportunities.

For an example of the drag of discrimination, how much ambition to complete high school and to move toward qualification for the primary market can we expect from blacks when, on average, in 12 poverty areas in 1968, those who were high school graduates averaged only $8.33 a week more than those who never entered high school? The white differential was $25.[13] One researcher even finds racial employment and wage discrimination in the unskilled labor market.[14]

---

[11]Robert Klitgaard, "The Dual Labor Market and Manpower Policy," *Monthly Labor Review,* November 1971, p. 46.

[12]Bennett Harrison, "Additional Thoughts on the Dual Labor Market," *Monthly Labor Review,* April 1972, p. 37.

[13]Bennett Harrison, "Education and Unemployment in the Urban Ghetto," *American Economic Review,* December 1972, p. 804.

[14]David Taylor, "Discrimination and Occupational Wage Differences in the Market for Unskilled Labor," *Industrial and Labor Relations Review,* April 1968. Taylor explains his finding of higher discrimination against material handlers than janitors on the grounds that the latter are in a dead-end occupation and the former occupation may lead to advancement. This hypothesis closely fits the dual market theory, even if it overstates opportunities for material handlers.

The poverty area work force displays some labor market characteristics which, considering the conditions it faces, appear surprising and reveal great resistance to a disadvantaged environment. For one thing, their intensity and method of job search is little different from that of other job seekers. A study of selected poverty areas found that, compared to job seekers in nonpoverty areas of the same cities, there was a not unexpected tendency for residents in the low-income zones to make more use of the public employment service with less help from private agencies. But the ranking of search methods for both groups was the same. The largest number sought jobs directly from employers; these were closely followed by workers who were referred to openings by relatives and friends and by those who relied on newspaper ads.[15]

The most significant characteristic of the labor force behavior of those who gain the least from work, either in satisfaction or earnings, is their willingness to work. When the data are studied carefully, the picture that appears is one of active participation in the labor force, comparable to those for whom work provides so much more in job stability, chance for advancement, and earnings.

A comprehensive Census Bureau study of low-income areas in over a hundred cities[16] reports an overall 1970 labor force participation rate of 57.1 percent, which is a little below the 61.3 percent for the nation as a whole.[17] All the difference occurs among males, with 73.1 percent for the poor areas and 80.6 percent for the nation. In fact, the female rate is actually slightly higher for the poor areas, 43.7 percent compared with 43.4 percent.

This participation pattern for the sexes can be explained by the high percentage of blacks in the poverty areas—almost 50 percent—among whom the female participation rate is characteristically much higher than for whites. The breakdown by sex and age still leaves some unexplained differential. The participation for each of the four sex-race components is a little lower in the poor areas. Even though the average age for whites is much higher than in the nation—explaining part of the lower average participation rate for whites—the rate for prime-age white males is some seven or eight percentage points below that of the nation.

But data on those not in the labor force reveal a sharp difference in attitudes towards work between the two groups and the seriousness of hidden unemployment or, at least, unfulfilled desire to work in the poor

---

[15]Harvey Hilaksi, "How Poverty Area Residents Look for Work," *Monthly Labor Review*, March 1971, pp. 41–45.

[16]*Employment, Profiles of Selected Low-Income Areas*, U.S. Bureau of Census, 1972.

[17]Since, at 8.7 million, the total population sixteen years of age and over in these areas is only 6 percent of the country, the figures for the nation as a whole, which of course includes this group, suffer from little downward bias when used as a basis of comparison.

areas. We have noted above that in 1972 only 4.5 million of the 56.5 million, or only about 8 percent of those not in the national work force, expressed a desire for work.

In the poor areas, though, showing completely opposite attitudes toward work, 1.7 million, or 63 percent of those out of the work force, state that they would like to work.[18] As might be expected, poor health places very high among reasons for not seeking work. The important point these data make is the comparatively large number who would like to work but who are not counted in the labor force.

A study of selected poverty areas concluded that because so many of the residents out of the labor force who expressed an interest in work cited ill health as the reason for their nonparticipation and so few had much substantial previous work experience, their actual potential for work falls well short of their expressed desire.[19] This conclusion makes sense, but it does not weaken the argument that, contrary to wide-spread—if not popular—belief, candidates for the secondary labor market show no generalized inclination to "live off welfare" but look to work as a means of support no less intensively than those with the opportunity for the better jobs. However, employers are not anxious to hire or train them as long as better-qualified workers are available.

Unemployment in the Secondary Labor Market

Low earnings rates in the poverty areas, our proxy for the secondary labor market, are augmented by high unemployment rates in aggravating weak economic status. In 1970, when the national rate was 4.9 percent, the unemployment rate in the poverty sectors was an almost double 9.6 percent.

Developers of the dual labor market theory point out that secondary workers move in and out of (dead-end) jobs frequently and that there are plenty of job openings for these workers, even if they are not good ones. As one critic of the theory puts it though, "It is *secondary* labor shortage that employers bemoan and lack of *primary* jobs that appalls ghetto residents."[20]

This picture of rapid turnover explains high unemployment rates in the presence of numerous vacancies and describes a strong labor market for bad jobs. As a consequence of these conditions, we should expect a

---

[18]Values are not strictly comparable with the whole nation, since poverty-area data on nonparticipants excludes those sixty-five and over, making the percentage who want jobs somewhat higher.

[19]Hilaksi, "Unutilized Manpower in Poverty Areas of 6 U.S. Cities," *Monthly Labor Review*, December 1971, pp. 45–52.

[20]Klitgaard, op. cit., p. 47.

higher unemployment rate in poor areas, which does occur, but a lower average period of unemployment, which does not happen. The data in Table 7-3 show that residents of poor areas suffer from both more unemployment and more time out of work per period of unemployment.

Making a rough estimate of the average length of unemployment from the data of Table 7-3, we find that the average length is 1.44 times greater in the poor areas than in the nation as a whole (11.7 weeks compared with 8.1 weeks). Multiplying this factor by the unemployment ratio, 1.96 (derived from a 9.6 percent unemployment rate in the poverty areas and 4.9 percent in the nation), yields a result of 2.82. This represents the ratio of annual time lost from work from unemployment in the poverty areas to that of the nation as a whole. There may be openings for secondary jobs, but the overall labor market for them is weak on two counts: unemployment is high and lasts longer.

Policy Recommendations

Unfortunately there will always be bad jobs. But steps could be taken to end the pigeonholing of people even if not to break up labor market segmentation. The training of minorities, together with stronger antidiscrimination laws and practices, would help break the concentration of particular populations in the secondary market. But these measures, which would blunt many sources of poverty, are painfully slow in being implemented.

Unionization has developed in various sectors of the secondary labor market. We have hospital workers', hotel workers', and department store clerks' unions. These organizations do prop up wages as they strengthen the bargaining power of their members and at least raise earnings if not job satisfaction.

Raising the minimum wage has been of questionable help. Missing the monopoly power of unions, those "protected" by rising minimums often find that their jobs disappear. There has been a decline in laundry

Table 7-3 Duration of Unemployment, Nation and Poverty Areas, 1970

Duration of unemployment	Nation, percent of unemployed	Poverty areas, percent of unemployed
Less than 5 weeks	52.3	41.8
5 to 14 weeks	31.5	25.8
15 to 26 weeks	10.4	15.1
27 weeks or more	5.7	17.2

Source: Manpower Report of the President, 1973 and Employment Profiles of Selected Low-Income Areas, U.S. Bureau of Census, 1972.

workers and restaurant workers, and the occupations of porter and bellhop are archaic. But we can wonder at the benefit of higher wages if they are gained at the cost of higher unemployment.

One suggestion calls for easy (subsidized) transportation out of the ghetto to take advantage of job openings elsewhere. Without any other changes, though, the transported workers would, in the main, simply fill the secondary labor needs of distant firms. The commuters would play the role of southern Europeans in the labor markets of northern Europe—doing the dirty work among a population of primary workers.

The dual labor market is here to stay; competitive efficiency in industrial manpower development requires it. Steps to randomize the probability of membership in the secondary market call for more equality of opportunity. But the pessimistic result of the dual labor market would remain; secondary workers would be poverty prone. The social gain would lie in reducing the disproportionate share of particular demographic groups in dead-end, low-level jobs.

SUMMARY

The basic proximate cause of poverty is inadequate earnings. Two factors account for low earnings: low pay rates and incomplete work effort. The latter represents the shortfall from full-effort work caused by unemployment and involuntary part-year and part-time employment; it involves the work force groups whose poverty can be relieved by effective full employment policy.

Our estimates yield a poverty rate of about 4 percent if all measured underutilized labor supply were employed. Official data understate excess labor supply. The "hidden unemployed," those discouraged from job search, add to the number whose poverty could be reached by the increase in available jobs. A further addition would come from at least some of those, not counted in the labor force because they are not now seeking work, who state that they "want a job." Of course, many millions would remain out of the labor force, no matter what adjustments are made to the data. Their poverty is best attacked by income supplement programs.

We might conclude that the "working poor," as we have narrowly defined them to include only the full-effort potential work force, those whose incomes are low because of low pay rather than because of periods of no pay (unused labor supply), pose a minor social problem since their poverty rate would be so low. But this view ignores the fact that the task of achieving full effort for a substantial segment of the labor force is not an easy one. The very nature of many jobs makes them temporary, unattractive, and low-paying.

One hypothesis maintains that competition in industry has led to the creation of a dual labor market. In the primary market there are no poverty problems; entry jobs given to those with prior education and perhaps generalized training lead to further company training and possible promotion. Secondary, dead-end jobs are low-paying and, what is most important, carry no competitive forces to induce employers to raise wages as a means of attaining a more stable, productive work force.

Firms and industries employing much secondary labor tend to locate where the workers are, and they find a ready supply in the poverty (ghetto) areas of cities. If the schism in the industrial labor market were not sufficient to bar easy movement out of the secondary into the primary market, inequality of opportunity (which leads to weak human investment, residence in areas far removed from the bulk of entry-level primary jobs, and continued discrimination) makes this mobility almost impossible.

Currently, as expected, unemployment rates are much higher in poverty areas than in the rest of the country. It is widely believed that, partly because of the very instability of secondary jobs, there are always many openings for such jobs. Therefore many feel that unemployment in these secondary job markets would tend to be only short-term for the most part. However, the average duration of unemployment is relatively high in poor areas. Thus, the holders of secondary jobs suffer three strong forces that induce poverty: their earnings rates are low, their unemployment is high, and their length of time between jobs is long.

Unfortunately, the prospects of attacking poverty through labor market reform are not promising. Unionization helps some in raising wages in dead-end jobs, but only for those who are organized; and higher minimum wages have a self-defeating element in pricing secondary workers out of the market. Stronger pressures against discrimination can randomize secondary labor market participation and poverty, which would certainly represent a social advance. But as Thurow so aptly puts it, in a labor market, when "instead of people looking for jobs, there are jobs looking for people,"[21] even prior training and education would not reduce the number of bad jobs.

Thus it seems that if the attack on poverty is to be an all-out effort, there will have to be income supplements for many workers. Do we have the economic knowledge, political will, and social consciousness to adopt such policies in a society which still associates need only with those who are unemployed or who cannot work?

[21]Lester Thurow, "Education and Economic Equality," *Public Interest,* Summer 1972, p. 68.

Chapter 8

Poverty and the Economy

Up to now we have been discussing various characteristics associated with poverty—educational level, race, sex, age, and labor force status. Disadvantages in any of these attributes can lead to poverty, and thus these individual economic handicaps are rightfully considered causes of poverty. In this chapter we examine the effect on poverty and the poor not of qualities which induce poverty among individuals and population subgroups but of the state of the overall economy.

Two important economic phenomena form the basis of the present discussion of the relationship between poverty and the state of the economy—growth and inflation. To some extent, this chapter serves as a transition to the next section on policies to combat poverty. Since economic growth would obviously reduce poverty, programmed growth might serve as an effective antipoverty measure. But certainly the question of whether national policy should be geared to growth is based on many other considerations besides poverty alleviation, if this element is considered at all. In any case, the policy tie between growth and poverty alleviation is much looser than that for manpower programming or income maintenance, the topics of the following chapters on combating poverty.

Although growth can only help the poor and tends to reduce poverty, the effects of inflation are unclear. But the consideration of poverty effects in inflation policy is even weaker than in decisions and priorities on growth. Thus, in this chapter we are concerned about the effects of growth and inflation on poverty. However, we do not suggest that poverty effects influence efforts to regulate growth or inflation rates, nor do we argue that they should do so.

POVERTY AND GROWTH

Detailed analysis is not required to support the argument that bad times increase the incidence of poverty. Unemployment and involuntary part-time work keep the income of millions below the poverty line. But less certain are the positive effects of a strong economy. Full employment will mop up the poverty among those with earnings potential high enough to yield above-poverty incomes when their labor supply is absorbed by the market.

Growth, measured by increased output per capita, results not only from technological improvements but also from full utilization of existing factors of production. Even if technological improvement has only a neutral effect on labor demand, so that the wages of the lowest paid rise no faster than the earnings rate of those with the best jobs, the increase in low earnings consequent to growth will push many workers above poverty. Furthermore, besides reducing unemployment among the potentially poor, there is persuasive evidence that, during strong economic periods, pay rates for those at the bottom of the industrial wage scale rise higher than for those at the top, thus narrowing the wage structure.[1]

In summary, several aspects of growth reduce poverty: unemployment is reduced; wages, even corrected for price changes, rise throughout the occupational structure in response to technological advancement; and lowest wages tend to rise the most.

But is there not a limit to the extent to which growth can reduce poverty? Will the beneficial effects of growth reach those outside the labor force? In short, is there a poor population, whose incomes remain unstimulated by growth, large enough to make growth an ineffective mechanism for removing poverty from the list of major socioeconomic problems? We can all share a wistful yearning for a negative answer to this question. Would it not be convenient, or fortuitous, if this most

[1]See Melvin Reder, "Wage Differentials: Theory and Measurement," *Aspects of Labor Economics*, National Bureau of Economic Research, 1962.

serious national failing were to be corrected in passing, as a by-product of policies aimed at the national goal of a strong economy, without any conscious effort to meet the problem head on?

The data, unfortunately, do not yield clear-cut answers to this question. While poverty certainly yields ground to growth, there seems to be a tendency for resistance to further cuts in the poverty count even as the economy continues to strengthen. That is, a hard-core residue of poverty remains impervious to the softening agent of a strong economy. But the question remains as to the size of this core. Is it small enough to be dissolved by a simple, inexpensive transfer mechanism, inexpensive because of the small size of the core? Finally, there are the important questions of whether we can depend on a policy of growth to be maintained, even if growth is found to be an effective force against poverty, and whether growth can treat the poverty problem only cosmetically by reducing absolute poverty while leaving relative deprivation untouched.

The "Backwash" Hypothesis

Early modern writers on poverty, emphasizing the negative, perhaps for dramatic effect or because of lack of hard data to the contrary, wrote pessimistically about the permanence of poverty in their conceptualization of a "culture of poverty," of "islands of poverty," of "the other America." In the main, the poor were considered immune to the stimulating effects of that prosperity and growth which gave a fillip to the buying power of those in the mainstream of economic life. These economic outcasts formed what Gallaway so aptly calls "the 'backwash' of American economic life."[2]

Gallaway is interested in the crucial question of the size of the backwash. If it is large—that is, if the reduction in poverty associated with a percentage growth in per capita output is small—or if the limit to poverty reduction from additional economic expansion is approached at a high poverty rate, then growth can be considered an inadequate means of eliminating poverty. Specific antipoverty measures must be adopted even in the framework of an economy enjoying sustained strength.

Gallaway's techniques for estimating the backwash population is to project poverty rates on the basis of growth rates for levels of unemployment. It is no surprise that he finds that high unemployment rates retard poverty reduction even with rising per capita income. His statistical method differs somewhat from that used by the Council of Economic Advisers[3] in relating poverty rates to growth, but the underlying approach is

---

[2]Lowell Gallaway, "The Foundations of the 'War on Poverty,' " *American Economic Review,* March 1965, p. 122.
[3]*Economic Report of the President,* 1965.

the same. Both try to predict future poverty rates, specifically for 1980, on the basis of growth rates using past growth-rate–poverty-rate relationships as a guide to their predictions. Gallaway notes that his 1980 projections for the poverty rate lie substantially below those of the Council because he assumes a steady future growth, measured by median family income, while the Council's computations are based on a declining growth rate.

Both the Council's and Gallaway's estimating equations assume nonlincarity in the growth–poverty reduction relationship. That is, they both assume growing resistance of poverty to the ameliorating influence of economic expansion;[4] both assume a "backwash" population, though they differ as to its magnitude. Based on this differential approach to growth, Gallaway's analysis led to a much lower estimate for 1980 poverty, 6.4 percent if (high) 1947–1956 growth rates were maintained, as compared to 10 percent for the Council.

In response to criticism of his estimating equation, Gallaway admitted that his method overstated the direct effect of even steady growth on poverty.[5] But in a later study, he argued that the increased response of social security receipts to changes in average income make his prediction of a low poverty rate for 1980 based on steady growth still realistic, even if for the wrong reasons.[6]

But the whole controversy over expected poverty rates for 1980 has an academic flavor. If it represented a cutoff date on the War on Poverty, 1980 would have some importance. Perhaps writing in the agitated period of the middle and late 1960s, these analysts felt a sense of urgency in chopping down the poverty count. But as 1980 nears, its significance wanes as a target date for the limiting effect of growth on poverty reduction. Growth beyond that date could still cut into poverty, albeit with diminishing depth. The weakened effect of growth on poverty should not weigh in the decision on programmed growth because, to repeat, even students of the growth–poverty count relationship do not argue that policy decisions on growth should be based on so distant a consideration as its effect on the poverty rate.

---

[4]W. H. Locke Anderson, in "Trickling Down: The Relationship between Economic Growth and the Extent of Poverty among American Families," *Quarterly Journal of Economics,* November 1964, pp. 511–524, reaches the same conclusion through a different method. By examining poverty subgroups, he finds that growth above a certain level has little impact on most because only tails of their distribution would be affected. For the favored white worker group, only those few at the bottom would be affected; and for workers in the disadvantaged groups, only those few at the top would be reached.

[5]Henry Aaron, "The Foundation of the 'War on Poverty' Reexamined," *American Economic Review,* December 1967, pp. 1229–1240, and Gallaway, "Reply," ibid., pp. 1241–1243.

[6]Lowell Gallaway, *Poverty in America,* Grid, Inc., Columbus, Ohio, 1973.

In any case, perhaps because of diminished influence of growth on poverty, as the poverty data show, the rate has seemed to develop strong downward resistance, around 10 percent, at least temporarily. 1973 was a prosperous year by current standards. But since we expect and hope that the present economic setback is temporary, the challenge to the poverty rate will be resumed when our economy strengthens and grows.

Gallaway is correct in assuming that the size of the backwash that does not easily disappear with growth has important policy implications, but perhaps not the ones he considers. He argues that a 6 percent backwash rate calls for simple income transfer while 10 percent needs selective antipoverty programs for effective treatment. In reality, the nature of the backwash population should carry as much weight as its size. Realistically, at the lower rate, most of the poor would be out of the work force and not likely to enter; these would best be aided by transfers. But even at the lower rate, efficiency would call for upgrading of the working poor and expanded employment opportunities for the underemployed and unemployed rather than simple income transfers for all. The size of the backwash would affect antipoverty policy, though this would be by its impact on long-run budgetary allocation for training, job placement, and income maintenance, assuming long-run, if not always steady, annual growth and reduction in the count and percentage poor—the antipoverty goal.

Practical Antipoverty Limitations of Growth

Up to now we have considered the quantitative influence of poverty on the growth rate. Now we examine the modification or—more closely—the attenuation of this influence resulting from the probable limitations to growth as a policy and the harmful effects of growth-induced poverty reduction on relative poverty.

Declining Popularity of Growth   For some years now, growth has joined motherhood and feeding the birds as activities that were once of unquestioned virtue but which have now come under a cloud because of their negative environmental impact. Threats to supplies of scarce resources and to the "quality of life," as the ecological Cassandras point out, can come from an increase in population or greater consumption per capita, the latter being both the measure and purpose of growth. We are continually reminded that we Americans use four times our share of this energy source and five times that, with "share" being measured by our percentage of world population. It is not that we have not always used more than our share, at least since we have been the most industrialized economy, but that we have now become more aware of, and perhaps even a little embarrassed about, our advanced stage of development and consequent strong demand for the world's available goods and services.

Whatever the source of our diffidence, it is unlikely that we will follow a national policy of planned economic growth. But in our free-enterprise economy, with productivity and potential output levels determined by private decisions, planning for slower growth will require the imposition of impediments to private business expansion. Restrictions to unlimited expansion are being imposed, and we can expect that the rise in median family income will slacken and opportunities for the amelioration of poverty to be reduced as a consequence of dampened growth.

Prosperity, Recession, and Poverty   But if growth is no longer so popular, maintenance of a strong economy still is. *Growth* refers to the raised potential for per capita or per family income, but the state of the economy determines how much of that potential is realized. When the economy is strong and resources are close to their full employment, per capita income is at its highest, with—obviously—opposite conditions prevailing during slumps.

The poverty rate is somewhat sensitive to moderate swings in the unemployment rate, even if median family income is little affected, because unemployment tends to be concentrated among those at the lower end of the income distribution. Normal changes in unemployment would therefore have little effect on median income. The Council of Economic Advisers has recently noted that poverty is much less related to unemployment since there is increased concentration of poverty in families out of the work force.[7] But this does not mean that an increase in unemployment, particularly the sharp recent rise, would not add seriously to the poverty count. Not yet having the actual data on hand, the Council expects to find a steep rise in poverty for 1974 with further increases in 1975.

The Council also notes that since World War II, there has been a tendency for income inequality to widen during recessions. This adds to the burdens of the poor in that they not only suffer a reduction in their incomes but a worsening in their relative position. The Council bases these results in the disproportionate suffering that shorter hours and reduced employment in general bring to those at the lower end of the income scale during downturns.

In detailed econometric studies, Miner agrees with the Council's reasoning for earlier periods but notes that the poor actually improved

[7]*Economic Report of the President,* 1975, p. 119.

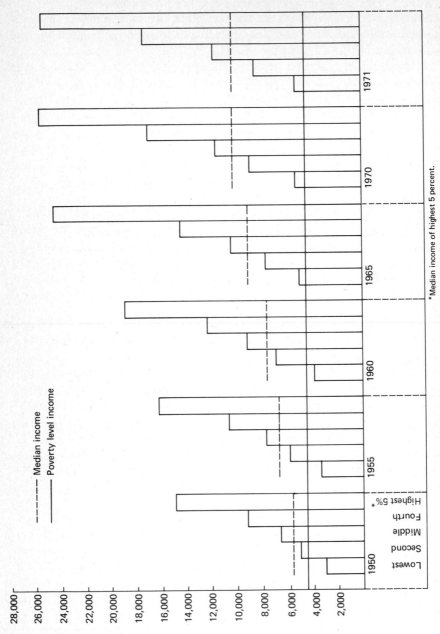

Figure 8-1 Average income for each fifth and the highest 5 percent of families, median national income, and poverty level income, in constant 1971 dollars for selected years. (*Source: Statistical Abstract,* 1974.)

*Median income of highest 5 percent.

their relative position during the slight recession of 1970.[8] Miner cites the development and expansion of transfers as a source of recessionary income support for the poor.

We know the income distribution was more unequal during the Great Depression of the 1930s than it is today, but that was a pretransfer era. During the current deep recession, with our growth in transfers, the poor might actually be experiencing an improvement in their relative position. This provides small consolation to the poor as their number swells, but it can explain a weakening interest in the issue of poverty. Recall the recent ill-advised comment of the Council's Chairman on the serious impact on stockholders and other high-income recipients of the recession's stock market losses and profit erosion.

In an earlier period, Harrington noted that poverty concern was a product of prosperity and not bad times; when with everyone struggling for economic survival, there was less interest in or guilt about the most unfortunate. Regardless of cyclical attitudes or change in relative incomes, recessions are particularly bad times for the poor.

Growth and Relative Poverty

Stability in the income distribution as our economy has grown since 1950 confirms the reduction in official poverty and the worsening of the relative position of the poor. The bar graph of Fig. 8-1 shows these facts over the period. Note that the median family income in constant (1971) dollars rose by 84 percent over the period, from $5,600 to $10,300. The almost proportionate rise in the upper limits of each quintile over the period reflects both the constancy in the income distribution and the push of millions of families over the unchanging poverty line. But of course, at the same time, those that remain below the line have fallen away from the median.

Table 1-3 (page 15) showed that Fuchs's measure of relative poverty has remained almost constant over the period 1950–1972, meaning that if the poverty line had moved proportionately with the median, growth would have left his poverty rate unchanged. Thus, the fall in the official count has been at the expense of the worsening relative position of those who remain poor.

Gallaway, in noting these trends, expects that "the poverty definition will probably have been adjusted by the end of the decade [of the 1970s]." He adds that "If this does happen, we will merely recycle

---

[8]Thad W. Miner, "The Effects of Macroeconomic Fluctuations on the Distribution of Income," *Review of Income and Wealth,* December 1973, pp. 385–406, and "The Distributional Impact of the 1970 Recession," *Review of Economics and Statistics,* May 1973, pp. 214–224.

through another period in which economic growth can be remarkably successful in eliminating poverty."[9]

In other words, Gallaway envisions step adjustments in the poverty rate in response to the pressures of worsening relative poverty as growth continues with an unchanged income distribution. In fact, his prediction of adjustment in the official definition is purely speculative, since it has not changed since its inception almost 15 years ago. Even if the rate did rise each time the poverty line drifted a certain distance away from the median income level, a treadmill effect in poverty reduction would develop each time the rate jumped in response to a higher level, then fell and rose again when the drop resulted only from a rise in average incomes, thus necessitating a further jump in the line, and so on.

Obviously, if the concept of relative poverty has any practical significance, and especially if it grows in public acceptance (as it very well may as our society becomes more egalitarian in principle), more than passive dispersion of the benefits of growth throughout the income distribution is needed to solve the problem of poverty. Thus the backwash population may be small or large, depending on future growth rates, the response of the official poverty count to growth, and the definition of poverty used. Nevertheless, antipoverty policy calls for special programs, whether to develop earning power or simply to transfer income, focused on those at the bottom of the income distribution.

INFLATION AND POVERTY

Inflation is often considered a type of tax, and one that falls heavily on the poor. According to this view, if prices rise 10 percent, then each family spending unit suffers a 10 percent reduction in its purchasing power. While this loss might take the form of a proportionate 10 percent tax, the poor are least able to adjust to any real income reduction.

But this explanation of the effects of inflation is much too simplistic and often quite incorrect. For one thing, inflation does not distribute its burden equally among income classes. But more important, the description of inflation as a tax looks only at one side of the economic picture. Also to be considered are the economic changes occurring with the inflation, so that price increases must not be looked at in the abstract.

For example, in a full-employment situation, if the government wishes to finance extra expenditures, say defense outlays, and does so through taxes, then the effect on consumer purchasing power is obvious; it is reduced to finance the production of war goods instead of an equal amount of consumer goods. Similarly, in this case, financing the defense

[9]Gallaway, op. cit., pp. 57–58.

outlays through new borrowing will lead to an inflationary "tax." Prices will rise on the reduced supply of consumer goods.

But borrowing can stimulate a less than fully employed economy. If it does, although prices may rise, real income in the form of still higher wages, profits, etc., may also increase. What was noted above about defense expenditures can also apply to transfer payments. If, in a tight economy, transfers are financed by borrowing instead of taxes, the redistributive effects occur just the same, this time through the price mechanism. Prices will rise for all, but recipients will experience a rise in real income from the transfer, eroded somewhat by the inflation, and taxpayers will find their income reduced, not directly by the tax collector but indirectly through the rise in prices.

Take the current situation. Antirecession policy is proceeding with both federal borrowing and increased transfers. Estimates for the 1975 fiscal year deficit are running up to $100 billion. The rise in transfers should help the poor, but inflation may also accelerate to dampen these gains and weaken the purchasing power of taxpayers. But with so much slack in the economy, production and real income will probably be stimulated by the tax cuts. Thus money income gains might exceed price increases.

To study the effect of inflation, though, there is no need to speculate about the future. All we need do is compare price increases over a time period with movements in money incomes. If the latter exceed the former for a particular population group studied, then that group has improved its *absolute* economic level. There is no implication in this analysis that inflation "caused" the improvement, but there is in it a tacit acknowledgment that price rises do not occur in the abstract. If prices of goods rise, so do factor prices, in particular wages, and the relationship between price changes and money income changes are the measurement of the economic effect of inflation.

This relationship will be studied for the poor to note the effect of price changes on absolute poverty and on the relative position of the poor. But inflation also has a differential effect on the spending as well as on the income side. The market basket of the poor differs from that of more affluent households, and we will want to take into account differences in price changes of goods and services bought by those at various levels of the income distribution in calculating the absolute and relative impact of inflation on the poor.

Price Changes and Income Changes

The analysis of this section will be limited to the direct relationship between price and income changes without regard to the possibility of a causative link between the two. In a rather recent study of the effect of inflation on the poor, Hollister and Palmer claim that inflation stimulates low incomes because of its favorable effects in reducing unemployment and underemployment, which fall so heavily on the poor. It is testimony to the rapid changes in our economic structure that this 1972 argument[10] is already somewhat out of date. More recently, the Phillips curve negative relationship between the price level and the unemployment rate has been denied, with prices and unemployment chasing each other upward. We can no longer have confidence that rising prices will ensure fuller employment, especially of the poor.

In studying the direct relationship between income and inflation, the first step is to note the movements in income of the poor during an inflationary period. Fortunately for this study if not for the state of the economy, we have a recent clear experience of rising prices for the period from 1967 to 1974, when the price level rose by 47 percent.

At first view the comparison seems an easy one to make; just compare the changes in average poverty income over the period with consumer price movements. But such a comparison involves a serious error of circular reasoning. The change in the price level itself determines the official poverty line, so that we could experience a rise in average poverty income, and a substantial increase at that considering our recent

---

[10]Robinson Hollister and John Palmer, "The Impact of Inflation on the Poor," in Kenneth Boulding and Martin Paff (eds.), *Redistribution to the Rich and the Poor,* Wadsworth, Belmont, Calif., 1972, pp. 240–269.

Table 8-1 Poverty Income Index Components, 1967–1974

	Earnings index component			Social security index component[†]		
Year	Minimum wage	Index	Weighted index component[*]	Average monthly payment[§]	Index	Weighted index component
1967	$1.60	100.0	36.0	$ 85.37	100.0	33.0
1968	1.60	100.0	36.0	98.86	115.8	38.2
1969	1.60	100.0	36.0	100.40	117.6	38.8
1970	1.60	100.0	36.0	118.10	138.5	45.6
1971	1.60	100.0	36.0	132.17	154.8	51.1
1972	1.60	100.0	36.0	162.35	190.2	62.8
1973	1.60	100.0	36.0	166.42	194.9	64.3
1974	2.00	100.0	45.0	187.29	219.4	72.4

[*]Source of index components: *Statistical Abstract of the U. S., 1974.* Weights are components' share of family income of those below $4,000.
[†]Retirement and disability income.
[‡]Aid for Families with Dependent Children—administered by Social Security.
[§]Source of all average component income data: *Social Security Bulletin,* February 1975.

strong inflation, without any increase in money income in a single poor family. This would come about as the rise in the price level pushed the poverty level up to include new higher-income poor families.

Another method that has the same attraction of simplicity, but which also contains a serious analytic flaw, would merely observe changes in the poverty rate during the recent inflation and conclude that inflation had a minor effect on the poor since this rate has not changed much, showing a slight downward drift, over the past several years. Such a method would make sense only if inflation were the only factor affecting the poverty rate, which is certainly not the case.

To avoid these errors, we will construct an income index of the poor composed of the annual values of the elements of income, weighted by their share in poverty income. The income sources included in Table 8-1 account for about 90 percent of the income of the poor. Only dividend, interest, and private pension receipts are omitted because of lack of data.

Weights for 1972 are used, and, of course, an inaccuracy appears in the application of these weights to other years. But the shifts in relative importance of income components of the poor over time should not substantially affect the results.

The use of the minimum wage as a measure of the earnings changes for the poor introduces another computational inaccuracy. Actual wage levels of the poor may move somewhat apart from changes in the minimum, but certainly a large number of poor wage earners have their pay rates tied closely if not precisely to movements in the minimum wage.

In any case, within the roughness imposed by data limitation, we

AFDC index component‡			General assistance index component‡			Unemployment insurance index component		
Average monthly payment§	Index	Weighted index component	Average monthly payment§	Index	Weighted index component	Average weekly payment§	Index	Weighted index component
$39.50	100.0	16.0	$39.40	100.0	10.0	$41.25	100.0	5.0
42.05	106.5	17.0	44.70	113.5	11.4	43.43	105.3	5.3
45.15	114.3	18.3	50.05	127.0	12.7	46.17	111.9	5.6
49.65	125.7	20.1	57.85	146.8	14.7	50.34	122.0	6.1
53.30	134.9	21.6	64.80	164.5	16.5	54.02	131.0	6.6
53.95	136.6	21.9	72.20	183.2	18.3	56.76	137.6	6.9
56.96	144.2	23.1	83.58	212.1	21.2	59.00	143.0	7.2
62.63	158.6	25.4	93.68	237.8	23.8	64.14	155.5	7.8

reach the interesting conclusion that the income of the poor has grown in real terms during a period of strong inflation. This improvement occurred despite relative stagnation in an important element of income, counting for over one-third the total—wage earnings. Measured by the minimum wage, these earnings rose only once in the period; even with the jump from $1.60 to $2 in 1974, the overall period increase of 25 percent was much below the 47 percent growth in the price level.

But as Table 8-1 shows, sharp gains were registered in social security and in general assistance receipts, although this latter component contributes comparatively little to the income of the poor.

Table 8-2 includes the annual sums of the various weighted index components to arrive at the Poverty Income Index for each year (1967 as base). These indexes are deflated by the Consumer Price Index (CPI) to derive a Poverty Real Income Index. Note the 18.6 percent gain in real income for the seven-year period. Admittedly, the greatest annual gain in real income occurred in 1972, a year of relative price stability, when fairly rigid wage and price controls were imposed. But still in only two years, 1969 and 1973, did real income fall below the previous year's level.

It is interesting to note that the annual growth in real poverty income of about 2.4 percent comes close to matching the national average annual productivity growth. In a competitive economy, we expect wages to keep step with productivity gains; but there is no close market tie between poverty income and productivity, since so much of poverty income—about two-thirds—is derived from sources outside of the labor market.

We can only conclude that inflation does not interrupt the tendency for transfers to keep pace with taxpayers' income growth. An overstatement might be made in concluding that inflation actually strength-

Table 8-2 Poverty   Real   Income   Index
(1967 = 100)

Year	Poverty Income Index	Consumer Price Index	Real Poverty Income Index (PII/CPE)
1967	100.0	100.0	100.0
1968	107.9	104.2	103.6
1969	111.4	109.8	101.5
1970	122.5	116.3	105.3
1971	131.8	121.3	108.7
1972	145.9	125.3	116.4
1973	151.8	133.1	114.0
1974	174.4	147.0	118.6

Source: Table 8-1.

Table 8-3   Real Income of Average Wage Earner and the Poor, 1970–1973

(1970 as Base)

Year	Average weekly earnings of full-time wage and salary worker	Average Earnings Index	AEI deflated by CPE	Poverty Income Index	Real Poverty Income Index
1970	$130	100.0	100.0	100.0	100.0
1971	138	106.7	101.8	107.6	103.2
1972	144	110.8	102.9	119.1	110.6
1973	159	122.3	106.9	123.9	108.3

Source: Statistical Abstract of the United States, 1974.

ens poverty income, in that we would need to know how real poverty income behaves in less inflationary times; but there is nothing in the data, which show a healthy growth in real income during one of the most nagging periods of inflation in our economic history, to indicate that inflation poses any particular income problems for the poor.

In fact, there is some indication that the poor actually showed slightly more income growth than the average wage earner. Table 8-3 presents data for the brief period 1970–1973 that allow comparison of real income for the poor and the average wage earner.

The poor lost a little ground in 1973, but at 108.3 the Real Poverty Income Index was still over a point above the real income level of the earning work force. There is no need to make a forceful argument about this small difference, and adjustments made in the next section will remove it; but the data do indicate that inflation does not worsen relative poverty. The poor gained at least as much as the fully employed work force during an inflationary period.

Poverty Price-Level Changes during Inflation

The above method of estimating real income of the poor by deflating money income changes by movements in the CPI calls for adjustment. The CPI measures price levels of the market basket of the typical urban (middle-class) worker, while the average poor household buys a different—or at least a differently weighted—bundle of goods. The poor spend a relatively larger share of their income on the basic necessities— food and shelter—and less on clothing, transportation, and recreation.

Thus differential price changes in spending components can cause deviation between price level changes applicable to the poor and movements in the CPI. Data in Hollister and Palmer on expenditure weights for the poor allow construction of a "poor man's price index." This index can be compared with the CPI to yield a closer measure of the relationship between inflation and purchasing power for the poor and the rest of the population.

Table 8-4 shows that in recent years inflation has hit the poor man's dollar a little harder than that of the rest of society. In fact, the negative effects on relative spending power of the poor occurred only in the last years for which data are available, 1973 and 1974. This abrupt change is easily attributable to the large jump (about 30 percent) in food prices during those two years, with food accounting for about 35 percent of the poverty family basket, only 28 percent of the average family's expenditures, and 22 percent of the wealthy family budget. At the same time, and because food weighs more lightly in their market basket, spending power of the wealthy suffered less damage from the sharp inflation of 1973–1974.

Over the entire period, though, Table 8-4 does not show much differential in price effects for the three widely separated income groups studied. We should not minimize the worsening differential for the poor in 1974, and it would be illogical to cite the recent tempering of inflation as an argument against the view that sharp inflation hurts the poor the most. It could be argued, though, that this recent inflation in atypical fashion focused on price rises in essentials.

In any case, the overall picture of the effects of inflation on the poor is not a gloomy one. Adjusting the Real Poverty Income Index in 1974 to deflate the Poverty Income Index by the Poor Price Index instead of the CPI, as is done in Table 8-2, would reduce the 1974 value from 118.6 to

Table 8-4 Price Indexes for Poor, Average, and Wealthy Families, 1967–1974

(1967 as Base)

Year	Poor Family Price Index	Typical Family Price Index	Wealthy Family Price Index
1967	100.0	100.0	100.0
1968	103.5	104.2	103.5
1969	109.3	109.8	109.1
1970	115.8	116.3	115.4
1971	120.5	121.3	120.4
1972	124.9	125.3	124.2
1973	134.8	133.1	132.1
1974	150.2	147.0	146.0

Source of Weights: Hollister and Palmer, "Source of Spending Component Price Relatives," *Monthly Labor Review,* 1974.

Table 8-5 Real Income of Average Wage Earner and the Poor (Calculated by Deflation by the Poor Price Index) 1970-1973

(1970 as Base)

Year	Average Earnings Index (deflated by CPI)	Real Poverty Income Index (deflated by Poor Price Index)
1970	100.0	100.0
1971	101.8	103.4
1972	102.9	110.5
1973	106.9	106.5

Source: Tables 8-3 and 8-4.

116.1. This would still represent a substantial gain in real income for a strong inflationary period.

The effect of the Poor Price Index adjustment on real income of the poor wipes out the relative gain of the poor. Table 8-5 shows this adjustment, which slightly alters the figures of Table 8-3. When 1974 data are available for the average worker, they will probably show a slight worsening of the relative position of the poor.

But because of the unusual nature of the 1973-1974 inflation, we cannot conclude that inflation tends, by its nature, to weaken the relative position of the poor. In any case, there is no evidence that inflation carries forces that weaken the *absolute* real income of the poor. Reducing inflationary pressure for other reasons undoubtedly has merit, but as Hollister and Palmer conclude, national policy makers "will at least no longer be able to claim that they are trying to stop inflation in order to protect the poor."[11]

Why in the face of data to the contrary does the average person still feel that inflation hurts the poor the most? First, people probably consider inflation only in the abstract, as an erosion of purchasing power, without taking into account the other side of price rises—higher money incomes. The poor are least able to tolerate losses.

Then, those who consider the effect on incomes at all will realize that while wages and salaries have some tie to the price level, a great share of the income of the poor does not. Minimum wages tend to rise, albeit with a lag, in step with the price level, and social security benefits have been

[11]Hollister and Palmer, "The Implicit Tax of Inflation and Unemployment: Some Policy Implications," *Redistribution to the Rich and the Poor.* We cannot agree with these writers, though, that inflation control will necessarily impose a heavy burden on the poor, because they adhere to the Phillips curve view that price stability can be bought only by a weakening of the economy. As noted above, recently the negative connection between price changes and unemployment seems to have greatly loosened.

recently "indexed" (tied to changes in the CPI). But welfare payments—whether AFDC, other categorical programs, or general assistance —which make up almost half of poverty incomes, do not increase automatically with prices. Thus a large share of the average poor family's income appears fixed, subject to the buffeting blows of inflation.

But such is not the case. Whether because of social or political pressures, the same forces that push up on the minimum wage have operated just as effectively in raising transfer payment schedules. That taxpayer opposition to these increases weakens as the real burden of a given transfer falls with rising taxpayer money income is perhaps the most important explanation of why they take place.

But whatever the reason, the money incomes of the poor have more than kept pace with price increases. We have noted many disadvantages the poor suffer and many reasons for their poverty, but on balance, inflation is not one of them.

SUMMARY

While it is not suggested that national economic policy is or should be dependent on antipoverty goals, certainly the incidence and severity of poverty is influenced by important national economic characteristics. The pace of economic growth, the state of the economy, and price-level changes each have their particular effect on the level of poverty.

There are three reasons for not relying on growth alone as a means of solving the poverty problem. In the first place, although the poverty rate responds favorably to economic growth, studies show that these positive effects tend to diminish as average income rises. A backwash, whose size may be uncertain, but whose presence is undenied, does not share in the benefits of growth. Those out of the work force and those in low-paying dead-end jobs will need income transfers or manpower development to alleviate their poverty, no matter what attainable level of productive capacity is reached.

In the second place, even if growth does contribute to poverty alleviation, it is unlikely that we will follow a policy of vigorous growth. The opposition of environmentalists will restrain growth.

Third, growth alone reduces absolute poverty but lowers the relative economic status of the poor. This result is not inconsistent with stability in the income distribution and in the poverty rate, measured by a changing relative poverty standard. Those who remain poor according to the official poverty definition drift further and further away from the average income as this level rises. While we may debate whether absolute or relative poverty has more social relevance, certainly the latter will become dominant as the income disparity between the poor and average family widens.

Obviously, bad times are very hard on the poor. They are the first to lose their jobs and they face stronger taxpayer resistance to needed transfers. But the issue of the relative status of the poor during recessions has only academic interest. Studies of income distribution changes when the economy weakens miss the qualitative measurement of losses to those least able to sustain them. In other words, the importance of relative poverty is not uniform through the business cycle. In bad times there would be little comfort to the poor to learn that their income losses were relatively less severe than those of the more affluent, if such were the case, and the need for recovery to alleviate poverty would be no less pressing if their relative status improved while they along with everyone else suffered income losses. In good times, though, the relative status of the poor has considerable weight in the importance of poverty as a socioeconomic problem.

Contrary to popular belief, inflation has more or less neutral effects on the poor. The real income of the poor, even taking into account that their market basket is heavily weighted with essentials—food and shelter—goods that have risen highest in the current inflation, has grown at more or less the same pace as that of the rest of the population. Price rises in the abstract weaken the purchasing power of everybody, but while price increases are reflected in higher earnings for the nonpoor, the poor have had their money incomes outrun price advances in the 1967–1974 period even though their incomes are much less dependent on earnings. Transfers have kept up with the price index.

Inflation may be bad for the economy, but poverty rates and the status of the poor are little likely to be affected by price-restraining policies. In fact, the recent disassociation between price movements and the unemployment rate suggests that even indirect effects of price changes will no longer operate on poverty.

Part Three
Combating Poverty

Chapter 9

Manpower Development and Planning

Manpower* development, as the term is applied to government policies, plans, and programs designed to upgrade the productive capacity and employability of those with the weakest earnings potential, represents a belated and insufficient effort to overcome the disadvantage of ineffective preparation for work during schooling years. There is no need here to reiterate the argument of Chapter 3 that European school systems do a better job than ours in career development. But a supporter of that view cannot help noting that manpower programs in Western Europe are limited to emergency expansion of public service jobs to reduce recessionary unemployment and under normal economic conditions, to special programs such as workshops for the physically and mentally handicapped.[1]

*The word *manpower*—rather than "nonsexist" alternatives like *workers* or *work force*—is used in this text because it is routinely used in the literature and by the U.S. government. In this customary usage *manpower* refers to workers of either sex.

[1]*Special Job Creation for Hard-to-Employ in Western Europe*, U.S. Department of Labor, Manpower Research Monograph no. 14, 1970. This monograph discusses these programs in several countries.

Manpower planning, as contrasted with development, may simply entail services to facilitate the employment of those out of work in jobs at their current skill levels through placement efforts or job creation. Unfortunately, except for periods of recession, those most in need of these services are actual and potential labor force members with very low earning power, so that this type of manpower planning without development may reduce unemployment rates but may not do much to raise income above the poverty level.

Prime subjects for manpower development and planning are those with low earning capacity when they do work and who are most susceptible to unemployment and underemployment. These are the disadvantaged—handicapped by age, discrimination, and economically deprived childhoods accompanied by inadequate education and training.

But inadequacy of early manpower preparation and labor market barriers of age and discrimination cannot justify despair or neglect of the millions of adults whose low earning capacity testifies to these handicaps. Manpower development and planning represents one of the only two broad alternatives to poverty alleviation. If the poor cannot be lifted out of poverty through development of their earning power—which under our system means an increase in the value of their labor services to their employer—or by removing discriminatory barriers placed in the way of the realization of their earnings potential, then the only remaining alternative is income transfers.

PROBLEMS IN MANPOWER PLANNING

Program Weaknesses

It is easy to be critical of manpower programs that evolved from manpower development policy. Given the conditions and circumstances under which they operate, it is inevitable that such programs receive poor marks in rigorous application of formal cost-benefits tests despite such optimistic acronyms as WIN, PEP, JOBS, and so on.

For one thing, the people receiving human investment in the form of manpower development are usually the least likely to be upgraded easily. They suffer from serious labor market disadvantages, whether from weak early cognitive skill development, unsatisfying work experience, age, or discrimination. A program cannot be faulted because its clients cannot be easily served. But in fact, program administrators do often resort to "creaming," that is, enrolling and generally servicing those most qualified for early employment.

Another factor operating against successful benefit-cost ratios is the age of potential participants. Returns from human capital are obviously greater the longer the amortization period, which means the longer the worklife after training. But the work period after training is shorter than for schooling investment, since—except for the Neighborhood Youth Corps—manpower programs enroll those who have terminated their schooling.[2] but again, programs, perhaps because of cost-benefit considerations, reach for those likely to yield the maximum return from job upgrading and improved job placement—that is, the young. Over half of program participants in 1971 were under twenty-two years of age.[3]

Another factor limiting the cost effectiveness of manpower programs is their limited budgets. Geared to service as many people as possible with funds available, programs often must skim through training and upgrading. Human investments, like their physical capital counterparts, must usually be substantial to bring about heavy returns. That is, investments are most effective when lumpy; although the costs of only a little training are low, the returns in improved earning power are comparatively even lower.

Finally, programs are often seen in terms of simply getting people off the welfare rolls, and they stress job placement over training. For example, the 1972 adjustment in the Work Incentive Program (WIN II) made just this switch in emphasis. Of course, increasing employment in itself yields income, but if efforts have really been directed to increasing incomes through raising employment instead of upgrading the skill level of the work force, they have been eminently unsuccessful. It is estimated that all manpower programs in 1971 served to raise employment by 600,000. Their effect in reducing unemployment was even less, since the programs drew 400,000 additional workers into the labor force.[4]

Emphasis on job placement rather than training does nothing to raise the potential earning power of program participants. Striking evidence of this can be found in a study of programs in poverty areas which finds that in 1968–1969, the average hourly earnings of those who completed special manpower programs was the identical $2.16 attained by those who never completed or participated in a program.[5]

Conflicting Program Goals

One wonders why there should be any conflict at all over the goals of manpower policy. Is not its purpose to alleviate poverty by raising the earning power of the poor through skill upgrading and placement in such

---

[2]This chapter deals only with federally financed programs. As such, it excludes consideration of apprenticeships and nonsubsidized on-the-job training programs.

[3]Sylvia Small, "Statistical Effect of Work-Training Programs on the Unemployment Rate," *Monthly Labor Review*, September 1972, p. 10. There is some exaggeration here of emphasis on younger trainees in that the program with the most participants, the Neighborhood Youth Corps, is directed specifically to youth.

[4]Small, op. cit., p.7.

[5]Roberta McKay, "Job Training Programs in Urban Poverty Areas," *Monthly Labor Review*, August 1971, p. 39, Table 2.

jobs? Should not the entire policy be focused on improving the chance of the have-nots to escape poverty through work instead of through welfare? Is there any dispute with the assessment of Mangum that "the priority concern of contemporary manpower policy is the minority left over in a strong economy that has proven its ability to offer adequate opportunity to the majority"?[6]

Yet the preliminary discussion of program results hinted that this apparently simple goal is somewhat elusive and not always followed. The conflict arises over the criteria of program success and the some-times ambivalent public and political attitude toward poverty alleviation.

Since programs are administered by people who are, through legisla-tors, ultimately responsible to taxpayers, it is only natural that they wish to show "good results." Success depends on public attitude at the time.

If times are good and poverty alleviation is the main goal, then "creaming" is a tempting practice which assures a maximum upgrading of participants. We can wonder how strenuous are the efforts to reach the hard-core poor in good times from the fact that in 1971—except for WIN which is attached to a major transfer program (Aid for Families with Dependent Children, or AFDC)—none of the federally assisted work and training programs had as many as 40 percent of their participants on public assistance.

Furthermore, of those receiving Manpower Development and Train-ing Act (MDTA) training, over 50 percent were educated at least through high school completion.[7] Admittedly MDTA, which started in 1962, predated the Johnson administration's War on Poverty and was not origi-nally specifically an antipoverty program. But the shift in emphasis of all manpower programs since the mid-1960s towards the poor should have resulted in a heavier representation of the disadvantaged in the program almost a decade later.

When times are bad and public interest shifts from the poverty rate to the unemployment rate, manpower policy follows the trend. Job place-ment and labor market services are stressed over training, which may increase weaker earnings potential but is less likely to lead to employment in a short run characterized by labor surplus. But preoccupation with short-term goals such as job placement has minimal long-run impact on moving people out of poverty by upgrading their skills and earning capaci-ty.

Consider WIN II. The 1972 amendments were not introduced in a weak economic climate, but the switch in emphasis from training to imme-diate placement represented a response to other motivations that had nothing to do with long-run solutions to poverty. For one thing, the train-

[6]Garth Mangum, *The Emergence of Manpower Policy,* Holt, New York, 1969, p.9.
[7]Office of Management and the Budget, 1973.

ing experience under WIN I had not been very successful. That is, the cost per successful placement was very high. The agency had three alternative responses to this problem and its accompanying public and political criticism:

1   It could try to improve its cost-per-trainee placement ratio by closer relationship of training to manpower needs. In reality, though, high costs per placement were much less attributable to administrative inefficiency than to the nature of the program, which called for quick training of those least susceptible to adaptability to short courses—mainly welfare mothers. Many had no work force experience, had pressing home responsibilities, and would be difficult to place even if properly trained.

2   It could try to convince the public and its Congress that if they were so strongly attached to the "work ethic" and so anxious that clients "work their way off welfare" that they called for labor force effort from those least likely to have successful work experience, then they should be willing to pay the price for this policy. But the public likes to have it both ways; it wants work to substitute for welfare but does not want to pay for its preference. That is, a work preparation and placement program that costs more than an equivalent transfer program is subject to abusive criticism even if it satisfies society's work ethic sensitivities.

3   It can take the easy course of abandoning training for job placement. This is a futile exercise in the pursuit of poverty relief. Most WIN recipients have such weak skill development that their earnings, even full time, could not lift them out of poverty if they were placed in jobs without further training. But while poverty might not be much reduced, expensive training would be curtailed, welfare costs if not the welfare population would be substantially lowered, and the work ethic adherents would be satisfied. It might not be much of an antipoverty program, but it would quiet the critics.

Needless to say, despite the fanfare and the rhetoric, WIN II represented the conscious choice for alternative three. While, to repeat, the introduction of the revised program in 1972 was not motivated by weakness in the economy, it is interesting to note that in our current recession, which features antipoverty cutbacks, WIN is the only existing manpower agency that is receiving expanded funding.

Before looking more closely at WIN as an example of the difficulty of making a manpower program an effective antipoverty vehicle, it should be noted in this discussion of the conflicts in manpower policy that strong arguments have been made in support of the view that this policy should not focus entirely on poverty reduction. In our more orderly economy of a few years ago, when prices and the unemployment rate moved in opposite directions (as they are supposed to), the important national economic problem involved moving from a fairly strong economic position to an even stronger one, with lower unemployment without inflation.

A structural bottleneck hypothesis developed which saw labor market imperfections and the mismatch between available worker skills, or lack of them, and industrial labor needs as the generators of inflationary pressure in a strengthening economy. Thus what was needed to allow for a successful noninflationary full employment policy was a manpower development policy aimed at widening bottlenecks by training and improving labor market services, such as is provided by the Public Employment Service.[8]

At present, of course, we still have inflation, but unemployment itself is very high, so that the labor bottleneck theory of inflation has little current substance despite manpower shortages in a few highly skilled crafts. But it will be revived if we ever return to a tight labor market under inflationary conditions. Then the anti-inflationists will have their case disputing the appropriate use of scarce manpower resources. Inflation-easing and antipoverty measures may not seem necessarily competitive. But it is only during strongest booms that shortages develop for the meager skills that can be grafted on the majority of the poor through the brief training periods of the typical manpower program. The bottleneck adherents really have in mind retraining and the refinement of skills of those who already possess substantial human capital.

The Work Incentive Program

WIN is studied as an example of the difficulties and shortcomings of manpower development becuse it is the only program treating welfare clients exclusively. These are the AFDC recipients, the largest welfare group, numbering some 11 million recipients. Furthermore, the WIN group has been studied more thoroughly than any other manpower program. Finally, the results sharply point out the basic failing of manpower programs designed for the poor, whatever their emphasis—whether training or job placement. These households are poor because of very low long-run earning capacity; brief and tentative efforts cannot suffice to effect radical changes in this capacity.

WIN I Two amendments to AFDC were instituted in 1967 to provide a work component. First, the program included referral for training and placement of employable clients for the purpose of allowing AFDC recipients to "become wage-earning members of society and return their families to independent and useful roles in the communities."

The potential work population was limited because so many of the re-

---

[8]This view is expressed forcefully by Charles Holt, C. Duncan MacRae, Stuart Schweitzer, and Ralph E. Smith in *Manpower Programs to Reduce Inflation and Unemployment,* Urban Institute, 1971.

cipient households were headed by women—with dependent children, of course. Nevertheless, both the referred population and the number of successful later placements at the end of the assessment, orientation, and training sequence were much fewer than anticipated.

The second amendment provided the actual work incentive by the disregard "stipulation" of $30 minus one-third. This exempted the first $30 and additional earnings up to one-third total earnings from an offsetting reduction of AFDC benefits. While this was certainly an improvement over previous arrangements, which in effect placed a 100 percent tax on earnings by reducing benefits one dollar for each dollar earned, it still left a tax rate of 67 percent on earnings above $30, which a detailed study of the program notes is a rate "applicable to the general populace only at incomes above $140,000."[9] Another study complains, "If the entire bureaucracy were to conspire against them, AFDC recipients could not be confronted with fewer work incentives than the current system [WIN I] provides."[10] Exemption of work-related expenses under WIN make these descriptions of the weakness of WIN's work incentives somewhat exaggerated.

What the writer of the first study calls the "WIN funnel" had indeed a small opening into the labor market. In the four years of WIN I's existence, from 1968 to 1972, 2.8 million persons were assessed. Of these, only 627,000 were found appropriate for referral to training, the others being excluded because of ill health, age, school atendance, or demands of home duties. Of the 483,000 who were actually referred, 286,000 were enrolled in training and 170,000 left the program, either completing training, dropping out, or dropping out to take a job.

A mere 36,000 could be considered successful completions in that they were still employed at least three months after WIN placement. This is indeed a small percentage of the 11 million AFDC recipients. Even relating it to those assessed, it represents a little over 1 percent of the total AFDC work-age population.

The cost per successful placement was estimated at between $3,000 and $5,000. These enormous costs were only slightly offset by the meager earnings gains of successful participants. The median hourly earnings gain for males over their earnings in previous jobs was 25 cents per hour and about 60 cents for females. This would average out to about $800 per year, which would still fall far short of costs unless those placed worked full time for many years, an unlikely prospect for most.

[9]Sar Levitan, Martin Rein, and David Marwick, *Work and Welfare Go Together*, Johns Hopkins, Baltimore, 1972, p. 80. Data in this section on WIN I are from this study.
[10]Jon Goldstein, *The Effectiveness of Manpower Training Programs: A Review of Research on the Impact on the Poor*, Subcommittee on Fiscal Policy, Joint Economic Committee, U.S. Congress, 1972, p. 50.

Of greater negative significance than the dollars-and-cents cost-benefit relationship were the minimal reductions in the welfare rolls. In the two-year period 1969–1971, AFDC actually grew by a million cases; but a defender of WIN could argue that the increase would have been higher without the program.

The Labor Department estimated that only 40,000 WIN terminees left welfare through 1971, that is, after three years of operation. This is less than 2 percent of the AFDC adult population. Furthermore, the actual decline in AFDC recipients that occurred because of WIN was undoubtedly less than 40,000. Many terminated WIN before completion of training and found jobs on their own. To say that WIN fell short of its primary goal of reducing welfare through work is an understatement.

WIN II   In 1971, further amendments to the Social Security Act (under which AFDC operated) established WIN II. If the slow process of training and placement of WIN I was unsuccessful in removing many AFDC families from the welfare rolls through work income, then the rules had to change. Two steps were taken in WIN II to accelerate the transfer from welfare to work.

1   Registration for WIN became mandatory for all AFDC recipients except those who were specifically exempted, for reasons noted above. For failure to register, the penalty of exclusion from AFDC benefits was imposed on the individual but not on other family members.

2   The emphasis of the program shifted from preparaton for work to job placement.

How successful was WIN II in its first year of operation? In summary, the results for the one year, mid-1972 to mid-1973, were very close to the four prior years' totals of WIN I with respect to the number successfully placed and the number removed from welfare. Table 9-1 compares the record of both plans.

Perhaps WIN II deserves credit for duplicating WIN I's four-year results in successful placement and welfare reduction in one year. But as Table 9-1 shows, WIN II more than matched the earlier program's cost. For some inexplicable reason, WIN II's one-year costs were so high even though its training component was much smaller (less expensive). As a result, WIN II's costs per successful placement were slightly higher and cost per participant removed from welfare was substantially higher. Further, these estimates do not include costs of tax credits to firms who retain WIN placement for more than a year.

There are lessons to be learned from both WIN programs:

1   A little training does not improve the employability of welfare clients much.

Table 9-1 Results of WIN I and WIN II

	WIN I, 1968–1971	WIN II, fiscal year 1973
Participants	286,000	354,000
Job openings filled	125,000*	137,000
Continuously employed (at least 90 days)	60,000*	65,000
Removed from welfare rolls	40,000*	34,000
Program costs	$250 million	$285 million
Cost per successful placement	4,166	4,385
Cost per participant removed from welfare rolls	6,250	8,382

*Data include those who left WIN I before completing the program and thus might exaggerate WIN I contribution to employment and poverty reduction.

Source: WIN I data from Levitan et al., Work and Welfare Go Together; WIN II data from "WIN II: A Progress Report," Manpower Report of the President, 1974.

2   When the program operates as an elaborate employment agency, including work-orientation social services, it does a slightly better job in placing clients in jobs. But the jobs are not good ones, and the welfare reduction is about the same as that under a training emphasis and lower placement efficiency.

3   Straining the work ethic philosophy to include welfare clients with few employable skills and limited prior successful work experience is a very expensive practice.

4   The implication of both programs that welfare clients have significant alternative work options is erroneous. (The high labor force participation rate in poverty areas, noted in the last chapter, should have provided sufficient information to show that most people prefer work to welfare.) This notion is especially inapplicable to AFDC men. Of 300,000 male registrants, only 100,000 could be classified as unemployed; the others were exempted from the labor force because of disabilities. Less than half the registrants could be placed in jobs, despite the placement priority given to males.

5   If society insists on believing that welfare recipients are primarily work shirkers, with many households headed by able-bodied males who choose to be supported instead of working for a living, it is paying a very high price to find out that it is mistaken.

Evaluating Manpower Programs

As was noted previously, the principal problem in evaluating manpower programs is the specification of program goals. If the single goal of economic efficiency were to be tested, then the decision on the merits of any program would be simple indeed. Benefits would consist of the increase in earnings resulting from the training program. These benefits would then have to be discounted to take into account the long period over which they accrued. Costs would be measured by training, placement, and other program expenses.

If discounted benefits exceeded costs, then the program would be economically inefficient. A simple transfer of funds to welfare recipients equal to the program costs would generate more income for them, and with the money received they could call forth more demand for goods and services than would be produced by their efforts after participating in a manpower program. That is the attraction of transfers; there is no uncertainty of the income gained by the recipients. In the case described, the resources invested in the manpower program would be put to more productive use elsewhere.

While the test to which a program should be put to judge its economic efficiency is simple enough, measuring the relevant variables is another matter. Difficulties of measurement plague all studies of the economic efficiency of human investments, but those associated with manpower programs are particularly severe. Returns are hard to measure because there is no record of the length of time successful participants remain at work. There is information on continuous employment up to three and even six months, but in all cases economic efficiency demands a much longer period—several years—for returns to catch up with costs.

Then there is the problem of assigning cause to the higher incomes that might follow participation in a program. Did the program itself lead to higher earnings or even job placement, or would the clients have found these jobs on their own in any case? Weisbrod warns that returns assigned to manpower programs during good times may be spurious in that strong labor demand is just the economic background favorable for the employment of these marginal workers, who might easily have found work without program participation.[11]This would especially be the case for a program such as WIN II, which focused on placement.

A very serious weakness in the measurement of returns is in estimating the employment and earnings participants would have experienced had they not gone through the program. If a control group of nonparticipants is used to estimate what would have been, much is left to be desired, since the actual participants are selected as likely candidates for successful placement from a group heavily weighted with those of very weak labor force potential. When creaming is practiced, it is especially unrealistic to assume that the control group's work history parallels that of what participants would experience.

Despite these problems, efforts have been made to measure the cost-benefit ratio of manpower programs. A detailed review of many such

---

[11]Burton Weisbrod, "Benefits of Manpower Programs: Theoretical and Methodological Issues," North American Conference on Cost-Benefit Analysis of Manpower Policies, Madison, Wis., 1969.

studies for several of the larger programs yields discouragingly negative results.[12]

But is it any surprise that data on manpower programs show them to be economically inefficient? We have already noted the negative factors that lead toward this result: weak labor force potential for the majority of the participants, meager training funds allocated, and brief programs.

Nevertheless, this does not mean that manpower development represents an unwise use of antipoverty funds. The goal of these programs is never simply positive cost-benefit results. Other considerations make it desirable to "pay" for the programs with economic inefficiency. There is the satisfaction of the work ethic philosophy of taxpayers. Of at least equal importance is the revealed preference of the poor for work over welfare, and while the welfare population is not reduced much by the programs, many remain on reduced welfare who gain satisfaction, to say nothing of higher income, from a combination of work and supplementary welfare. Then there is the feeling of self-esteem and even community acceptance from work—the sociological benefits of earnings over transfers described in Chapter 1.

In recounting these benefits from work resulting from training that cannot be derived from transfers, Cain and Hollister note that they lie outside the cost-benefit calculation and, being nonmeasurable, cannot be included in them.[13] These imponderables make a mathematical calculation of appropriate decisions on manpower programs impossible. They add an implicit amount to returns, and their qualititive strength can make an economically inefficient program worthwhile.

Thus, in the final analysis, the decision to continue, change, or abandon a program must be made subjectively. The ultimate decision depends on how strongly society values these nonmonetary benefits; cost-benefit analysis can give some indication as to how strong these attitudes must be to justify continuation of an economically inefficient program.

THE SCOPE OF MANPOWER PLANNING

Federally supported manpower programs had their modern origin with the introduction of Manpower Development and Training (MDTA) in 1962. Since then many programs have developed, but they still command a much smaller share of antipoverty funding than do income transfers. From a trickle of $60 million in fiscal year 1964, funding for employment and training services of the poor grew to $2.4 billion in fiscal year 1972;

[12]Goldstein, op. cit.
[13]Glenn Cain and Robinson Hollister, "Evaluating Manpower Programs for the Disadvantaged," North American Conference on Cost-Benefit Analysis of Manpower Policies.

but this was still less than 20 percent of the $12.2 billion of cash outlays to the poor in that year.

Furthermore, in recent years this gap has not been closing. Then too, it must be noted that training and maintenance allowances form a large segment of training costs. While these stipends count in manpower investment, in effect they also represent cash transfers to the poor.

Programs, Enrollments, and Funding

The Labor Department has consistently administered most of the manpower programs. Table 9-2 presents a brief description of these Labor Department programs. This table describes a host of categorical programs. Some like the Neighborhood Youth Corps (NYC) and the Job Corps are geared to youth, while Operation Mainstream, one of the smaller programs, is the only one specifically designed for the older worker. Since 1973 most of these programs, though still funded mainly with federal money, have consolidated administration at the local level under the Comprehensive Employment and Training Act (CETA).

All have unemployment or underemployment as an eligibility requirement. Existing manpower programs are not designed for in-job career advancement. The same taxpayer who would balk at funding the further occupational development of those at work uncomplainingly subsidizes the most important part of the career preparation of millions, their college education, without a means test for eligibility.

A few programs require poverty status for eligibility, but only WIN is limited to welfare recipients. There have been changes in eligibility requirements over the years—Table 9-2 only reports requirements as of the last year recorded. The trend has been toward the poor, and the otherwise disadvantaged; though the Public Employment Program (PEP), with its emphasis on filling unfunded public jobs whatever their level, often operates against the trend. There is some overlapping, and many are eligible for and actually do participate in more than one program. But still each one has its own identity and focus.

In any case, the major handicap under which these programs operate—apart from the serious labor force problems of their enrollees which they are trying to overcome—is the shortage of funds available for their efforts. Table 9-3 presents the data on available funds and number enrolled during the period fiscal years 1963 – 1974. Program history is one of slow and fairly steady growth with some ups and downs in individual programs, mainly a weakening in the relative dominance of MDTA in participants and less so in funding.

It is interesting to note that more than one-third of the participants have been in the NYC Summer, a program that involves no training at all and which provides marginal job experience and income. More funding went into this program in 1974 than into MDTA institutional training, still the most thorough carreer preparation component.

The funding expansion since 1972 is greatly misleading. The figures are swelled by PEP, a temporary antirecessionary program. While the jump in total funding since 1972 is undeniable, there has been no carrythrough into more recent years. In fact, there has been stagnation in federal outlays in all manpower programs since fiscal year 1973 and a significant decline in real terms, considering the recent inflation.

Table 9-4 shows this decline. While fiscal year 1975 was funded before the sudden onset of the deep recession beginning in late 1974, it remains to be seen whether manpower funding will suffer further cutbacks in a period of budgetary stringency. If the much milder recession of 1971–1972 is any guide, the direction of funding will probably be toward public employment.

Manpower Programs in Recession

There is some question as to whether manpower programming is feasible during recession. The problem with manpower programs during recessions is that they operate under a situation that acts against them no matter what their emphasis. If they stress training, bad times lead to the worst frustration—trained workers with no opportunities to apply their new skills. If they concentrate on job placement in the manner of WIN II, then the programs find it difficult to place untrained, marginal workers in a loose labor market.

One way out is through public employment. The government does not have to answer to stockholders who want employment dictated by business needs. Furthermore, the government, ever since the Full Employment Act of 1946, assumes the responsibility of adopting policies that will lead to a full-employment economy. What better way could this goal be achieved than by having the government stand as an employer of last resort to absorb an excess supply of labor?

When the (federal) government employs workers directly or funds state and local employment of the unemployed without regard to their productivity, there is some question as to whether such an arrangement should be called a manpower program at all. At least that part of placed workers' wages which exceeds their contribution to output really constitutes an income transfer.

But if the experience of the previous emergency public employment program following the mild recession of 1970 is any guide, there is little to

Table 9-2   Comparable Description of Manpower Programs Administered by the Department of Labor, 1962–1973

Program	First year of operation	Type of training	Objective
Manpower development and training (MDTA-Institutional)	1962	Skill center or school	Occupational training for unemployed and underemployed persons along with supportive services
Manpower development and training on the job[2] (MDTA-OJT)	1962 (ended 1971)	On-the-job training	Occupational training in a job, for unemployed and underemployed persons combined with instruction
Jobs-Optional (JOP)	1971 (MDTA-OJT merged into JOP in 1971)	On-the-job training	Training on the job for disadvantaged and nondisadvantaged persons in entry-level jobs and upgrading of employees into higher skill shortage occupations
Neighborhood Youth Corps—in school and summer (NYC-In School and NYC Summer)	1965	Work	To provide opportunities for students in low-income families to earn enough to enable them to stay in school
Neighborhood Youth Corps—Out of School Program (NYC-Out of School)	1965	Work and on-the-job training with supportive services	To provide work experience and on-the-job training to school dropouts to encourage them to return to school or acquire skills to improve employability
Operation Mainstream	1968	Work and supportive service	Work-training and employment, with supportive services, to chronically unemployed poor adults
Public Service Careers	1969	To train on the job for government work	To help disadvantaged adults to qualify for jobs with state and local government and private nonprofit agencies
Concentrated Employment Program (CEP)	1968	Outreach, counseling, medical, educational, & other supportive services, work training, and placement	To coordinate and concentrate federal manpower efforts to attack problems of the hardest hit of the disadvantaged in urban or rural neighborhoods that have serious unemployment or subemployment

Method	Eligibility requirements for participants	Benefits
Training or retraining in skills needed in the local labor market at skill centers or vocational training schools outside the regular school system	Unemployed household head or member or household with unemployed of underemployed head. Must have one year of work experience.	Eligible persons receive training subsistence, and transportation allowance
Contract with public or private employers	Unemployed and underemployed persons; at least 2/3 must be "disadvantaged"; perference to persons over 18 years old	Employer pays beneficiary the going wage for such work in the area
Contract with private employers or nonprofit companies	Unemployed or underemployed persons; 50 percent must be disadvantaged poor certified by State Employment Service or other group designated by Regional Administrator of Manpower	Employer pays beneficiary the going wage, but his additional training costs are reimbursed under contract with the government
Private or public nonprofit agency sets up jobs to perform public service for community, using students part time or during summer	Students from low-income families in grades 9–12 or ages 14–21	Jobs–part time or in summer to fit student schedule
Private or public nonprofit corporation sets up full-time jobs for community service, full time, and provides training on the job and in institutional setting, counseling	Unemployed out-of-school youth 16–17 years old	Jobs and training for youth
Federal funding of 90 percent of cost of state and local community beautification projects or other community services that do not replace existing programs	Poor adults, 22 years old or over, and chronically unemployed; 40 percent must be over 55 years old	Jobs, especially in rural areas
Federal funds to enable state and local governments to train disadvantaged people in subprofessions in health, education, etc.	Unemployed or underemployed persons, 18 years old or over; or people who are so discouraged that they have not looked for work	Permanent employment in public service agencies and upgrading of current employees
Federal funding to develop delivery of a variety of manpower programs through a single sponsor–generally a community action agency	Residents of CEP target areas who are disadvantaged, and who meet criteria for JOBS program (above)	Education and other supporting services and work training to aid in placement in a permanent job

Table 9-2 (cont.)

Program	First year of operation	Type of training	Objective
Job Opportunities in the Business Sector, (JOBS), federally financed	1969	Actual work on the job with supportive services	Encourage private industry to hire, train, and upgrade hard-core unemployed and underemployed
Work Incentive Program (WIN)	1968	Work or training for people on welfare	To move men, women, and out-of-school youth from welfare rolls into meaningful permanent employment at or above the minimum wage
Job Corps	1965	Training away from home	Training to enable beneficiary to become productive citizen; also placement in jobs or school or the Armed Forces; remedial services are stressed
Public Employment Program (PEP)	1971	Work at temporary jobs	To create transitional employment when the unemployment rate has equalled or exceeded 4.5 for 3 consecutive months

Source: Small, "Statistical Effect of Work-Training Programs on the Unemployment Rate."

Method	Eligibility requirements for participants	Benefits
In cooperation with National Alliance of Businessmen provides technical assistance and grants to offset added costs of remedial education	Poor persons who do not have suitable jobs and who are: (1) school dropouts, (2) under 22, (3) 45 or over, (4) handicapped, or (5) subject to special obstacles to employment	Jobs, training, and remedial education for hard-core unemployed
State Employment Service officers will provide placement or on-the-job training day care and other supportive services to welfare recipients. Employers will be allowed a 20 percent tax credit for wages paid WIN recipients for the first 12 months of employment, provided the employer retains the welfare recipient in a job for an additional 12 months	AFDC recipients referred by welfare officers to the State Employment Service	Public and private jobs for employable adults on welfare with pay at the same rates as other employees
Government funding to train and care for disadvantaged youth while paying them $30—$50 a month	School dropouts 14—21 years old who are unemployed, underprivileged, and in need of a change in environment	School and work training—in a residential facility
Federal funds to help state and local governments hire people to perform needed public services	All unemployed and underemployed persons, with priority consideration to be given Vietnam veterans and young persons entering the labor force	Jobs for unemployed persons at the going rate for such jobs

Table 9-3 Enrollment and Funding of Labor Department Manpower Programs, Fiscal Years 1963–1972

(millions of dollars) (enrollment in hundreds of thousands)

	Total*		FY 1974		FY 1973		FY 1972		FY 1971	
	Enrollment	Funding	Enrollment†	Funding	Enrollment	Funding	Enrollment	Funding	Enrollment	Funding
Total	91.4	$14,370	4.4	$2,140	9.3	$2,750	15.6	$2,700	11.5	$1,500
MDTA	24.1	3,600	1.8	400	1.8	380	2.3	420	2.1	340
Institutional training	15.3	2,900	1.1	310	1.2	300	1.4	350	1.4	280
JOP-OJT	8.9	700	0.7	90	0.6	80	.9	70	0.7	60
NYC	54.0	3,700	1.8	670	6.6	420	8.6	520	7.0	430
In school	11.9	n.a.	1.4	90	1.1	60	1.0	70	0.8	60
Out of school	5.6	n.a.	0.4	110	0.4	110	0.4	120	0.4	120
Summers	36.4	n.a.	n.a.	460	5.1	250	7.2	320	5.8	250
Operation Mainstream	1.6	500	0.4	110	0.3	80	0.2	80	0.2	70
Public service careers	1.1	306	n.a.	30	n.a.	40	0.2	60	0.4	90
CEP	n.a.	1,100	n.a.	150	n.a.	130	n.a.	150	0.9	170
JOBS	3.6	800	0.3	60	0.3	70	0.6	120	0.6	170
WIN	3.8	900	7.9	250	n.a.	210	1.5	170	0.6	60
Job Corps	1.1	900	0.2	150	0.2	190	0.2	200	0.2	180
PEP	1.9	2,500	n.a.	280	n.a.	1,240	1.9	1,000		

*Enrollments refer to slots available. Some are not filled, but some are filled by more than one participant after turnover.

†Enrollment figures for FY 1974 are incomplete. For example data from the large NYC Summer program are not available.

Source: Manpower Report to the President, 1975.

Table 9.3 (cont.)

	FY 1970		FY 1969		FY 1968		FY 1967	
	Enrollment	Funding	Enrollment	Funding	Enrollment	Funding	Enrollment	Funding
Total	10.1	$1,400	9.1	$1,000	8.2	$800	8.1	$800
MDTA	2.1	340	2.0	270	2.3	300	2.7	300
Institutional training	1.5	290	1.2	210	1.3	220	1.3	220
JOP-OJT	0.6	50	0.8	60	1.0	80	1.4	80
NYC	6.0	360	5.4	320	5.4	280	5.1	350
In school	0.9	60	1.0	50	1.4	60	1.4	70
Out of school	0.5	100	0.5	120	0.6	100	0.8	150
Summers	4.6	200	3.9	150	3.4	120	2.9	130
Operation Mainstream	0.2	50	0.1	40	0.1	20	0.1	20
Public service careers	0.3	90	0.1	20	0.1	10	0.1	20
CEP	n.a.	190	n.a.	110	n.a.	90	n.a.	80
JOBS	0.6	150	0.5	160	0.3	90	0.1	30
WIN	0.7	80	1.0	100	0.1	10		
Job Corps	0.2	170						
PEP								

Table 9-3 (cont.)

	FY 1966		FY 1965		FY 1964		FY 1963	
	Enrollment	Funding	Enrollment	Funding	Enrollment	Funding	Enrollment	Funding
Total	8.1	$600	5.1	$400	1.3	$140	0.6	$60
MDTA	2.8	340	2.3	290	1.3	140	0.6	60
Institutional training	1.6	280	1.7	250	1.1	130	0.5	60
JOP-OJT	1.2	60	0.6	40	0.2	10	0.1	
NYC	5.3	260	2.8	130				
In school	1.9	n.a.	1.0	n.a.				
Out of school	1.0	n.a.	0.6	n.a.				
Summers	2.4	n.a.	1.2	n.a.				
Operation Mainstream								
Public service careers								
CEP	n.a.	20						
JOBS								
WIN								
Job Corps								
PEP								

Table 9-4 Federal Manpower Program Funding, Fiscal Year 1972–1975*
(Billions of Dollars)

Fiscal year	Dollar outlay	Real outlay (dollar outlay in 1972 dollars)
1972	4.4	4.4
1973	4.9	4.7
1974 (estimated)	4.8	4.4
1975 (budget proposal)	4.8	4.0

*The largest activities outside of Labor Department management were in Vocational Rehabilitation and employment-related child-care services.
Source: General Accounting Office

fear in this direction. In fact, the two-year history of PEP led to criticism that it focused on the labor force elite among those thrown out of work by the recession, to the disadvantage of the hard-core unemployed.

While PEP was not specifically a poverty program, it certainly did not go out of its way to try to service the most disadvantaged workers. For example, only 27 percent of PEP participants had less than a high school education, compared to almost half of the unemployed. The average salary of PEP placements in fiscal year 1972, the first year of operation, was $7,000. This was some 20 percent less than the average paid to regular state and local employees, but it represents a wage that indicates any average skill and productivity level far above that characteristic of the hard-core unemployed. As a result of this emphasis on the easily employable, with a peak PEP employment of 185,000 in the summer of 1972, the program in effect reduced total unemployment by only 0.2 percentage points "on the heroic assumption that all participants would have been otherwise unemployed."[14]

In fairness to the program, PEP should not be criticized for carrying out the goals with which it was charged. It makes more sense to question the goal of gearing an *emergency* program to the long-run manpower needs of state and local governments. One of the stipulations of the placement arrangements with these governments was that the PEP-financed employee be hired with a view to permanent job attachment. Naturally, under these conditions, the public employer wanted a good selection of likely candidates.

The purpose of PEP was laudable. Here was an opportunity to staff public agencies with valuable personnel whom state and local governments could not employ during recessionary budget stringencies. The

[14]Sar Levitan and Robert Taggart (eds.), *Emergency Employment Act: The PEP Generation*, Olympus, Salt Lake City, 1974, p. 20. Data on PEP are from this source.

program promised an improvement in public facilities at a time when efficiency was threatened by imposed budget cutbacks.

But in servicing lower governments in this manner, federal financing lost sight of the major, pressing, truly emergency problem—the reemployment of workers forced out of their jobs by the recession. While it is true that there were also $5-an-hour workers unemployed, a program aimed for them is bound to miss the bulk of the unemployed, who are also those in greatest need of outside assistance to find new jobs.

It is still too early to tell the direction of public employment programs in the current deep recession. Emergency funding for public jobs is still in the legislative stage. But with an unemployment rate around 9 percent, it seems reasonable to assume that the lofty goals of PEP will be sacrificed to some degree in order to have the greatest impact on the unemployment rate. This means funding for relatively low-wage jobs and a relaxation of the implication that the state and local governments who employ these workers—whose pay is provided by the federal government—will be obligated to retain them when the emergency is over. Then their chances will be better in the private sector.

The problems of getting local and state cooperation in hiring federally funded workers during recessions seem minor compared to the difficulty of obtaining private-sector interest in joint manpower programs. Consider the experience of the NAB-JOBS program. The National Alliance of Businessmen (NAB) pledged to aid in the employment of those with severe labor force disadvantage among the poor. Under the JOBS program, the firms would provide on-the-job training, with the federal government paying the bill for extra training and related remedial instruction.

On the surface, the program appears very attractive to business, offering firms the opportunity to develop a skilled work force at very little cost. But even in good times placements fell far short of program participation goals. Firms were reluctant to enter a long-run relationship with workers whom they thought would not be as likely to reach as high a productivity after training as less disadvantaged workers trained outside the program entirely at company expense. That is, to many firms, subsidized costs of skilled work preparation would not compensate for below-average productivity gains for the covered workers.

But NAB-JOBS problems are even more severe during recession. JOBS trainees are hired for production jobs, which are the hardest hit. Then, the specific nature of the training makes it difficult for the workers to find other work if the firms that hire them must cut back. The firms themselves would feel some obligation to retain those specially hired workers, a fixed labor position in which no firm likes to find itself.

In recounting these weaknesses of NAB-JOBS during recession, Mestre concludes that "the program is morally commendable [but] economically misguided."[15] As Mestre implies, there certainly is a built-in inefficiency in the program. In effect, for hired workers the taxpayer assumes the costs of work preparation which profit-maximizing businessmen would not underwrite because of the dim prospects of sufficient increased productivity of trainees to recoup these costs.[16]

But there is a degree of economic inefficiency in all manpower programs. What makes the JOBS program particularly vulnerable during recessions is that, while programs which stress job placement face the difficulty of finding employment opportunities, JOBS tries to find training slots in an economy conducive to severe cutback in on-the-job training.

Comprehensive Manpower Planning

Over the years, manpower programs have been subject to the criticisms of too much centralized planning from Washington and too strict a separation of programs. These have prevented cooperation and the avoidance of administrative overlap. The Comprehensive Employment and Training Act of 1973 (CETA) was designed to solve these problems.

CETA in effect serves as a giant revenue-sharing program in which programs are consolidated and supported by a federal grant to governors, mayors, and county executives. Thus the programs come under local jurisdiction regarding program policies and, what is most important, distribution of funding among the individual agencies.

CETA has not been in operation long enough to be evaluated, but it holds promise for solution of administrative problems. For one thing, it will still local criticism of the impracticality of distant direction of programs designed to solve local manpower problems. Nevertheless, a study group finds possible shortcomings in CETA itself.[17]

The group regrets that many important programs fall outside CETA: WIN, vocational education and rehabilitation, and the Public Employment Service. It also fears that the disadvantaged will have less opportunities to participate in locally run programs. While it is true that federal guidelines will no longer apply to eligibility conditions, it remains

[15]Eloy Mestre, *Economic Minorities in Manpower Developmemt*, Heath Lexington, Boston, 1971, p. 73.

[16]Some firms were charged with hiring workers under JOBS whom they would have hired anyway. This practice gives the firms a welcome subsidy to meet their training costs, but it hardly reflects the spirit of an antipoverty program.

[17]*The Comprehensive Employment and Training Act: Opportunities and Challenges*, National Manpower Policy Task Force, 1974.

to be seen whether local leadership will be less inclined to focus on disadvantaged groups. There is no reason why they should be, considering the increased representation of minorities in local manpower planning. Finally, the group decries the low level of federal funding projected for CETA and the shortsighted policy of cutting back during recessions. But this is a shortcoming of federal budgeting and not an inherent weakness in the comprehensive planning concept.

No doubt a well-run CETA will do much to alleviate many of the administrative problems of uncoordinated planning and perhaps thus improve managerial efficiency, but it can do little about the two major problems facing manpower development decisions. It cannot overcome the shortage of funding that would permit meaningful improvement in the long-run employment and earnings prospects of those who have received little prior preparation for labor market success; nor can it help reach the social decision of whether manpower programs which have a losing cost-benefit relationship are superior to income transfers because of their substitution of work for welfare.

SUMMARY

The practical goal of manpower development and programs is to improve the earning power of participants through skill upgrading by training and through improved job placement services. This simple goal becomes confused and distorted by the intrusion of other considerations and purposes.

If the goal of inflation control is superimposed on the basic manpower development goal, emphasis would be placed on skill development to meet current labor market shortages. Given the limits of manpower funding, following this policy would require major training efforts aimed at those who already have attained a reasonably high skill level. Such programming would do little for poverty elimination.

If long-run poverty reduction is the goal, then the focus should be on the trainable poor. Realistic programming with limited funds would reach those comparatively few with the greatest prospect for skill development rather than spread scarce funds thinly and ineffectually over a large number of participants. Such creaming would increase the chances of poverty reduction through human investment in the most receptive subjects but would do little to cut into the mass of the poverty population.

If unemployment reduction is the goal, as it is likely to be during recessions, then the stress would be on placement over training. Improved labor market services may facilitate job attainment for program participants; but if this practice only puts them in jobs for which they qualified in the past, the chances are that they will still earn less than poverty level incomes.

Federally sponsored antipoverty manpower programs suffer from two elements that operate negatively on their chances for economically efficient performance, with efficiency measured by benefits of raised earnings greater than program costs: (1) Their funding is insufficient to allow the substantial investment in individual participants required to upgrade skills; this is especially the case when coverage is broad. (2) Their subjects are those with the least general educational (cognitive) skills—those skills which allow for the easy addition of new job-oriented learning.

Given these limitations, it is no wonder that cost-benefit studies show negative results for individual manpower programs. But the goal of making work a substitute for welfare has nonmonetary benefits. It provides the desirable societal aspects of work—status, self-esteem, work ethic philosophy. The desire for these seems to be shared by both the taxpayer and the recipients, as evidenced by the high labor force participation among the poor. Cost-benefit analysis cannot make the decision on the merits of continuing a program, but it can indicate the cost of satisfying these nonmonetary goals.

Recent efforts to consolidate program administration and to place decision making on funding allocations at the local instead of federal level may lead to more efficient operation. But it cannot overcome the basic problems of insufficient funding and weakness in prior human investment in participants. Manpower programs would be considered more successful, and perhps funding would be more generous, if the public accepted the fact that if work is preferred to welfare, then manpower programs are worth an extra cost above that imposed by simple income transfers.

Chapter 10

Income Maintenance

Most of the poor cannot be reached by manpower programs because they are not in the labor force and cannot be prepared for labor market competition by these limited efforts. Many suffer the handicaps of age, disability, and the demand on their time for home duties, especially in the rearing of children. Others have such little human capital and such weak skill development that their consequent earning power is too low to warrant employer demand for their services at minimum wages; they have been priced out of the labor market.

For all these nonworkers and their families, the only means of poverty relief is through income transfers. Unfortunately, that is all our transfer programs do—relieve poverty. They do not eliminate it because only in the rarest instance is the income supplement sufficient to push a poor household over the poverty line.

In the case of WIN we find about the only attempt to allow welfare payments to add to earnings, so that combined income may rise above the poverty level; and we saw how minor the antipoverty gains were in that case. Other public assistance programs impose a 100 percent tax rate on earnings. That is, for every dollar earned, there is a dollar reduction in welfare benefits. Since the basic stipend is well below the poverty level, the recipient family can never work its way out of poverty unless its working members earn enough to put them above the poverty level. But the program itself has nothing to do with this achievement.

Furthermore, the transfer programs impose a strict means test. For example, most general assistance formulas administered by local governments provide no support until all assets are divested, especially earning ones, except for owner-occupied dwellings and the barest essentials of furnishings, etc. Then the difference between the maximum standard support and household earnings is provided. Since this support is offset by whatever earnings are attained, work incentives of recipients are in practice completely destroyed.

This chapter examines the scope and coverage of existing welfare programs. Then it studies new proposals for reducing poverty through the best-known noncategorical income-maintenance scheme, the negative income tax. Since, as we have seen, manpower programs have only a minor effect in eliminating poverty, and since current transfer programs do not provide enough to pull recipients above poverty, and since proposed income maintenance plans might do the job but have not been instituted, we can wonder about the strength of our commitment to the War on Poverty.

OUR WELFARE SYSTEM

Conflicting Welfare Philosophies

Two schools of thought regarding income distribution determine views on the goal of income transfers. Friedman, who champions the cause of free market capitalism, differentiates them as *egalitarian* and *liberal*.[1]

The egalitarian believes that income redistribution policy should be aimed at equalizing incomes that have been made unequal at the source of earnings by our system of distribution, which pays workers in accordance with the value of their production. Differences in human investment, family background, wealth, luck, and motivation lead to differences in earning capacity and actual earnings. Thus, equality to the egalitarian means what Friedman calls "equality of outcome," or material equality, which can only be brought about by the massive redistribution of earned income. Obviously, success in aproaching this goal would reduce and probably eliminate poverty in passing, as lower incomes were pushed up toward the average.

The Friedman-type liberal also believes in equality. But he is think-

---

[1]Milton Friedman, *Capitalism and Freedom*, University of Chicago Press, Chicago, 1962.

ing of equal opportunity, not of results. The market system should be freed of impediments and monopoly elements, and handicaps of discrimination should be removed from all individuals in their struggle for material well-being within the free market system. Then those who are more successful will capture a greater share of the national product. The plight of those who bring up the rear will, in Friedman's words, induce the liberal to "regard private charity directed at helping the less fortunate as an example of the proper use of freedom. And he may approve state action toward ameliorating poverty. . . ."

This grudging concern over poverty may be a step ahead of Malthus, but it still has a nineteenth-century flavor. The liberal wants to express an attitude of fairness by calling for the removal of all barriers to equality of opportunity in his ideal of a meritocracy. But removing the last traces of overt discrimination would still leave many disadvantages handicapping the poor in their efforts to work their way out of poverty. This "liberal" philosophy may in practice be one that is now popularly characterized as conservative.

The liberal's credo tacitly accepts institutionalized discrimination, whether racism or sexism, by its defense of inherited wealth and differential capacity to finance human investments through education as part of the system. Given the unequal distribution of assets at birth, income distribution in later life cannot be much affected by measures designed to "equalize opportunity."

The force of the attack on poverty reflects the prevailing strength of the two attitudes on income distribution. The facts of the matter point clearly to consensus preference for the "liberal" position. At least redistribution through transfers to the lowest income groups has done little to lift them out of poverty, much less move them close to the national average. With a 100 percent tax on earnings for most categorical programs and with a support limit well below the poverty level, the redistribution message is clear, despite frequent efforts to substitute antipoverty rhetoric for adequate redistribution action. The poor will not starve, at least not rapidly, but neither will they be lifted out of poverty by taxpayer generosity.

Coverage and Amount of Public Assistance

Many public assistance programs began during the Great Depression of the 1930s. There have been changes, ameliorations, additions to and subtractions from the program roster over the years, but the principle of inadequate support to prevent more than poverty relief remains intact.

In the late 1960s there was a substantial increase in the number of public assistance cash recipients—an increase resulting almost entirely from the expansion of a single program, AFDC. Expanded coverage did lead to a substantial increase in cash public assistance outlays, but there was no improvement in the adequacy of support. In fact, there was just stability in the real purchasing power of average recipients for the programs as a whole.

Table 10-1 presents the coverage of the major cash payment public assistance programs for 1967, 1970, and 1973. As it grew in coverage, AFDC, which was the largest program even at the beginning of the period, has come to include close to 80 percent of all welfare recipients. While all the total growth in coverage may center on one program, an important consequence that this concentration does not deny is the much larger percentage of the poor that is reached by public assistance transfers. Unfortunately, this growth has not carried through in the most recent years. Early 1975 AFDC recipients (about 11 million) form a group no larger than that of 1973, a much stronger year for the economy.

Three reasons can account for this fact—that coverage reaches a limit well below the number poor:

1 Many of the poor are ineligible for the categorical programs which have the most funding, Note that General Assistance, the welfare program that probably first comes to mind to the average person fortunate enough to earn an adequate income, includes comparatively few recipients. These are the poor who, not fitting into any federally funded plan, must depend on the meager limitations of local funding.

Table 10-1   Number of Public Assistance Cash Payment Recipients by Major Programs, 1967, 1970, 1973
(Numbers in Millions)

Program	1967	1970	1973
Total*	8.8	13.8	14.6
Old Age Assistance†	2.1	2.1	1.8
Aid to the Permanently or Totally Disabled	0.6	0.9	1.3
AFDC recipients	5.3	9.7	10.8
Families	1.3	2.6	3.1
Children	4.0	7.0	7.8
General Assistance	0.8	1.1	0.7
Percentage of poor covered by public assistance	31.6	54.3	60.8

*The total is of the four major programs. Recipients of Aid to the Blind and other minor categorical programs would increase the total by about 100,000.
†Discontinued after 1973 and replaced by Supplementary Income Program.
Source: Social Security Bulletin, February 1975.

Table 10-2 Average Monthly Payments, Current and 1967 Dollars, for Major Public Assistance Cash Payment Programs, 1967, 1970, 1973

Program	1967		1970		1973	
	Current dollars	1967 dollars	Current dollars	1967 dollars	Current dollars	1967 dollars
Old Age Assistance	$ 70.15	$ 70.15	$ 77.65	$ 66.78	$ 76.15	$ 57.21
Aid to the permanently and totally disabled	80.60	80.60	97.65	83.95	109.75	82.46
AFDC families	161.70	161.70	187.98	161.64	195.21	146.66
AFDC Recipients	39.50	39.50	49.65	42.61	56.96	42.79
General Assistance	39.40	39.40	57.85	49.74	83.58	62.80

Source: *Social Security Bulletin*, February 1975. The Consumer Price Index is used as the deflator to calculate average payments in 1967 dollars.

2   Many of the poor are unaware of their welfare opportunities. The government has not been the best advertiser of its own programs, and the poor are not the easiest group to reach through normal communication channels.

3   Of probably greatest weight, many of the poor are ineligible for assistance because their incomes are too high. The very fact that this statement can be made dramatizes the failure of welfare to serve as an effective antipoverty weapon. If it were designed to eliminate rather than alleviate poverty, the earnings maximum for support eligibility would be at least at the Poverty Line.

Looking at the data on average payment, it is no wonder that AFDC is the largest program. Apart from the facts that most poor families have children present and local general assistance and federally financed categorical programs are reluctant to fund recipients eligible for other plans, the financial motivation for joining AFDC is strong. It provides the largest average payment per household. While Table 10-2 shows that the amount per child does not compare favorably with the per recipient stipends of other programs, poor families can consolidate expenditures. Furthermore, children can be supported more cheaply than adults. Therefore the higher cash payment per household makes AFDC an attractive program, at least compared to General Assistance payments.

None of the programs is very generous. AFDC gives the most per family, but at a $195.21 average in 1973, this would provide less than $2,400 per year, or roughly half the Poverty Line income. The only positive feature of these programs is that they are not getting any more unsatisfactory. Table 10-2 shows that despite variations in the individual programs and despite strong inflation over the period, they are maintaining their low level of inadequacy. The drop in real purchasing power AFDC families experienced from 1970 to 1973 is compensated for by a reduction in family size, so that purchasing power of payments per person did not fall over the period. In fact, transfers per recipient under the program actually expanded in real terms over the period.

But the spotty record during the current inflation gives no indication of any concerted movement toward a change in transfer policy that would suggest a goal of poverty elimination. Welfare groups are more organized and their needs more publicized, but what is needed to make transfers effective in reducing the poverty count is a change in taxpayer philosophy that makes this the public assistance goal.

Total Outlays to the Poor

While public assistance programs are designed specifically for the poor, these are not the only source of public funding that reaches them. They receive unemployment benefits and veterans' compensation. Further-more, they receive food stamps and other payments in kind.[2] Then they are also recipients of major health benefits and other human investment outlays in education and training. The total in 1972 came to more than $28 billion. Table 10-3 details the components.

If we exclude the education and manpower outlays as contributing to future and not current income (in that they are human investment expend-itures), the total comes to about $24 billion, or roughly $1,000 per poor in-dividual. It is interesting to note that this is exactly the figure suggested by Senator McGovern during his ill-fated 1972 presidential campaign as the income guarantee that should be provided every American. This proposal was greeted with severe criticism and in fact was retracted for reasons of political expediency, but it is no more than was actually provided the poor in 1972. The emphasis on "rights" against the public treasury and "guar-antees" proved unpopular; perhaps the public is unaware of the costs of poverty alleviation, or perhaps they do not want to be reminded of the amount.

But once again, if the approximate $4,000 of outlays per poor family is considered a major solution to the problem of poverty through transfers, this conclusion needs much modification. The $4,275 Poverty Line for 1972 refers to cash income needs. Table 1-1 shows how meager a budget for life's necessities this amount actually allows. The other sup-plements are welcome but do not make meeting daily living expenses any easier.

Consider federal health outlays. Without Medicaid (designed specifi-cally for low-income families) and Medicare for the aged without regard to income, low-income families would not begin to finance their medical expenses. With hospital costs running $150 per day and nursing care reaching $1,000 per month per patient, how much of these expenses could the poor meet? For that matter, even families with incomes well above the Poverty Line could not pay these costs. They too are subsidized by feder-al health outlays.

The point of this discussion is that the Poverty Line refers to income and not to special costs defrayed. Expressed differently, if the poor were guaranteed a Poverty Line income and all supplements were eliminated, they would still be poor, and perhaps even poorer by any objective stand-ard that measured their capacity to maintain an adequate standard of daily living while they paid for all their health expenditures.

Some upward adjustment should be made in poverty alleviation to the public assistance cash payments noted above. Veterans' compensa-

---

[2]The prior discussion centered on AFDC. For a detailed study of the impact of other programs on the poor, see Sar Levitan, *Programs in Aid of the Poor for the 1970s*, Johns Hopkins, Baltimore, 1973.

Table 10-3 Federal Outlays Benefiting the Poor, 1972
(Billions of Dollars)

Total	$28.3		
Cash payments	12.2	Education	$ 2.0
Social security*	5.8	Early childhood	0.3
Public assistance†	4.6	Elementary and secondary	1.0
Veterans' compensation	1.1	Higher education	0.4
Unemployment benefits	0.7	Other	0.3
Income in kind	3.2	Manpower	2.4
Food stamps	1.7	Skill training	1.3
Child nutrition	0.5	Work support	0.9
Other food programs	0.3	Labor market services	0.2
Housing subsidies	0.7		
Health	6.2	Other‡	2.3
Medicaid	3.3	Community action	0.7
Medicare	1.8	Social services	1.4
Other	1.1	Other	0.2

*Includes AFDC, net of WIN.
†Excludes AFDC.
‡Mainly child care, human investment, and home maintenance service.
Source: Statistical Abstract of the U. S., 1974.

tion and unemployment benefits add to the incomes of the poor, even if they give even more to those with higher incomes. Income in kind should also count as contributing to purchasing power. Thus the total for 1972 would be adjusted upward, from $12.2 to $15.4 billion, by including these items. This is some improvement, but it still comes to about $625 per poor individual and would provide the average poor family almost exactly half the poverty level income. No matter how much we adjust the data, the current transfer system will always be described as a system of poverty aid and not one of poverty elimination.

THE NEGATIVE INCOME TAX

History and Mechanics

The idea of the negative income tax is usually credited to Friedman.[3] He suggested that those whose incomes were so low that they pay no taxes receive a subsidy based on the amount of their unused deductions and exemptions. In estimating these unused taxpayer benefits at $20 billion in 1969, Lampman argued as if the poor were deprived of financial privileges awarded the more affluent.[4]

[3]Friedman, *Capitalism and Freedom,* op. cit., chap. 12.
[4]Robert Lampman, *"Approaches to the Reduction of Poverty," American Economic Review,* May 1965, pp. 521–529.

While the logic of calling a tax offset a categorical benefit to taxpayers that is denied to others may be questioned, in that what is involved is a reduction in cost to one group which the other does not incur at all, the emphasis on unused deductions and exemptions serves a psychological purpose. It removes the "stigma effect" of welfare. Now, the recipient is just another taxpayer, albeit a negative one. His receipt of a subsidy is intended to create no more psychological impact to himself and others than the arrival of tax refunds to fortunate positive taxpayers.

Friedman suggests that the negative income tax plan replace the entire group of public assistance programs. Friedman's estimate of the money available for the substitution is overly optimistic, since he includes in his calculation farm price supports, which give aid mainly to the non-poor; but the $28 billion, or adjusted $24 billion for 1972, would give the negative tax plan substantial initial funding.

This is more money than the amount of unused exemptions and deductions, and in fact more recent negative tax plans have abandoned the funding limitation imposed by these imaginary tax offsets. But even taking the $24 billion value, if the plan were to operate in the manner of current income support programs, there would be some savings from a reduced bureaucracy with the the substitution of a single all-purpose program. But basically the same problem of income inadequacy would remain.

What is needed is a system that allows work earnings to supplement the income subsidy, and the only way to bring this about is to eliminate the 100 percent on earnings tax feature which all current assitance plans except WIN have. Negative tax plans impose a lower tax rate on earnings than the work-prohibitive 100 percent rate. In fact, it can be said without exaggeration that the distinguishing feature of these plans is not their income guarantee but their adherence to Friedman's principle that "an extra dollar earned always means more money available for expenditure." The big question; though, is how much more? What tax rate should be imposed on earnings? This issue and other problems associated with the plan make the negative income tax conceptually simple but difficult to program, and so far it has been impossible to gain enough political acceptability for such a plan to enact it into law.

Issues and Problems of the Negative Tax

The negative tax plan starts the poor recipient off with a basic stipend. This is the amount that will be received if he or she does not work at all. Of course, the plan recognizes that many recipients will not work under any conditions, and this basic stipend is designed to support those not likely to participate in the labor force.

The size of this stipend determines the degree of certainty with which poverty is eliminated by the plan. Obviously, if it is set as high as the Poverty Line, then the plan would wipe out poverty. But the cost of the program would be higher than if a lower basic stipend were provided. Furthermore, there would be a tendency to weaken work incentives with the higher tax rate on earnings that would have to be imposed in order to avoid granting subsidies to those with relatively high earnings.

In fact, the basic weakness of a stipend at the Poverty Line for a negative tax plan which maintains some degree of work incentive is that it requires subsidies to those not in need. This is a program feature which hurts its chances in Congress.

To explain this feature of a negative tax plan, consider a basic stipend of $5,000 per year, the approximate level of the current Poverty Line. If a 50 percent tax rate on earnings were imposed, then the household earning $3,000, still well below the Poverty Line, would receive a total income of $6,500; this would be made up of $3,000 earnings and $3,500 subsidy. But such a program would not operate without subsidies to those earning more than $5,000. Who would work to earn, say, $5,700 if he could net $6,500 by earning only $3,000?

On the other hand, a low basic stipend would permit tapering off the subsidy at or even below the Poverty Line. But such a program, while it would even permit a low marginal tax rate to maintain work incentives, might be ineffective in substantially reducing poverty.

The above discussion points to an obvious conflict in taxpayer goals for income maintenance plans. The taxpayer seeks three results from these plans: (1) substantial benefits to the poor; (2) low program costs; and (3) low level of work disincentives. Unfortunately, he cannot receive all three from any feasible plan. The two variables that determine the mix of results for these three elements are the basic stipend and the tax rate on earnings. Table 10-4 presents two hypothetical negative tax plans with the same break-even point. At this income level the subsidy disappears, but alternatives involving different basic stipends and tax rates help to explain the difficulties in selecting the most desirable plan.

The break-even point in this example is set at the $5,000 Poverty Line. Such a plan, as noted above, does not guarantee the elimination of poverty, but it does avoid subsidizing those above the Poverty Line. Note that to reach the same break-even point, plan A, with the higher basic stipend, requires a higher tax rate on earnings.

From the table it can be seen that the recipient prefers plan A to plan B. At any earnings level, which with assumed identical market wage rate means equal labor effort, the recipient has a higher income because of the larger subsidy.

Consider the $3,000 earner as a full-schedule, 2,000-hour-per-year

Table 10-4 Two Hypothetical Negative Income Tax Plans with Some Break-even Income but Different Basic Stipend and Tax Rates on Earnings

Plan A (Basic stipend, $2,500; tax rate, 50%)			Plan B (Basic stipend, $1,500; tax rate, 30%)		
Earnings	Subsidy	Income	Earnings	Subsidy	Income
$ 0	$2,500	$2,500	$ 0	$1,500	$1,500
1,000	2,000	3,000	1,000	1,200	2,200
2,000	1,500	3,500	2,000	900	2,900
3,000	1,000	4,000	3,000	600	3,600
4,000	500	4,500	4,000	300	4,300
5,000	0	5,000	5,000	0	5,000
6,000	0	6,000	6,000	0	6,000*

*Positive income taxes beyond the break-even level are omitted, but in any case the tax rate at $6,000 would be less than the rate for either plan.

worker who earns $1.50 per hour. Under plan A, he or she would gross $4,000 and under plan B only $3,600 while working the same hours. That this worker might cut back his or her labor supply more sharply under plan A and actually end up with lower income than under plan B is a possibility. But this would be the worker's free choice, reflecting a preference for a reduced work load over extra income, and he or she would still be more satisfied under plan A.

But there are two sides to these plans, and the taxpayer may not be so pleased with plan A. For one thing, the cost is higher for any given reduced work effort by the recipient. But more against plan A in the taxpayer's view is that the recipient's work incentive will be more seriously weakened by this plan, a harmful effect in its own right to taxpayers who want welfare recipients to share their work ethic philosophy. In addition, reduced work effort means higher subsidy and increased cost.

But why are work incentives weakened more by plan A than plan B? Why are they weakened at all by a negative tax scheme? Consider once again our $3,000-per-year earner. Under plan A he or she nets only $500 for the last 667 hours of work, or 75 cents per hour. Under plan B he or she earns a higher $1.05 for this extra effort to raise income above $2,900, as compared to the 75 cents per hour to raise income above $3,500 under A. With no plan at all the worker nets $1.50 per hour to raise his or her income from a still lower $2,000.

A higher income at a constant wage rate tends to weaken work incentive, as a more comfortable financial position allows the choice of more time off from work. There is nothing like inheriting a million dollars to destroy one's work incentives. At the same time a lower net wage rate—as in plan A compared to plan B, and plan B compared to no-subsidy conditions—discourages the preference for (poorly rewarded) work over free time. Thus, given the work-free time unsubsidized choice of $3,000 and 2,000 hours of work, plan B would weaken work incentives somewhat because of its higher income and lower net wage at full-schedule effort. Plan A would weaken work incentives even more because it yields a still higher income and lower net wage at any given labor effort. Obviously, then, the most destructive to work incentives of all possible plans would be a basic stipend at the Poverty Line with a 100 percent tax rate, in the manner of our current public assistance formulas.[5]

But it is not only those below the Poverty Line whose work incentives are affected by negative tax plans. If the formula leads to support of those with incomes above the poverty level, a new group of recipients appears that have never shared in any of our public assistance programs.

But even plans A and B of Table 10-4, which do not subsidize the nonpoor, may weaken work incentives and lead some of the nonpoor to become welfare recipients. Consider the $6,000-per-year worker who earns $3 per hour for full-schedule effort. Under plan A, for the last 667 hours of effort, his or her income rises from $4,500 to $6,000. This increase of $1,500 represents a reduced net wage of $2.25 per hour. If this worker chose to work the additional 667 hours when they netted $3 per hour from a base of only $4,000, he or she might not choose to work this much if the net were only $2.25 per hour for these extra hours from a higher base of $4,500. Thus, the negative effect of the plan on work incentives may induce some of the nonpoor to cut down their hours and enter the program. The likelihood of this happening is greater under plan A than plan B for reasons discussed above.

But this entire analysis of the harmful effects of negative income tax plans on work incentives is basically static in that it assumes stable preference relationships between income and free time. It is by no means certain, though, that these relationships are stable over time. Conlisk suggests the possibility that as income rises, spending "needs" become modified and may actually lead to more effort to meet these expanded consumption goals.[6] In any case, enough uncertainty has risen over the direction of work incentive effects to lead to empirical testing of negative tax plans.

[5]Michael Taussig, "Negative Income Tax Rates and the Elimination of Poverty: Comment," *National Tax Journal*, September 1967, p. 329. Taussig makes the telling point that concern over the work disincentive effects of negative income tax plans should be lessened by recognition that these plans are suggested as alternatives to the current welfare system, which discourages work much more than the most poorly conceived negative tax plan would.

[6]John Conlisk, "Simple Dynamic Effects in Work-Leisure Choice: A Skeptical Comment on the Static Theory," *Journal of Human Resources*, Summer 1968, p. 325.

Before looking at a few of these tests, it should be emphasized that preoccupation with effect on work incentives[7] is stimulated by more than its importance to work ethic satisfaction. Work disincentives also make program costs higher. Thus, on the surface, it may appear that taxpayers would prefer plan B over plan A. It costs less and does less damage to work incentives. But then, no plan at all would cost even less and leave work incentives untouched. In other words, we should not lose sight of the fact that the whole purpose of these plans is to improve the economic level of the poor. Plan A does a better job toward this purpose. The welfare trade-off remains regardless of program; how much do we wish to pay for poverty reduction?

Measuring Work Incentive Effects of Income Transfers

Three approaches have been used to estimate the effects of income transfers on labor supply: (1) Simulation models of these effects are studied from responses of labor supply to different levels of nonemployment income. (2) Analysis is made of the work incentive effects of those public assistance programs, such as Old Age Insurance and AFDC-WIN, that impose benefit reductions less than earnings. Because of the 100 percent tax put on earnings for other programs, there is no need to study their effects. When work cannot lead to extra income, involved analysis is not required to conclude that work incentives will be seriously reduced if not destroyed altogether. (3) Controlled experiments have been conducted to study the effect of negative income tax formulas on labor supply. The best-known and most elaborate of these is the Graduated Work Incentive Experiment, known as the New Jersey Negative Income Tax Experiment.

In general, the results were not uniform, but neither were they conflicting. Instances when the added transfer of a negative tax actually led to an increase in work incentive were rare indeed, but there was great variation in the degree of disincentive measured by reduced labor force participation and in hours of work, variation that ranged from close to zero, or statistically insignificant declines, to reduction in work effort so substantial as to be clearly attributable to the income support program. The usual pattern was for the primary (male) breadwinner to be less affected by subsidies than secondary family workers.

In their review of simulation studies of predicted reductions in labor supply of males in response to income maintenance plans, Cain and Watts reported a range in reduced labor from 37 percent with a $2,400 income

[7]For a thorough study of static work incentive effects of alternative plans with different basic subsidies, break-even income levels, and tax rates, see Christopher Green, *Negative Taxes and the Poverty Problem*, Brookings, Washington, D. C., 1967.

guarantee and tax of 50 percent to 3 percent with a $3,000 guarantee and the same tax rate.[8] These wide differences need explanation, especially since static theory would argue for greater work disincentive with the higher guarantee (basic subsidy). Part of the answer lies in the population studied. Prime-age males, the group studied in the lowest estimate of work reduction, would be expected to show less labor supply reaction to subsidies. But more significantly, Cain and Watts point out that these studies have difficulty in isolating the effects on poor households. Studies showing greater work disincentives may be heavily weighted with poor males who, because of the unpleasant jobs they have, may be expected to reduce their work effort more when aided by subsidies.

Garfinkel reviews studies of the labor supply effects of categorical assistance programs that impose less than a 100 percent tax on earnings.[9] AFDC mothers are found to react to income guarantees and reduced stipends in accordance with static theory. That is, in states where pressure to work in order to stay in the program is not very strong, there is a tendency to withdraw from work the greater the expansion in nonwork income support.

Male Old Age Insurance recipients also reduce their work effort in response to the reduction in pension benefits they receive as they earn more from work. The step movement in the reduction leads to bunching of work responses at earnings levels just below the level that would lead to a drop in pension receipts. It is always difficult to relate effect to a particular cause in economics, but only the least daring researcher would look for other causes than the removal of the retirement test at age 72, perhaps as a bonus for longevity, for the reappearance of these older men in the work force.

AFDC mothers and older men form two groups that can be expected to react in accordance with static theory. Their work attachment is marginal, the jobs they hold are often not personally satisfying, and their consumption needs are fixed and not prodded by vague desires to move up the socioeconomic ladder. All these factors lead toward a stronger interest in meeting income targets determined by consumption needs than toward aspirations for rising up the income scale. Thus the provision of subsidies effectively reduces labor supply of these groups.

The New Jersey Negative Income Tax Experiment represents the most comprehensive effort at testing the effects of a negative income tax on labor supply. Now completed, the findings have been studied and

[8]Glenn Cain and Harold Watts (eds.), "Toward a Summary and Synthesis of Evidence," *Income Maintenance and Labor Supply*, Rand McNally, Chicago, 1973.
[9]Irwin Garfinkel, "Income Maintenance Programs and Work Effort: A Review," *How Income Supplements Can Affect Work Behavior*, Studies in Public Welfare, Joint Economic Committee, Subcommittee on Fiscal Policy, 1974.

analyzed in detail.[10] The administrators of the programs and reviewers of its results were well aware of the shortcomings of the experimental technique.

In the first place, as with all experiments, there is the danger of a Hawthorne effect causing unusual responses. This refers to the tendency for subjects of a study to react abnormally or unnaturally because they are aware they are being tested. In the case of a negative tax plan, since the direction of this possible bias was not known, it could have led to stronger or weaker negative labor supply responses to the program.

Then the temporary nature of the project was bound to affect the results. If the subsidy was considered a windfall which did not represent a continued income guarantee, there would have been a check on the tendency to cut down work effort and an even stronger influence against leaving the labor force. Although the four-year length of the project mitigated against this weakness of a temporary experiment, undoubtedly some force was created in the direction of job and hours maintenance. This would not have been felt in a permanent program.

Comparison with a control group which received no subsidy from the program was made difficult by the fact that many families in this group were on some form of welfare. Those on AFDC already belonged to a program that has roughly the same features of a negative tax plan—a basic subsidy and partial retention of earnings, although with a much higher tax rate. Thus, differences between experiment subjects and the control group were not as large as would have been the case were the latter completely unsubsidized.

Another serious handicap to the analysis of results arose from the budgetary limitations of the study. With only a little over a thousand families in the project, including the control group, and a breakdown of households by race among several formulas with different guarantees and tax rates, some of the components had few subjects indeed. This reduced the accuracy of statistical analysis.

Nevertheless, the experiment still represents the best record we have of the effects of a negative tax program under something approaching realistic conditions. The results, on balance, provided support for those who favor a negative income tax in that there was little evidence of work reduction. Males and black wives did not alter their work effort significantly, and the only pronounced reduction in labor force and hours came from white wives.

These results are encouraging to hopes that a negative tax plan would

[10]The conceptual problems in testing are discussed, and findings reported in two series of symposium articles entitled "The Graduated Work Incentive Experiment," *Journal of Human Resources*, Spring and Fall 1974.

not incur sharp additions in costs from growth in program participants because of work cutbacks in response to the benefit provisions. But an experiment of this nature cannot yield conclusive results. We will never know what will happen until a national program is undertaken. So far we have had no such plan, despite much interest in the concept. But the Family Assistance Plan introduced in Congress in the first Nixon administration almost became our first experience with a negative income tax plan.

The Family Assistance Plan (FAP)

FAP came very close to enactment into law. It passed the House of Representatives in April 1970 but was rejected by the Senate.[11] A brief look at the proposal satisfies more than academic interest, since any new attempt at passing a negative tax bill will probably take the same form and face similar problems.

FAP was a negative income tax program, pure and simple, limited to poor families with children. The basic stipend paid $500 per adult and $300 per child, or a total of $1,600 for a two-parent, two-child family. In order to maintain work incentives, the first $720 of earnings were exempt from taxation; that is, the basic benefit was not reduced. For higher earnings, the tax rate was set at 50 percent, so that the break-even point of the plan was at an income of $3,920 ($1,600/.5 + $720).

The most obvious shortcoming of the plan is in the inadequacy of income support. The break-even income itself was just a little above the 1970 Poverty Line. Thus a family with no earners or with little income from work would remain in poverty. The skimpy benefits introduced a serious operational flaw in the plan. At the time, only eight states provided standard AFDC benefits less than $1,600. Obviously, FAP had to promise more if it was going to attract participants. FAP required states to supplement the program up to the AFDC level.

But then, to keep the break-even point low, states were allowed to impose a tax rate of 80 percent on earnings for the supplemental part of the benefits. What FAP in effect degenerated into, then, was a modified AFDC program with a tax rate on earnings for most participants that was actually higher than what AFDC imposed.[12]FAP did hold the promise of

[11]For a lively account of the ins and outs of the political background leading up to FAP and its ultimate rejection, see Daniel Moynihan, *The Politics of a Guaranteed Income: The Nixon Administration and the Family Assistance Plan*, Random House, New York, 1973.
[12]For discussion of these shortcomings of FAP, see D. Lee Bawden, Glen Cain, and Leonard Hausman, "The Family Assistance Plan: An Analysis and Evaluation," Public Policy, Spring 1971, and Robert F. Smith and Joseph Heffernan, "Work Incentives and Wefare Reform: The FAP Experience," *Mississippi Journal of Business and Economics*, 1971.

expanded benefits for those living in states providing meager AFDC benefits.

An operational plan needs a higher base stipend. Then the trade-off between work incentive and costs implied in the decision regarding the tax rate to be established can be decided in accordance with social and political preferences at the time. But there is no capacity for negotiating this issue and still arriving at meaningful poverty reduction unless the guarantee is closer to the Poverty Line than $1,600 was in 1970.

One appeal to conservatives of the negative income tax is that if adequate enough and if coverage is expanded to the poor without children, it can substitute for the whole range of current categorical and general assistance programs. Conservatives find the concept of welfare somewhat distasteful in any case, and this one-program system has the same attraction as a single loan consolidating several small obligations; it seems less painful, no matter that the interest rate is higher. In commenting on Nixon's last attempt at welfare reform with a higher basic benefit and expanded coverage, *The Wall Street Journal* revealed still another conservative bias satisfied by the negative income tax. It notes that in replacing other programs with expanded FAP, "armies of welfare workers would no longer be needed."[13]

But this new plan was proposed by President Nixon in early 1974, with a targeted congressional approval date in 1976. Hindsight tells us this was rather unrealistic timing for a Nixon administration proposal. Now we must wait for some unknown future date to learn whether a practical, all-purpose income maintenance program can be implemented.

SUMMARY

Two schools of thought contend over welfare policy. Egalitarians seek a movement toward the elimination of disparities in income. The move toward equality would wipe out poverty in the process. Liberals, at least according to Friedman's classification of the group, want income to be distributed by a freely operating market system which pays workers in accordance with the value of their production. They do believe in removal of barriers to equality of opportunity but do not support redistribution as an aspect of national economic policy. They give reluctant support to welfare to keep the poor from destitution.

The income inadequacy of our current welfare programs indicates consensus leaning toward the liberal position. In fact, given the low level of transfer support and the minor success of manpower programs (dis-

---

[13]*The Wall Street Journal*, March 18, 1974, p. 28.

cussed in the last chapter), one wonders how vigorously the War on Poverty is being waged.

Besides the low level of benefits provided, current public assistance programs also fail to reach a large segment of the poor. Furthermore, the individual programs—except for AFDC, admittedly by far the largest one—discourage work by imposing a 100 percent tax on earnings.

The negative income tax has been suggested as a welfare reform measure that will reduce poverty, replace the numerous individual categorical and general assistance plans, and maintain work incentives by imposing a tax rate below the prohibitive 100 percent rate.

But these plans have intrinsic conflicts in meeting welfare goals. If the basic stipend, or income guarantee, reaches the poverty level, then subsidies must be given to the nonpoor if the tax rate is to be set below 100 percent. At any given break-even income level, a lower guarantee with a lower tax rate will cost less than a plan with a higher subsidy and tax rate; but it will yield less income or satisfaction to the poor, hardly a welfare program achievement.

Static theory concludes that a negative tax plan will reduce work incentives, but dynamic aspects of raised consumption goals after higher income is attained may stimulate work effort in the drive for higher income. Statistical studies of simulated labor supply responses to a negative tax plan, analysis of AFDC and Old Age Insurance programs which impose less than a 100 percent tax on earnings, and the New Jersey Negative Income Tax Experiment indicate only mild support for the static theory. A slight reduction in work effort is found, but only among secondary family workers. These findings suggest that a negative tax plan would not incur significant increases in projected costs because of work reduction and consequent expanded benefit demand from those who were motivated to reduce their labor effort.

The Family Assistance Plan was the closest we have come to a full-blown national negative tax program. To be successful, a future plan that passes Congress must raise the income guarantee, or else it would merely provide an expanded AFDC. At this writing there is no clear indication that the American public wants to pay the cost of poverty elimination through redistributional transfers.

The message in these two chapters is that current manpower development and planning efforts and inadequately funded income maintenance programs cannot eliminate the social blight of poverty. Possible future success toward this end depends on combined application of the two methods.

Workers and potential labor force participants among the poor need strong doses of human resource development, supportive employment services, and income maintenance during the process of upgrading and placement to move them permanently off welfare and out of poverty. Small doses and minimal skill training only waste scarce resources. Successful manpower development requires not only adequate funding but also careful forecasting of future skill needs and efficient program administration.

If development and planning is successful, then the reduced number of welfare clients can escape poverty as limited total taxpayer generosity can be focused on their income maintenance needs.

Chapter 11

Summary and Conclusions

Although each of the previous chapters ends with a brief summary of major findings, a purpose can be served by an overall review of the salient issues and unsolved problems of poverty. A comprehensive summary can move through the various steps from concepts to causes to treatment of poverty and result in a brief unified review of the many sides of the problem. In addition, released from the confines of the subject matter of individual chapters, a final summary can trace out the impact on the particular groups with high incidences of poverty, of the various causes of poverty and can point out the remedies most appropriate to the factors inducing poverty for each group.

Consequently, this summary chapter contains the following two sections: first, a brief review of important issues and findings of each of the chapters with an emphasis on those aspects often overlooked or misconceived by the general public; second, a brief presentation of causes and appropriate means of reducing poverty among its principal sufferers—blacks, women, the young, and the old.

MAJOR FINDINGS AND CONCLUSIONS

Concepts and Definitions

Designating the Poor   Those sensitive to the feelings of others cannot help but take offense at the word *poor* when it is used without clarification to classify a large group of people whose income does not reach acceptable levels. Unfortunately, although we are all aware of the general meaning of the word when it is applied in an economic context, there might be a tendency to associate its other usages with population subgroups at the bottom of the income distribution.

That is, as an adjective, *poor* also means inefficient, or of low quality, as in "poor performance," "poor grades," or even "poor excuse for a man." In each of these examples there is a strong suggestion that the poverty described is attributable to faults in the people to whom it relates. The early history of public attitudes toward poverty, extending up to the 1930s in this country, shows enough evidence of attributing the causes of poverty to the poor themselves without encouragement from supporting descriptive terminology.

Expressions such as "low-income population" have not caught on as substitutes for *poor* in describing income inadequacy. This simply means that in using *poor* in its economic sense, we must separate out any lingering connection with its other uses. These chapters have presented enough evidence to make untenable the view that there is any inherent deficiency in the poor as a group to account for their economic misfortune. While there are certainly *individuals* with low native earnings potential and low economic motivation, forces beyond their present control explain the presence of most people within the poverty population. This population is not classified for the purpose of satisfying academic curiosity but in order to designate those people who should be subjects of public concern and programs to improve their economic status.

Definitions—Absolute Poverty   The poverty standard set by the Social Security Administration has many shortcomings. First, the income level is *inadequate*. Based on an Economy Food Plan for temporary emergencies, the Poverty Line income allows only the sparest standard of living.

Second, the level is *inflexible*. It maintains the same standard of living in that it adjusts only with the price level. Thus it fails to consider rising consumption aspirations in its maintenance of a constant low purchasing power for the Poverty Line.

Third, preoccupation with the Poverty Line can lead to *biased antipoverty policy* in favor of the least poor, to the disadvantage of those in most desperate need.

Fourth, emphasis on an income standard ignores the *sociological and psychological damage* of poverty. The poor need money, but they also need meaningful employment to strenghthen their self-esteem and position in society. Transfer payments can be designed to lift many out of poverty, but they cannot provide the noneconomic benefits that go with satisfying work.

Relative Poverty   Poverty has not only an absolute quality of deprivation but also a relative quality of low income in comparison with the more numerous and affluent nonpoor. Thus, if many escape officially measured poverty simply because of more or less equal increases throughout the income distribution, they will still feel economically deprived compared with the rest of society.

Attempts to introduce a relative measure of poverty, the simplest being a moving poverty line at half the median income, have not received public acceptance. Nevertheless, these standards point out the lack of success in removing poverty as a social problem despite the steady decline in the official poverty rate, because as the percentage poor so measured has steadily declined, the percentage of the population lying below one-half the median income has been stubbornly stable over the years.

The Demography of Poverty

The poverty rate has been in a declining trend, falling from a 22.4 percent rate in 1959 to 11.1 percent in 1973. The most important proximate cause of poverty is low earnings, which under our present system of income distribution result from an inability to contribute much to the value of output. In addition, poverty obviously arises among consuming units, mainly families, whose members do not work at all or work less than full schedules.

The incidence of poverty falls heavily among a few population subgroups— among blacks, women who head families, the young, and the old. Incidence is a much more significant measure of poverty than a group's share of the total poverty population. The latter depends on the size of the group itself, while the former measures the tendency toward poverty within the group and indicates the degree of need for remedial action. For example, more whites than blacks are poor, since whites are about nine times as numerous; but the high incidence of poverty among blacks, their poverty rate being almost four times the white rate, suggests attack on barriers to adequate black income as an effective antipoverty policy.

Earnings capacity is expanded by human resource development

through education and training. Consequently it is not surprising to find that poverty rates fall as the level of schooling rises, with very high rates among those with little education.

Although education itself is not a demographic characteristic, two population subgroups, blacks and the aged, have schooling levels well below the average. This earnings handicap explains part of the poverty among these groups.

But that blacks and the aged have higher poverty rates than the rest of the population at *every schooling level*—with the one exception of grade-school attainment for the aged—suggests that little schooling is just one and not the only explanation of their high poverty rates. Blacks have their earnings potential blunted by discrimination. Older workers, though they might face less economic discrimination, have their earnings limited by incapacity and nonparticipation in the labor force.

High poverty rates among women, who as a group reach the same educational level as men, adds further argument against the expectation that rising educational attainment will solve the poverty problem among blacks and the aged. The main proximate cause of poverty among women who head households—the female group of high poverty incidence, since married women share the same income standard with their spouses—is inadequate labor market participation either in actual nonparticipation or less than full-schedule work.

The presence of children in these households and the consequent need to care for them prevents many of these women from working. But lower earnings when they do work full schedules also contribute to female poverty in that the rate for full-schedule women who head households far exceeds that of households headed by full-schedule men in which the man is the only worker.

Poverty is high for all households, regardless of race or sex of head, the greater the number of children. Since earnings are not related to family size, children add a strain on living-standard adequacy among low-income families.

Unemployment and part-time or part-year work also contribute to poverty. The high incidence of poverty among these groups and the low incidence among full-schedule workers suggests an easy solution to poverty through a successful full-employment policy. But work will not eliminate poverty unless it pays adequately. With the unemployed heavily weighted with those of low earning potential, employing these workers at their current earning capacity will do little to eliminate poverty.

Pinpointing groups with high poverty incidence shows us the areas of concern for antipoverty action. But successful policies and programs for these groups require closer knowledge of the causes of their poverty.

Causes of Poverty— Inadequate Education

The relationship between income and education seems clear enough, despite contrary arguments that schools do little to raise earning power. When occupations are related to their poverty rates, those jobs requiring the most schooling have the lowest poverty incidence; poverty is concentrated among jobs with low educational demands.

Despite this connection, there are many among the poor who have attained at least a high school education. Contrary to the European system, our educational process does not assure proper channeling of students toward the type of schooling best suited to develop their earning power.

But our schools do try to develop cognitive skills, which allow the application of reasoning to knowledge. This general education helps people to do many jobs that are not available without these skills. Whether or not schools actually succeed in helping people to develop and apply reasoning power, the educated have an employment advantage over the less schooled as long as employers believe that schooling does help. *Credentialism*, which uses education as an unjustified measure of work capacity, actually represents a form of employment discrimination.

The Coleman Report claims that the differential quality of schools does not contribute to differences in cognitive skill development, and the Jencks study goes one step further in denigrating formal schooling by claiming that cognitive skill development itself has nothing to do with earnings. Schools are damned whether they do or don't. The policy implication of these studies is devastating to the view that equalized schooling is a major step toward economic equality.

But the statistical methods which led to these conclusions are suspect. While it is true that there is no proof that more money put into the education of the poor will improve their cognitive skills or that even if it does, this development will raise their earning power, at least this line of attack on income inequality is worth the try.

Causes of Poverty— Racial Discrimination

Black earning power suffers from three types of discriminatory practices. There is first, *screening* for characteristics which, though related to productive efficiency do not conclusively determine ability to perform. This practice bars many blacks from employment. Low educational attainment and consequent unsatisfactory test scores keep many blacks from jobs they might fill adequately, despite indications from these screening devices to the contrary.

Overt discrimination, the exercise of prejudice to set conditions of employment unrelated to ablity to perform, affects blacks more seriously than does screening. The most obvious form of overt discrimination— wage difference based on race— may be little practiced; but more subtle, harder-to-detect forms of employment discrimination, such as slow promotion and placement in jobs below ability levels, are still wide- spread.

Institutionalized racism, disadvantage arising from past discrimi- nation and unrelated to current prejudicial attitudes, has the strongest im- pact on black earning power and is the most difficult to eliminate. Insti- tutionalized racism has as its source the vicious circle which moves from low earnings to poor neighborhoods, poor family income status, and poor schooling; to inadequate human resource development; to unsteady, dead-end jobs; and back to low earnings.

Treatment of all three forms of discrimination imposes costs as bar- riers are lifted. Eliminating screening raises costs when poor job perform- ance substantiates the validity of the screening device. Overt discrimi- nation benefits the favored group, such as white workers for whom com- petition is reduced by bias against blacks. But the law against this blatant form of prejudice, if effectively applied, would make any mercenary sup- port for its continuation inoperable.

Successful attack on overt discrimination, though, requires sustained pressure all along the circle of institutionalized racism, at a cost to be paid by society as a whole.[1] The evidence of the negative effect of discrimi- nation on black earning capacity is clear. Perhaps even more serious than the fact of low black economic status is its persistence.

Relative black family income is holding steady at a level less than two-thirds the white average. Black poverty rates have steadily remained at approximately $3^{1}/_{2}$ times the white rate and lie above the white rate for every job category. The black unemploynnt rate has been consistently twice the white level, with a much sharper racial difference among youths. Year after year, labor force participation of prime-age black males lies about 10 percent below the white rate. Some cause for optimism arises from the slight improvement in relative job status and from a narrowing of the gap in racial educational attainment, but these minor advances do not obviate the need for vigorous action in reducing discrimination to raise black income levels and lower black poverty rates toward white averages.

Causes of Poverty— Low Income of Women

Poverty among women takes the form of high rates for families they head. In fact, the ratio of poverty among these families to the rate for families headed by males is on the rise and has reached a level five times higher.

---

[1]Details of effective action in this area as well as for reducing poverty among women and the young and old appear in the following section.

Nonparticipation in the work force can explain a great deal of female poverty, and this nonparticipation arises mainly from the woman's role as homemaker. A very revealing statistic of the effect of this one element on female earnings finds that more women claim they are out of the work force because of home responsibilities than are actually at work. The presence of children and the tradition that child care is the woman's responsibility can account for heavy nonparticipation among female-headed families that include children. But why is the participation rate lower for single women than for single men?

Although women attain the same educational level as men, they hold less responsible jobs, customarily at the assisting rather than the decision-making level. Even when their education lifts them to professional status, sexism directs them to particular fields that pay less both because of overcrowding and the relatively low economic value of the jobs themselves. Women hold the vast majority of jobs in nursing, primary-level teaching, and library work.

While low female economic status in professional work in itself has nothing to do with poverty, this condition is indicative of the barriers to income adequacy faced by women. Sexism keeps the woman in the home, even when household duties are minimal. When she does work, opportunities arise mainly in low-paying jobs. While lower-echelon professional jobs and service-oriented white-collar work may yield incomes above the poverty level, downward pressure all along the occupational scale forces many women into the lowest-paid unskilled service jobs— domestic service and laundry work are examples. In other instances they are pushed out of the work force entirely; in either case, they end up in poverty.

There have been recent gains in female participation, especially in the preparation stages, in higher-level professinal jobs. But unless this easing of sexism extends to lower occupational classifications, and especially to change in the current exclusive assignment of women to child care and other household duties and in the attitude that woman's place is in the home even in the absence of heavy household duties, the problem of female poverty will remain unsolved and even unmitigated.

Causes of Poverty— Age

The incidence of poverty is high at both ends of the life cycle, for children and the aged. This poverty reflects the inadequacy of income during the working years to cover consumption needs in life's two major nonworking periods. But the prescription for poverty relief differs for the two groups.

Childhood Poverty Poor children need special help in human resource development to break the bonds of poverty formed by their low-income family background.

Some suggest population control as a means of checking childhood poverty. Statistics support the view that there are more children in black and other minority poor families than among the white poor. But this condition only reflects the higher poverty rates among blacks in general; the ratio of poverty among black children to black family heads is about the same as the white ratio.

The fact that low-income families have fewer children than the average — not more, as is popularly believed— makes population control among the poor a misdirected antipoverty policy. While some families with otherwise adequate income are driven into poverty when they have many children, the relatively small number of children low-income families have suggests that antipoverty policy would be more effective and fairer if it stresses raising incomes and earning potential rather than population control.

Old-Age Poverty Opportunities for human resource development are obviously limited for the aged poor, who would be better served by more generous transfer programs. The percentage poor among the aged has fallen steadily over the years. This decline has been a little greater than that for the population as a whole, although poverty among the aged is still about 50 percent higher than the overall average.

These slight relative gains reflect, on the positive side, the effect of an improvement in private pensions and especially social security benefits and, on the negative side, a reduction in labor force participation and earnings. The future for older poverty, measured by the official poverty rate, is encouraging; higher educational levels promise a more productive older population and transfer benefits seem to be on a rising trend.

Offsetting this optimism, though, employer demand for older workers at all skill levels appears to be declining and the steady rise in benefits may only match the growth in average income. If these trends continue, official poverty may decline for the aged, but their relative poverty will remain unrelieved as older incomes stay at about 50 percent of overall income— the relationship that has persisted over recent years.

Causes of Poverty—Unemployment and Underemployment

Official data underestimate the contribution of unemployment to poverty. Although the incidence of poverty among the unemployed is high, the comparatively small percentage of the work force unemployed makes for a low percentage of the poor who are unemployed. But official data only measure the monthly average of unemployment and fail to show that a much larger part of the work force has its annual income reduced by periods of unemployment during the year.

Thus a full-employment policy would actually reduce poverty more than official figures suggest. To be effective, such a policy must reach those who work less than a full year and/or who work part time involuntarily. It must also find jobs for those just off the edge of the work force: the "hidden unemployed" who do not seek jobs because they think they will not find them, and many of those who "want a job now" but cannot seek work because of home responsibilities, ill health, and other reasons.

The low earning capacity of those who do work also contributes to poverty, but the comparatively low poverty rate for those with some work experience suggests that finding fuller employment for at least the part-time and part-year workers would go a long way to reducing overall poverty. Unemployment and underemployment contribute more heavily to poverty than do low earning rates.

But given the nature of the labor market, a full-(schedule) employment policy is difficult to achieve. Segmentation leads to a dual labor market in which secondary jobs provide only sporadic employment at low wages.

Study of poverty areas in which secondary jobs dominate yields clear evidence that the secondary market represents a demand and not a supply phenomenon; circumstances and not deficiencies in the poor themselves determine poverty. Labor force participation rates in poverty areas are only a little below the national average, and the strong desire to work despite limited opportunities is further evidenced by the relatively large number who "want to work now."

Popular belief holds that although bouts of unemployment are more frequent in poor areas, the duration of unemployment is shorter, since workers move easily in and out of jobs that demand little training or work stability. That this duration is actually much longer in poor areas adds to the urgency of remedial antipoverty action.

Growth, Inflation, and Poverty

On the surface, economic growth seems to hold promise for softening the problem of poverty. With growth comes steadier employment and less unemployment, an increase in wages, and a rise throughout the income distribution. These gains will fall to the poor, too, and lift them out of poverty.

But several forces operate against these beneficial aspects of growth. Many of the poor are not in the work force and are unlikely to be drawn to work by expanded job opportunities. Then, too, a balanced expansion of income will leave the remaining poor relatively worse off than before. Finally, environmental concern has lessened the popularity of growth as a national goal for any purpose, not just for poverty reduction.

A prosperous economy at present full-employment output potential has strong consensus support as a national economic goal. Success toward this end will reduce poverty to minimun levels attainable at present productive capacity and distribution patterns but will miss the gains from growth.

Contrary to popular belief, data do not support the view that inflation has its strongest adverse effects on the poor. The income sources of the poor— low-wage earnings and transfer receipts— rise faster than the price level, even when these gains are deflated by a price index based on the market basket of the poor. Real income changes for the poor during inflation about match those for the rest of the population.

Combating Poverty—Manpower Development and Planning

In theory, manpower development and planning offer the opportunity for the most beneficial form of poverty reduction. Like transfer programs, they will serve to raise incomes over poverty levels. But they have many potential advantages over transfers. If successful, manpower development and planning would raise income through earnings, yielding the following benefits:

1   Reduction in welfare and burden on taxpayers
2   Satisfaction of work ethic philosophy, held by taxpayers and poor recipients alike, thereby treating sociological as well as economic aspects of poverty
3   Increase in total national production and net increase in standard of living rather than a simple redistribution of income— the method of income transfers

In practice, though, manpower development and planning have fallen well short of their goal of poverty relief through increased earnings of the poor. Costs per successful placement of program clients have been very high. Only a small number of participants have left the welfare rolls, and actual decline in real expenditures testify to public attitudes that social benefits have not been worth program costs.

But past mistakes can be corrected and more successful development and planning efforts can be made. The following suggestions would lead to better results:

1   Reduce administrative inefficiencies and program overlapping by more coordinated planning. The Comprehensive Employment and Training Act moves in this direction.
2   Acknowledge that many, probably most, of welfare clients cannot be readied for well-paying work by brief human resource development efforts. Either aid these clients through transfers or acknowledge

the high costs needed to prepare them for leaving welfare through work. Halfway measures of limited funding simply waste money.

3   Do not confuse manpower training and planning in general with antipoverty needs. While there has been a sharper focus in manpower efforts on the poor and disadvantaged, in a denial of the position that manpower activities should be directed against labor bottlenecks which strengthen inflationary pressures, emergency recession placement in public employment of the skilled unemployed directs funds from the chronically poor.

4   Coordinate training and labor market (placement) services. Emphasis on placement might reduce welfare costs but not the number poor and will, in most cases, yield only temporary relief, since these jobs in the secondary market are easily lost.

5   Maintain work incentives by allowing welfare supplements to low-wage earnings. Only WIN acknowledges this need, and only with grudging support.

Combating Poverty— Income Maintenance

The most revealing evidence of the inadequacy of transfer programs to reduce poverty is that many of the poor are ineligible for their benefits because their incomes are above the level of eligibility. Apart from skimpy stipends, transfers have, in almost all cases, the added weakness of imposing a 100 percent tax on earnings. This feature, designed to protect the taxpayer from contributing support to those who can earn enough to cover at least part of their basic consumption needs, destroys the work incentives of low-wage labor,

Suggested overhaul of the transfer system— to widen its coverage, to avoid bureaucratic program overlap, to maintain work incentives, and to do a better job in reducing poverty—features variation on a basic negative income tax plan. Under the negative tax, recipients have their basic stipend reduced as their earnings increase, but not on a dollar-for-dollar basis.

The stipend and the tax rate play crucial roles in satisfying, or trading off, the three principal goals of poverty relief, maintenance of work incentive, and low program costs. A high basic stipend and low tax rate will have the least harmful effect on work incentives and will strengthen incomes of the poor, but it may be costly. A low-cost program would have a low base stipend and a high tax rate, but it would be unworthy of the designation "antipoverty program."

We almost had a negative tax program, and despite its faults of inadequate funding and complicated formulas, the Family Assistance Plan would have been a bold attempt at implementing a new-style transfer mechanism. Experimental studies of negative tax plans which show only mild disincentive effects on labor effort from program funding might encourage further congressional efforts toward passing a negative tax plan. But new concepts of poverty relief must wait until preoccupation with the recession lessens and prosperity allows the majority to reawaken its concern for those not sharing in its benefits.

REDUCING POVERTY
AMONG HIGH-INCIDENCE GROUPS

Just as the problem of poverty is many sided, so too must be the measures needed to attack it. Antipoverty programs suitable for one group are inappropriate for another. In this last section, we relate treatment to poverty cause for the three highest incidence poverty groups— blacks, women (household heads), and the two subgroups suffering from age poverty: children and the aged.

Of course, many individuals belong to more than one high-incidence group. For an extreme example, older black women who head households have three characteristics closely related to poverty. But, on the realistic assumption that the independent effect on poverty of each feature of race, sex, and age outweighs the secondary contribution of any added influence, we can confine the discussion to these three features in the abstract.

Black Poverty

Blacks, and other minorities, face all three forms of discrimination: screening, overt discrimination, and institutionalized racism. In all three cases, elimination or at least reduction in these practices can widen earning opportunities for blacks. But at the same time it must be acknowledged that while society as a whole will be an economic gainer from their disappearance, to say nothing of resulting social gains, individual groups who profit from their practice will lose out from their discontinuation. This statement does not imply any support for their persistence nor sympathy with those who will lose out from the gains of prejudice. It is made to emphasize the difficulty of implementing measures that go against the economic interests of particular groups, no matter how antisocial the source of their advantage.

Screening, for example, has a particular negative impact on blacks. The use of educational attainment or test scores as an employment screen eliminates many capable blacks from consideration for certain jobs, even when racial prejudice plays no part in their exclusion. Firms point out that screening saves them money in that the hiring costs of testing and screening do result in a more able work force, even though some individuals with ability are screened out. The expenses of an inefficient work force and the difficult task of weeding out the incompetent after they begin work more than outweigh the loss of the good workers screened out.

Screening can be eliminated, but at a cost which should be assumed by society and not by the firms involved. Just letting prices rise as costs go up would not be fair, since the firms would still lose profits and the whole industry would suffer competitive losses to products not affected by screening. Tax concessions, on the other hand, which matched the added costs of screening elimination, would impose a cost on taxpayers as a whole and not on the complying firms.

There is no justification for screening in public employment when the costs of its elimination could fall directly on society as a whole in higher prices for public goods and services.

Overt discrimination, being the most obvious practice of prejudice, should be the easiest to eliminate. But here we are dealing with emotions, and strong action must be taken to suppress the crudest forms of prejudice. We have the Civil Rights Act and other specific antidiscrimination laws and directives, which must be strongly enforced.

As a result of these laws and prior industrial attitudes, wage discrimination is little practiced. But more subtle forms of overt discrimination remain. Screening, taking the form of credentialism, is often purposely directed towards blacks. Slow promotions and quick layoffs also have their racial overtones.

That some people will lose as competition from blacks stiffens should be of no national concern. Furthermore, it is not fair to malign in advance the attitude of those who gain from overt discrimination since they are not the ones who initiate discriminatory practices.[2]

The elimination of *institutionalized racism* requires concentrated public action. With no single group responsible for its current practice and with obvious costs associated with its elimination, the national purpose toward this end must be strengthened.

Will higher education open its doors to blacks with lower entrance credentials? Will firms hire them for training slots when they do not meet screening tests? Will banks take risks on loans to businesses in low-profit areas?

If the circle of institutionalized racism is to be done away with, it must be broken at many points. More money must be put into schools attended by poor children; delayed decisions on the benefits of busing are irrelevant to the present pressing need for better early schooling for blacks. Affirmative action in employment will be accepted and functional

---

[2]For example, the white worker gains from his employer's racial discrimination.

only when black incomes rise in general to allow for net expansion in employment, not just racial redistribution of jobs.

A complex, coordinated system of compensatory spending, business subsidies— the lack of success of NAB-JOBS can be attributed to its isolation as a program to break institutionalized racism— and tax benefits must be devised to assign the costs of eliminating institutionalized racism to society as a whole.

Female Poverty

Unlike blacks, women do not suffer from a comprehensive structure of institutionalized discrimination. Their family economic background and their education is the same as their brothers'.

But employment discrimination and assignment of women to roles outside the labor force suffice to push a larger percentage of women and the households they head into poverty.

Public programs in aid of poor women cannot change attitudes, especially those held by women themselves, but they can adjust to them. If the majority of these women claim that household duties, especially child care, prevent their labor force participation, then we should not argue over the reasonableness of their attitude but, instead, provide subsidized day-care centers.

We should encourage the expansion of job opportunities, by subsidies and tax reductions if necessary. A woman jockey may contribute nothing to poverty relief, but her presence widens the employment aspirations of other women. The telephone company might secretly grumble about the inefficiency of its linewomen, but if a woman can climb a telephone pole routinely, she should be able to bus tables and fix bicycles.

But all these steps will not serve the woman who is now poor, has children, is out of work, and has a sketchy labor force history. How should her poverty be treated? (The same concern should be expressed for all those needing assistance, whether men, blacks, teen-agers, or the aged.)

The case involves a decision for training and placement or for transfer payments. Currently, her prospects are not good; the likelihood is that training will be inadequate and transfers insufficient to lift her and her family out of poverty.

It is not enough to say we need more training and larger transfers. Given budgetary limitations, a choice will always have to be made between the two. We must recognize that training has a threshold element; a little training will not lead to a fairly good job and it will add nothing to the recipient's earning potential.

Those who, because of prior education and experience, have a good chance for improving their skill level by a fixed amount of training time and money should be placed in training. The others should receive (increased) transfers. In practice, this policy cannot be rigidly applied, and there are always marginal cases. But it sets up a more realistic and efficient basis for attack on poverty than the current implicit bias that everyone should work and that transfers represent only a last-resort stopgap against starvation.

Age and Poverty

Children Inequality of opportunity for children begins at birth, but at least early schooling can serve to help balance out chances for later economic success. The recent Supreme Court decision supporting the constitutionality of the property tax as the basis for public school funding has struck a blow against equality of educational opportunity. The decision gives school districts permission to have widely different expenditures per student, expenditures based on the size of property tax bases.

The controversy over the merits of busing children across district lines, still unsettled despite a Supreme Court decision discouraging the practice, misses the point of the disadvantages of low funding in particular districts and even more subtle differences within districts. Busing may randomize inadequate schooling racially, but it would still leave some children with less funding than others unless efforts were made, through equalization plans, to eliminate funding differences between schools.

But children need more than adequate school funding to escape poverty. Their education needs more direction toward labor market success than our schools now provide.

The data show that those fortunate enough to complete college will stumble out of poverty no matter how poorly they are prepared vocationally. But those who just finish high school, and especially dropouts, are not so lucky. They need expanded career education programs which will prepare them for work if not always for specific occupations.

Population control may have its own merits, but it has no particular value as an antipoverty measure. The data which show that low-income families have fewer children than the average indicate that the problem of poverty comes from not enough food, not from too many mouths.

The Aged Compulsory retirement ages act as an employment screening device for older workers. That laws against age discrimination permit firms to establish such ages makes attack against this practice a losing undertaking. In fact, the decline in the aged (over sixty-five) labor force represents both an expansion of income opportunities outside of

Table 11-1 Checklist of Needed Remedies for Reducing Poverty among High-Incidence Subgroups

Antipoverty action		Subgroups			
Area	Measure	Blacks	Women	Children	Aged
Discrimination	Enforce antidiscrimination (overt) laws more rigorously	X	X		X
	Reduce institutionalized discrimination by				
	affirmative action	X	X		
	tax reductions and subsidies to complying firms	X			
	Reduce screening by tax reductions to complying firms	X	X		X
Schooling	Increase school funding in poor areas			X	
	Strengthen career education			X	
Manpower development and planning	Enroll those with highest potential for raising earning capacity	X	X		
	Expand public day-care funding		X		
Transfers	Increase transfers in categorical programs or through negative income tax plan	X	X	X	X

work, mainly in pension income, and in reduced industrial demand for older workers.

In most cases, the only practical solution for existing aged poverty is through expanded transfers. Since social security income depends heavily on past earnings experience, improved transfers for the aged poor must look to other sources of funding.

If some form of adequate negative income tax formula is implemented, there would be no need for a categorical transfer program designed for the aged. But until we have such a comprehensive plan, the aged poor need special transfers which take into consideration that existing props to aged income—social security and private pension benefits—give little income to the poor.

The complex and various connections between appropriate antipoverty policy and causes of high poverty incidence among particular subgroups are summarized in the checklist of Table 11-1. To repeat the method of the above review, only the elements directly related to a particular group are recorded. For example, certainly black children — or, more precisely, youths— are in need of career education, but the check is placed in the "children" column to emphasize that the need applies to all young people, not just those belonging to any particular population group.

The purpose of Table 11-1 is to emphasize the ramifications of effective antipoverty action. More than money is needed to meet this many-sided problem. That we have given too little of this necessary ingredient to fight poverty raises questions about the strength of our purpose toward this struggle. But we need more than the will and good intentions to remove poverty from the top of the list of our socioeconomic problems; we also need knowledge and judgment.

INDEX

INDEX